To my Dear Friend Ellie -
For that dreaded day when inspiration wanes.
love
Wynne

SOFT SCULPTURE
and Other Soft Art Forms

Books by Dona Z. Meilach in Crown's Arts and Crafts Series:

COLLAGE AND ASSEMBLAGE
with Elvie Ten Hoor
CONTEMPORARY ART WITH WOOD
CONTEMPORARY BATIK AND TIE-DYE
CONTEMPORARY STONE SCULPTURE
DIRECT METAL SCULPTURE
with Donald Seiden
MACRAMÉ ACCESSORIES
MACRAMÉ: CREATIVE DESIGN IN KNOTTING
PAPIER-MÂCHÉ ARTISTRY
SOFT SCULPTURE AND OTHER SOFT ART FORMS
SCULPTURE CASTING
with Dennis Kowal

Also by Dona Z. Meilach:

ACCENT ON CRAFTS
THE ARTIST'S EYE
COLLAGE AND FOUND ART
with Elvie Ten Hoor
CONTEMPORARY LEATHER: ART AND ACCESSORIES
CREATING ART FROM ANYTHING
CREATING ART FROM FIBERS AND FABRICS
CREATING DESIGN, FORM, COMPOSITION
with Jay Hinz and Bill Hinz
CREATING WITH PLASTER
CREATIVE STITCHERY
with Lee Erlin Snow
MAKING CONTEMPORARY RUGS AND WALL HANGINGS
PAPERCRAFT
PRINTMAKING
WEAVING OFF-LOOM
with Lee Erlin Snow

SOFT SCULPTURE

and Other Soft Art Forms

With Stuffed Fabrics, Fibers, and Plastics

BY DONA Z. MEILACH

CROWN PUBLISHERS, INC., NEW YORK

Dedicated to Jan Wagstaff . . .
whose work ignited the spark
that resulted in this compilation

Library of Congress Catalog Card Number: 73-91153

Inquiries should be addressed to Crown Publishers, Inc., 419 Park Avenue South, New York, N.Y. 10016.

Printed in the United States of America
Published simultaneously in Canada by
General Publishing Company Limited
Designed by Shari de Miskey

Second Printing, June, 1975

Contents

Acknowledgments

GATHERING AND ASSEMBLING THE MATERIALS FOR THIS BOOK has been a gratifying endeavor, thanks to the cooperation and generosity of so many people. My sincere thanks to the approximately 375 artists and craftsmen who submitted photos or shipped work to me to be photographed. I cherish the trust that permits so many people whom I have never met to send me their artwork, large and small, to be photographed and returned: sculptures they have toiled and pondered over for countless hours, often weeks, maybe months. In many instances the pieces were shipped to me to be photographed, and then my instructions were to forward them to a gallery or museum exhibition. Each artist's name accompanies his work.

I am particularly grateful to Sheila Malkind, director of The American Craftsman Gallery, Chicago, for permitting me to photograph an entire show entitled *Soft Sculpture* held in her gallery in 1972. Thanks also to Sonia Zaks, of the Deson-Zaks Gallery, Chicago, for her recommendations and leads to outstanding "soft" artists.

The foresight of Foundation Woolmark, France, in supplying artists with wools, resulted in marvelous examples presented in the show *Woolmark* at the Galerie Boutique Germain, Paris, 1972. My thanks to the Foundation Woolmark and the Galerie for permitting use of the photos in this book.

I appreciate and am indebted to Tom Ladousa, Associate Professor of Art, University of Southwestern Louisiana, Lafayette, Louisiana, for the demonstration, photos, and examples of latex sculptures prepared especially for this presentation.

A special thanks to Jim T. Soult, director of the Richmond Art Center, Richmond, California, for allowing me to photograph the soft sculptures in a gallery show and for his generous time and effort in introducing me to artists in the San Francisco Bay area.

I spent a fascinating evening interviewing Jonathan Bauch and Charles Meyers, New York City, and I will always remember their warm hospitality.

The cooperation of gallery directors who responded to my request for people working in soft materials was amusing and delightful. Often, they knew immediately which artists were already involved in soft materials. More often, they didn't realize that these materials fell into a soft sculpture category. They appreciated having a "handle," or "umbrella," under which they could categorize the current output of some of the artists they represented.

Thanks to Sol Gurevitz, The Field Museum of Natural History, Chicago, for opening the photo archives to me so I could select stimulating examples of primitive art from their collection.

I want to thank my husband, Dr. Melvin M. Meilach, for his patience while I traveled about tracking down material, interviewing artists, and photographing artwork. He encouraged and aided in all aspects. I appreciate the counsel and criticism of Ben Lavitt, Astra Photo Service, Inc., Chicago, who will not permit me to use any photographs of my own, or of others, that fall short of the general high level of photography required in an art book. To my typist, Marilyn Regula, who can now decipher my scribbling without a magnifying glass, go my deepest admiration and thanks.

My admiration, too, to Brandt Aymar, my editor who allows me a free hand to develop and design the book, and to his ability to see it through production with such efficiency and quality.

Note: All photographs by Dona and Mel Meilach unless otherwise credited.

Foreword

WHEN I FIRST BECAME AWARE THAT SOFT SCULPTURES WERE peeking and burrowing their forms through the ever-present maze of exciting work being shown in galleries around the country, I spoke to the artists involved. In almost every interview, the artist imagined he or she was the only one who had begun to work in this medium; and many admitted that they had been inspired by Claes Oldenburg's approach. After hearing this story, perhaps a dozen times, in as many cities, I began to mention to each artist that others were, indeed, also working along the same lines. When the first look of astonishment had passed, the usual reply was, "Of course, ideas are in the air," and soon each artist began searching and discovering others in his own vicinity who were forming soft materials into sculpture. These artists unselfishly notified me of others, until, by deadline time, I had more examples of soft sculptures than I could possibly use in three books. There were probably as many people quietly working over their sewing machines and looms as there were jewelers, potters, and painters. Space limitations necessitated selecting representative work from different artists in the media that dominated: fabrics, fibers, plastics, and latex using an astonishing variety of techniques.

SOFT SCULPTURE and Other Soft Art Forms is the first comprehensive compilation of the activity in this contemporary art movement that necessarily utilizes established methods and approaches. It proves that the creative mind can, indeed, continually find untapped avenues of expression. There is no doubt that soft sculptures will continue to be among the many art forms emerging in galleries around the world and that they will eventually become an important adjunct in museum and private collections.

SOFT SCULPTURE is a trend-setting book; it is for the professional artist and craftsman, the teacher and student anxious to learn about the new trends, the people who are setting them, and their approaches. It is filled with avant-garde stimulating, imagination-firing ideas, and applications of well-known art materials and methods with which you already may be familiar.

SOFT SCULPTURE

1

The Development of Soft Sculpture

SCULPTURES IN ORANGE AND PURPLE. Sheila Hicks. 1969. 7' high. Wrapped yarns.
Courtesy, Hyatt Regency O'Hare, Chicago

THE TERM *SOFT SCULPTURE* GENTLY SLID INTO ARTISTIC LITERAture sometime during 1968–69. Until then objects that were made of soft materials, whether they were woven of fibers, poured in rubber, or made of stuffed fabrics, were not considered "sculpture" by hard-nosed aesthetes. The word *sculpture* was reserved for wood, stone, bronze, and other traditional sculptural media. Works composed of soft materials were more apt to be called "soft forms" or "objects." Two of Claes Oldenburg's early soft objects were "Soft Typewriter" and "Soft Calendar." In time, art critics conceded that art was becoming an expression of concepts regardless of the medium or technique used. When soft materials could no longer be disregarded as a viable movement, the term *soft sculpture* was applied.

Regardless of its nomenclature at the time, the decade of the 1960s marked the emergence of soft sculpture. Fiber and fabrics, plastics, and combinations of soft and hard materials worked their way into exhibitions. Among the early happenings were the weavings of Lenore Tawney, Sheila Hicks, and Claire Zeisler. The surfaces and shapes of their woven forms moved beyond the rectangle and two-dimensionality, into relief surfaces and then into the third dimension. The fibers assumed dimensional roles as they cascaded, protruded, and thrust away from their backgrounds in knotted, twisted, braided, wrapped, and flowing cords. The artist began to explore the quality of the material and to allow this quality to become the expression of the piece. At the beginning, the pieces assumed sculptural dimension, but they were, for the most part, two-dimensional concepts with the addition of depth.

In an article in *Craft Horizons,* March/April 1969, Jack Lenor

OBJECT. Meret Oppenheim. 1936. Fur-covered cup, 4⅜" diameter; saucer, 9⅜" diameter; spoon, 8" long.
Courtesy, The Museum of Modern Art, New York

Larson, a well-known fabric designer, cites an exhibition at the Museum of Modern Art entitled *Wall Hangings.* He points out that "some of the pieces were neither wall hung nor hanging at all." The same was true in a follow-up show at the Stedelijk Museum, Amsterdam. Though Mr. Larson refers to the pieces as "objects," he describes some of them as "sculptural," thus illustrating the ambivalence of the terminology applied to the works at this time. He predicted, rightfully, that these two shows held out great hope for additional exploration.

Fulfilling this prediction, weaving soon got off the floor and the wall and became completely sculptural in many cases. The woven form began to exist in space; it related to other three-dimensional forms in the environment rather than as an isolated object. In shows that followed, weavers added nonrelated components to their wools and synthetic fibers for greater exploration. They used offerings of the hardware store and cordage company to discover new textures, materials, and forms. The words *soft sculpture* were inevitable and welcome.

A 1969 exhibit at the Whitney Museum was reviewed by Virginia Hoffman in another *Craft Horizons* article (August 1970), which was entitled "When Will Weaving Be an Art Form?" She observed that this show was a beginning for weavers who were already thinking of weaving as an expressive force rather than simply as decoration. The exhibit included many "three-dimensional forms made by flexible joinings, fibrous materials, modules with fixed beginning or end, soft materials made hard and vice versa. . . ."

At the same time that weaving was moving away from the wall, soft stuffed fabrics were coming into prominence. The innovator was Claes Oldenburg who began moving from painting to his new medium in the early 1960s. By the middle of the decade his soft objects were commanding attention for their statements as pop art. Their obvious softness caused considerable comment, but there were other aspects of the works that attracted more attention. His reviewers stressed the translation of hard objects into soft materials such as vinyls and canvases; and their tactile quality. "From the standpoint of material and structure" said one reviewer, "Oldenburg draws. Free two dimensional pencil drawings are translated into marvelous architectural structures in cut, glued and painted corrugated cardboard. From these versions, patterns are drawn for the cutting of light canvas and after the stuffed canvas version is studied, the final vinyl piece is made. Each version, drawing, cardboard, canvas and vinyl, is a succinct statement of an approach to texture and structural clarity with the superb execution completely subordinated to the image."

While the weavers were exploring textures and tactile qualities and Oldenburg's influence was being felt in many areas, artists working with other soft disciplines began to explore the use of old materials and methods into new statements. Embroiderers, or "stitchers," began to rethink the flat surface. Fabric collage, usually worked as flat rectangular presentations, began to stress materials that provided relief dimensions. Alma Lesch and Marilyn Pappas employed fabrics with raw edges, with threads that hung away from the backing and, eventually, with materials that were bunched up and stuffed for a greater relief surface.

Lee Bontecou, a renowned sculptress, built up unusual relief forms using stretched canvas that was stitched and wired over a metal armature to create an undulating softness that gave the illusion of a hard material. John Chamberlain's use of wrinkled papers in his early collages stimulated a statement similar to his wrinkled metal automobile fenders and bumpers and more recently into Plexiglas forms that exploit the properties of a soft-hard medium.

Other artists too moved from hard to soft media, sometimes combining the two. William King was among the pioneers of this blend with his vinyl, canvas, and muslin over wood to create his own statement of "people"; several are illustrated in Chapters 1 and 4. Robert Morris piled heavy slabs of industrial gray felt in many ways. Christo began wrapping objects in soft materials, and David Lee hung clear sheets of plastic from rafters. The reviewer, again avoiding the word *sculpture,* made such statements as: "One change has been the emphasis on soft, amorphous Oldenburgian constructions, works that fold and change from day to day. . . ."

Kay Sekimachi, a California weaver, manipulated nylon monofilament into three-dimensional hanging shapes. They were innovative for their approach to form and the use of cast shadows, space, and

SENNIT GOD. Society Islands, Polynesia. Knotted rope over wood.
Courtesy, Field Museum of Natural History, Chicago

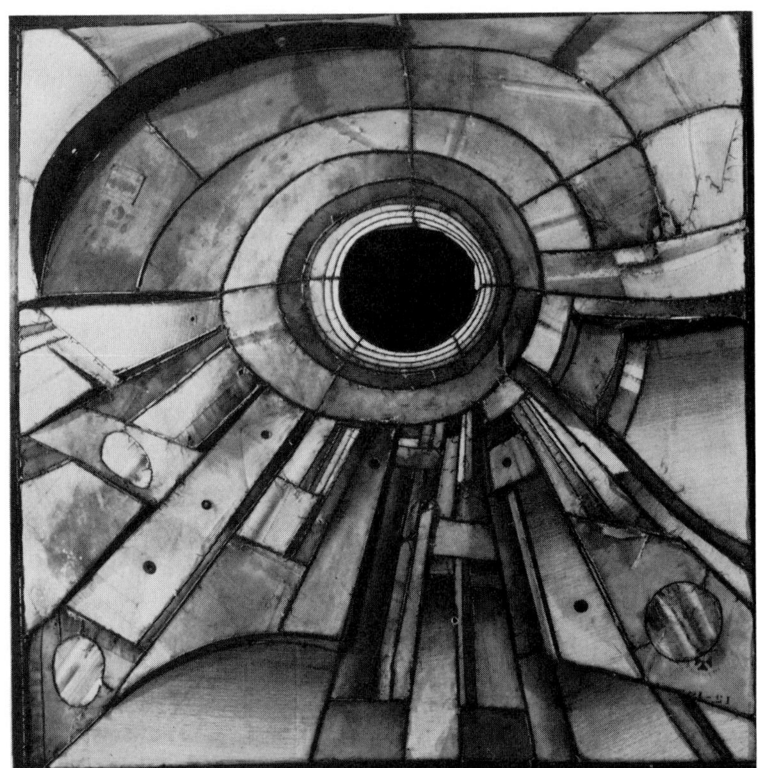

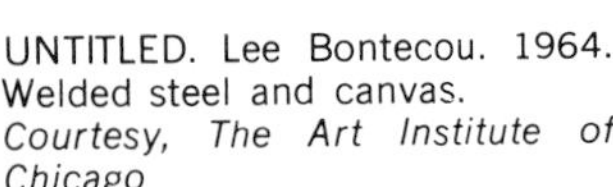
UNTITLED. Lee Bontecou. 1964. Welded steel and canvas.
Courtesy, The Art Institute of Chicago

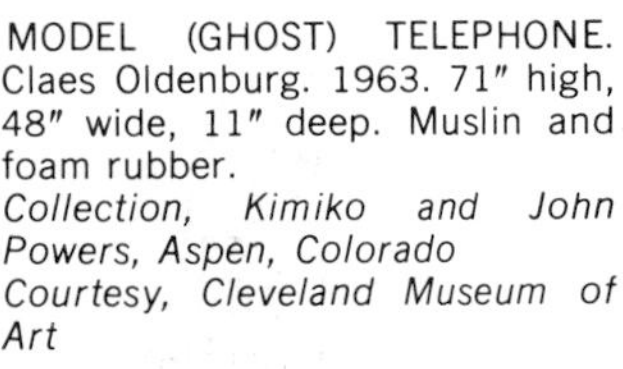
MODEL (GHOST) TELEPHONE. Claes Oldenburg. 1963. 71″ high, 48″ wide, 11″ deep. Muslin and foam rubber.
Collection, Kimiko and John Powers, Aspen, Colorado
Courtesy, Cleveland Museum of Art

material. The hangings were lightweight and transparent and among the early weavings to be defined as dimensional sculpture.

Clayton Bailey and Tom Ladousa, working with liquid latex, usually associated with mold making for metal sculpture, explored the potential of this industrially oriented process for stuffed soft forms and the techniques are illustrated in Chapter 9. Howard Woody's application of polyethylene in relation to atmosphere and environments is destined to be another direction that merits continued investigation.

As these inventive artists became excited about the direction of their media, they exposed them to classes and workshops. Their students of the late 1960s, now craftsmen in their own right, continued to carry the concepts of soft sculpture far beyond the expectations of the writers who reviewed the soft shows in the 1960s. By 1970 the activity of artists employing and delving further into statements offered by these versatile materials was astonishing.

In November 1971, the importance of weaving as sculpture burst upon the art world with the exhibition *Deliberate Entanglements* held at the University of California in Los Angeles; it toured several cities and was shown in major art museums the following year. Weavers who had already begun to explore spatial concepts were involved in monolithic and monumental works. The thirteen invited exhibitors who proved the trend was international included Magdalena Abakanowicz (Poland), Neda Al-Hilali (California), Olga de Amaral (Colombia), Tadek Beutlich (England), Jagoda Buić (Yugoslavia), Francoise Grossen (New York), Sheila Hicks (France), Ritzi and Peter Jacobi (Germany), Aurelia Muñoz (Spain), Walter Nottingham (Wisconsin), Kay Sekimachi (California), Dorian Zachai (New Hampshire), and Claire Zeisler (Illinois).

The exhibitors, as well known in the fiber arts as Marc Chagall is in painting, substantiated the direction of weaving as a three-dimensional art. The theme of that show, *Fiber as Medium,* was furthered by a follow-up exhibition at New York's Museum of Contemporary Crafts in January 1972 entitled *Sculpture in Fiber.* And in April 1973, another show, sponsored by the same museum, was entitled *Sewn, Stitched and Stuffed.* The first show exhibited woven and non-woven fiber forms; the second concentrated on stuffed fabrics as a sculptural medium. At the same time, several smaller shows with similar scopes were sponsored in museums and galleries throughout the country, which gave further attention and direction to the burgeoning movement.

Working artists were fired with enthusiasm. Soft materials began to appear at art and craft showings along with traditional media. Frequently artists combined soft materials with metals, woods, and clays, so that soft sculpture was not necessarily an entity for its own sake: the sculptures became entities in themselves. The importance was the message, the expressiveness and the concept that was brought to the viewer. In addition, the viewer was expected to contribute by responding and being involved.

Eventually, some of the soft pieces became environmental; the tactile senses were involved and the viewer was invited to touch, to change the object, to move the parts or the shaping. In an early interview Claes Oldenburg lamented the policy of many museums that do not allow a viewer to touch an object. He spoke of the necessity of being able to achieve a yielding surface, one which could be moved and still not affect the movement of the piece that is part of the inherent forming of the sculpture. He felt other people should be involved in the sculptures, not only the artist.

GIANT SOFT FAN. Claes Oldenburg. 1966–67. 10′ high 10′ 4″ wide, 6′ 4″ deep. Vinyl, wood, and foam rubber.
Gift of Sidney and Harriet Janis, Collection, The Museum of Modern Art, New York

ZILTI-DUSH-JHINI. John Chamberlain. 1970. 33″ high, 45″ wide, 37″ deep. Melted Plexiglas hardened.
Courtesy, Leo Castelli Gallery, New York

FATE. William King. 1964. 84½″ high. Burlap and aluminum.
Courtesy, Terry Dintenfass, Inc., New York

As the vitality of soft sculpture has heightened, the artist has, inevitably, explored beyond the use of fibers and fabrics to achieve his statement. Examples throughout the book illustrate the various materials that are called into play including leathers and furs, feathers, plastics, wire screening, soft metals, rubber, and so on. The techniques employed include mainly weaving and sewing, but also knitting, crochet, stitchery, knotting, braiding, and others. In short, any material, any technique is fair game. The ultimate question regarding any work is not only how it employs the media, but is it good sculpturally?

The artist who works in soft sculpture has ready inspirational sources among useful and ceremonial objects of primitive cultures. Several examples have been included in Chapter 2 and throughout the book to illustrate forms used by African and Oceanic craftsmen. Nature, always a prime source for form and pattern, is also an inspiration for soft sculpture. Sometimes, a new twist of thinking and seeing is required to translate visual images into soft art and, through photos and examples, you are encouraged to observe how artists have been able to accomplish this transition. You can readily adapt these images

CASCADE. Claire Zeisler. 1968. 30″ high. Natural jute. Wrapping and knotting.
Collection, Dr. Robert Sager, Peoria, Illinois
Photo, Jonas Dovydėnas

THE WAY TO DO IS TO BE. Janice Ring. 1972. 10′ high, 2′ wide. Jute, wool yarns, velvet fabric.
Courtesy, artist

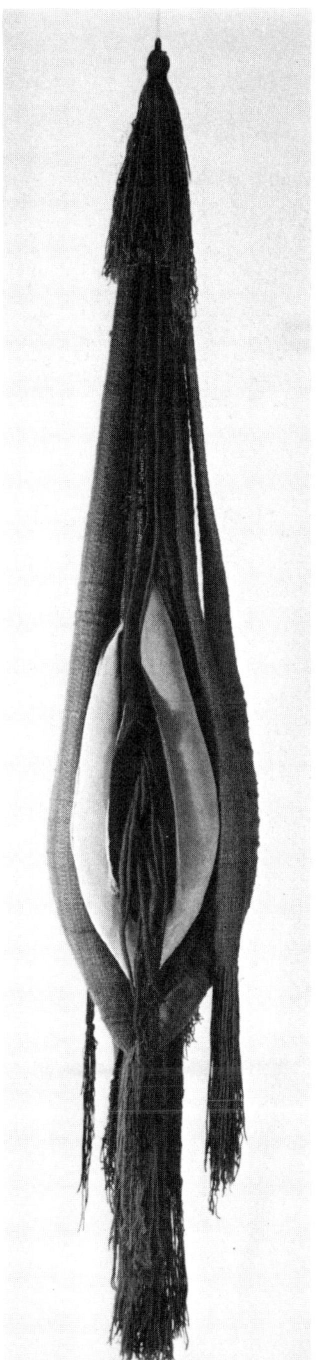

to your work in your own individualistic manner.

Art curators, restorers, and collectors whose orientation to art leans to traditional materials often find the concept of soft art disconcerting. They fear the materials may not stand the test of time. They recognize that it is an important movement, but they worry that the pieces will not last long enough to represent our culture two thousand years from now. The artists simply shrug their shoulders. The new materials are the media by which they experiment, create, and represent the time in which they are living. They feel that art should be bought and appreciated for our own lifetimes; what someone finds two thousand years from now is not their concern.

Soft sculpture, already a motivating form of expression for serious artists and craftsmen is, however, still in its infancy. There is a rich vein of materials and ideas to be tapped for the statements that will evolve from the 1970s and continue unabated to influence future creativity. As the curators worry about permanence, who knows? That may be the message of the art form itself as it relates to the environment and to the universe.

2

Construction and Ideas for Inspiration

THE APPROACHES TO THE CREATION OF A SOFT SCULPTURE ARE as numerous and varied as the artists who do them. Some artists work from drawings as carefully made up as a blueprint. Others prefer to let the work "happen"; the forms grow from the inside out. Each piece is individual and unique; therefore, it is impossible to provide instructions for duplication. Nor is it the purpose of this chapter to suggest that the reader duplicate the works shown. Its function is to show how some problems that usually are part of the creative process are met and overcome and some of the shortcuts for solving them.

Individual problems that arise generally deal with what to create, what materials to use, and the size of the piece. Small sculptures usually have simple solutions; larger pieces may require armatures and rigging to work with them as they increase in size and weight. Generally, each piece will dictate the type of armature or support required, and arriving at a solution may require technological help. Often it is necessary for the artist to have access to, or be versed in metal and wood work, so that many disciplines combine in the final creative endeavor.

Stuffing Materials

Characteristics of the materials used for stuffing different forms, weavings, and fabrics will be discussed in the related chapters. But for all techniques the stuffing and padding materials may be new to you, and the general rule is to use anything that will serve the purpose and is available and inexpensive. Much depends on the size and final presentation of the sculpture. The following materials, used for stuffing in the examples shown throughout the book, will lead you to a

FEATHER IDOL. Hawaii. Feathers combined with other materials and attached to backings and stuffed forms may be found in many primitive cultures and adapted to modern sculptures. *Courtesy, Field Museum of Natural History, Chicago*

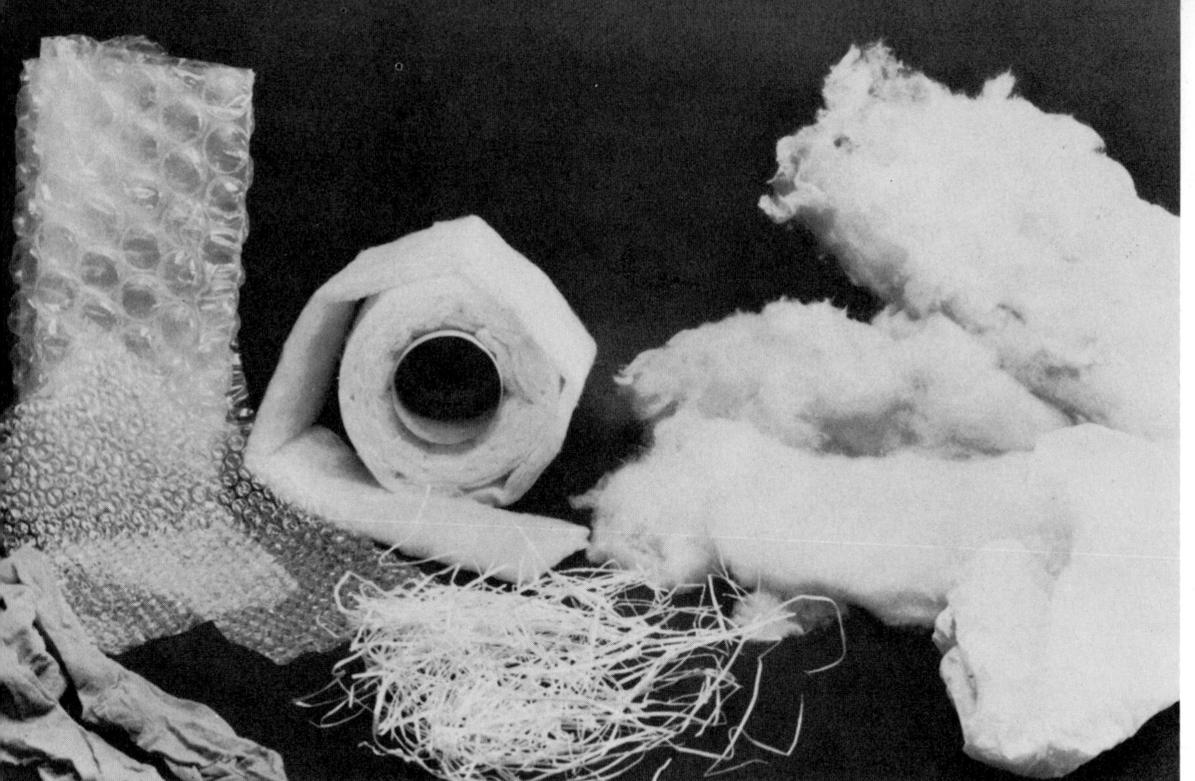

Soft materials used for stuffing include: Dacron batting, polyester, Styrofoam blocks and pellets, foam rubber, cotton batting, kapok, straw, nylon stockings, crumpled and shredded papers, rags.

search for new and used items that will suffice. They include second-hand mattresses cut up, foam rug padding, old pillow material, rock wool insulation, and other builder's insulation materials, feathers, cotton batting, Dacron batting, hay or straw, newspaper balls, old nylon stockings, polyurethane, polystyrene pellets and batting, bubble paper, cork, art foam, Styrofoam, steel wool, and lightweight rubber used in brassiere padding. For stiffening and quilting, interfacing is sold under several trade names such as Sta-Shape, Pellon, Milium, and so forth. Sewing counters, hardware stores, upholsterer's and builder's suppliers, and companies that make or sell packing supplies are logical suppliers of the materials. Foam particles are also sold in dime and discount stores and are used for stuffing pillows. Old nylon hose, rags, yarns, and clothes are also among the commonly used materials for stuffing.

Used materials can be culled from old furniture, bedding, and so forth and can be found at rummage and garage sales. An association with industrial firms that have waste foam, mattress padding, packing materials, and so on that may be discarded is very helpful. Many communities have "swap your throwaways" days when unwanted items, placed at the curbs, can yield all kinds of objects that the artist can creatively recycle at no cost.

Patterns

For those who like to work from a sketch, and methodically reproduce the sketch into paper patterns, the shortcut involves learning how to think of the object as simple shapes. Claes Oldenburg relates that he had to decide which object to make by observing how simple

they would be to re-create in fabric and then vinyl or other material. At the beginning it is advisable to create forms that require only a few pieces that can be assembled easily. Enlarge the drawing onto tissue or pattern paper (available at sewing supply counters) and then into fabric. If you are not sure of the assembly, make a model in muslin or scrap fabric before working in the final material.

Fabrics

Generally, one must grapple with problems of permanency when creating soft sculptures. It is unlikely, but not impossible, that sculptures created from cloth will last as long as those made from stone, wood, or metals. When selecting fabrics for stuffing, threads for weaving, and cords for knotting, you must consider the strength of the materials and their colorfastness. Almost all dyed fibers fade in time and with exposure to sun and light. With certain works of art, fading will not be important; but where permanent color is an essential quality of the work, you will have to select those fabrics that are guaranteed fast color. If you are designing your own fabrics, be sure you use quality dyes and follow all recommended procedures for fixing colors.

Assembly

In the early stages of a form, and in a model, one can baste, clip, or staple a piece together. For the final piece, more permanent hand or machine sewing is necessary. On many pieces the sewing must be very precise and require the work of a good seamstress. If you are using such fabrics as plastic-backed vinyl, leathers, furs, double knits,

Patterns for stuffed pieces can be cut from paper first, then transferred to fabrics. Four pattern parts are required to create the structure for a small stuffed airplane (part of a series of airplanes) used in a mobile. Benita Cullinan.

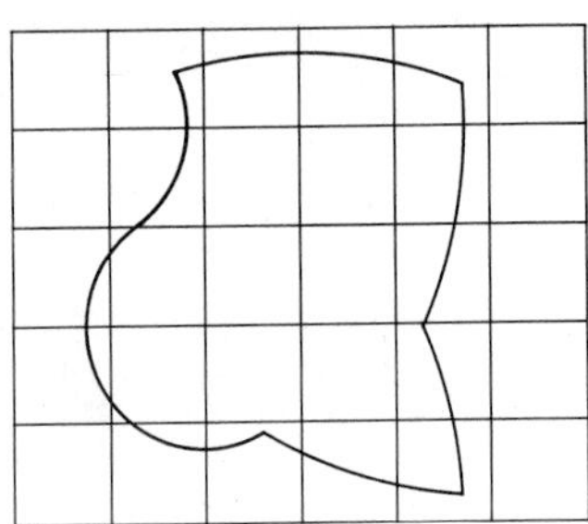

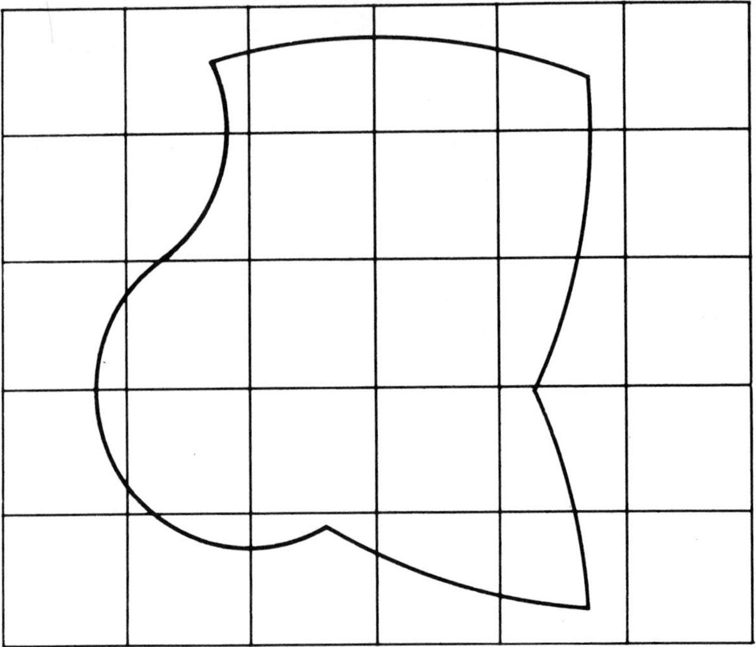

There are various ways of enlarging or reducing designs so all parts are in proportion. The easiest is to square off a pattern and then enlarge or reduce the squares and the parts within according to the size you want.

You can enlarge from a drawing by either of two methods:
a) Place a piece of screen wire over the drawing and square it off.
b) Transfer the original design to graph paper.
Once the piece is squared off, you then change the size accordingly. For instance, if your grid squares are ½" and you want to make the pattern three times the size, then make a new grid with squares 1½" each and draw the necessary portions in each comparable square.

You can also enlarge a drawing by having it photostated to any size you want. This is more expensive than tracing it yourself but it is quick and accurate. Photostats are made by services that reproduce blueprints: They can be found in the classified pages.

and others that may present sewing problems, a muslin pattern or a small mock-up for the piece in actual materials is suggested. Also, practice sewing on scraps of the material to assure proper needles, machine settings, and threads. A sewing machine is practically a must for stuffed fabrics. Fiber works can be accomplished by loom and by hand-working methods.

Armatures

Many concepts require that the soft sculpture be held or supported by a metal or wood armature. Throughout the book sculptures illustrate the use of these armatures in different ways. Some are completely hidden; others make a frank use of the armature and let parts of it show along with the woven or padded form itself. Jeanne Board-

RETURN TO QUIETISM. Janice Ring. 1972. 6′ high, 2′ wide. Wool yarn, burlap, raku beads, marine cord, velvet upholstery fabric. *Left* (detail).
Free-form pieces must often be constructed as they are worked; no basic technique may apply to every piece. This hanging was done on a frame and combined weaving with fabric. Weaving was done, the velvet form was manipulated, pinned, and stuffed, then sewn in place, and weaving continued. Additional woven portions were assembled later. Beads and macramé were added last.
Courtesy, artist

man Knorr exploits the design of the armature purposely and may build her sculpture on its form.

Other Materials

Portions of a relief or three-dimensional form may require stiffening of some kind, alone, or in addition to padding. This is especially true of stitcheries, crochet, and knit pieces that can be backed with heavy canvas such as those used for needlepoint and rug making; often the mesh can be used to work into. For collage reliefs, tent canvas, screen, muslin, and other materials can be selected depending on the fabrics and objects to be used on the surface. In every instance the artist must seek out the materials that are available and that can be manipulated to serve his needs.

FLOW AS LIFE FLOWS. Janice Ring. 4′ high, 6′ wide. Jute, wool, and silk yarns, velvet fabric, and Dacron stuffing. Details illustrate the use of multiple fabrics, yarns, and techniques in one work.
Photos, courtesy, artist

Detail of center stuffed form.

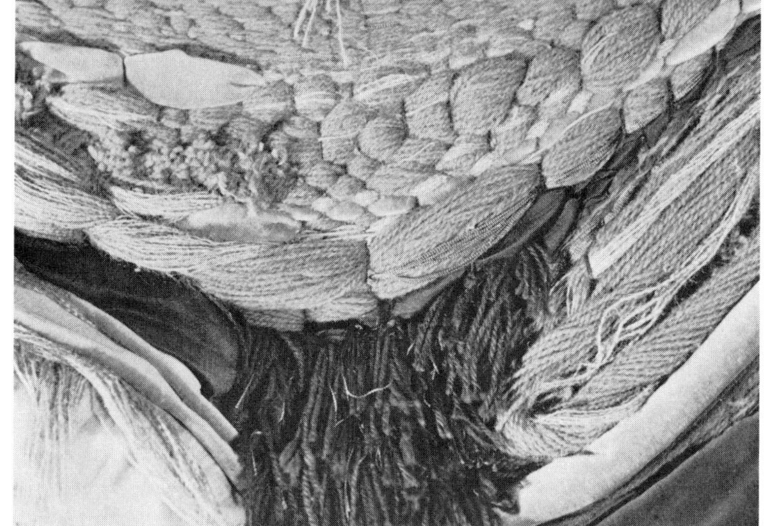

Detail of top woven area. A large clump of yarn was set in place and finger woven.

Detail of layered areas of fabric.

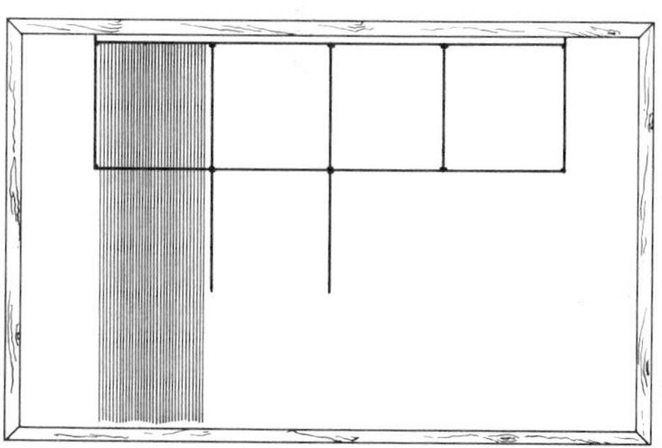

Setup for working includes a wood frame warped with nylon cable cord and jute. The warp is reinforced with steel rods to support the weight of the stuffed fabric forms. The steel form is mounted to the top of the frame. Fabrics are sewn invisibly into place and some areas of the fabrics are stuffed. An interfacing on the back of the hanging also acts as a support for the stitching and sewing.

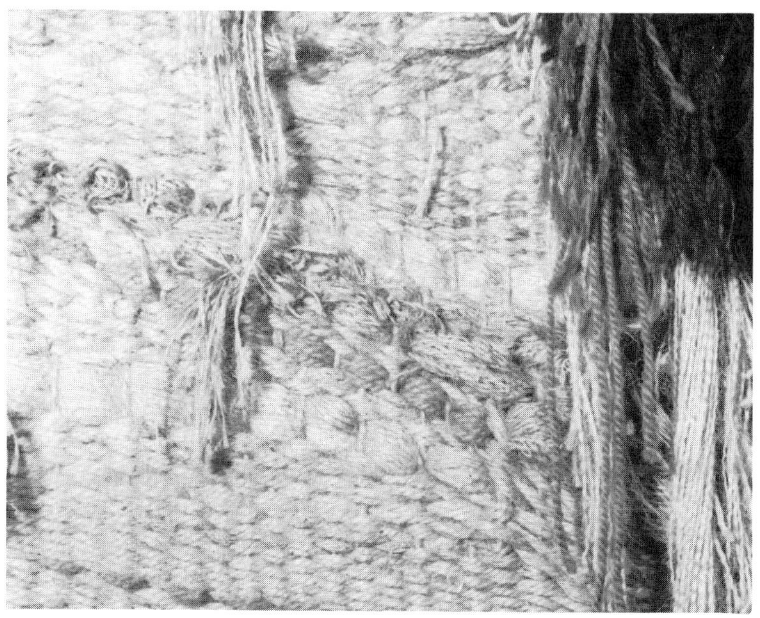

Detail of left side shows the use of various yarns and multiples of yarns and jute with loose and tight weaves.

Students at Roosevelt University, Chicago, prepare soft parts for an indoor garden under the supervision of instructor Don Baum. Pieces are cut and sewn on a machine.

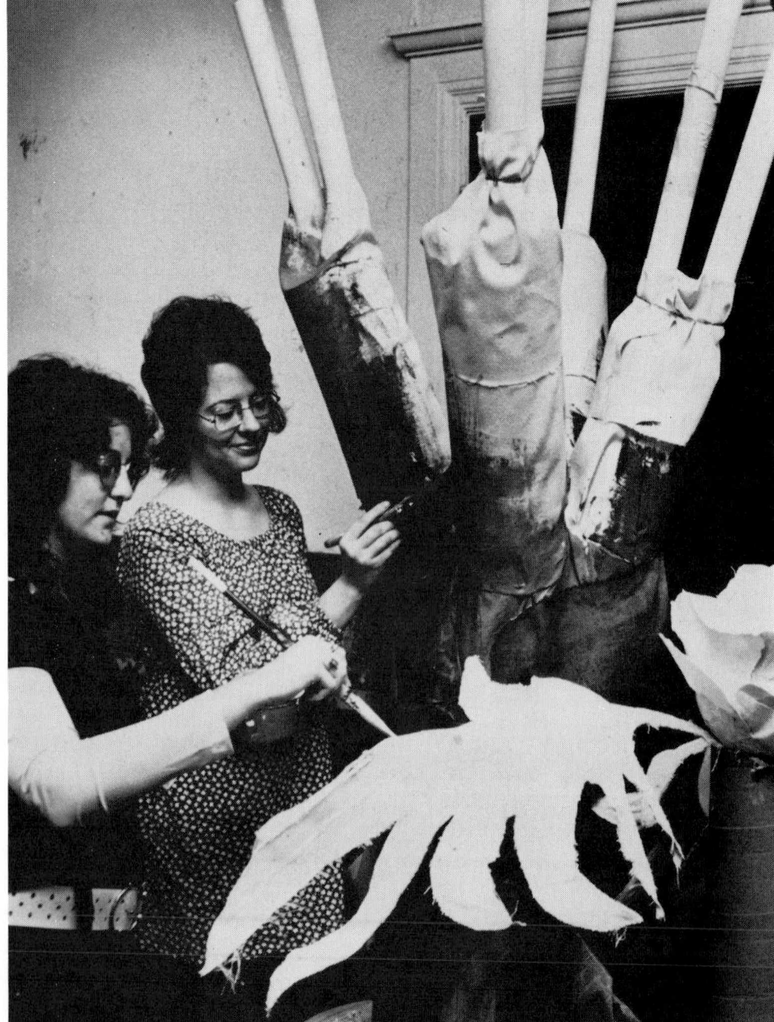

Assembly involves an armature of wood or wire where necessary, then stuffing and wrapping. The fabrics may be drawn upon and painted.

Photos, Allan Weber

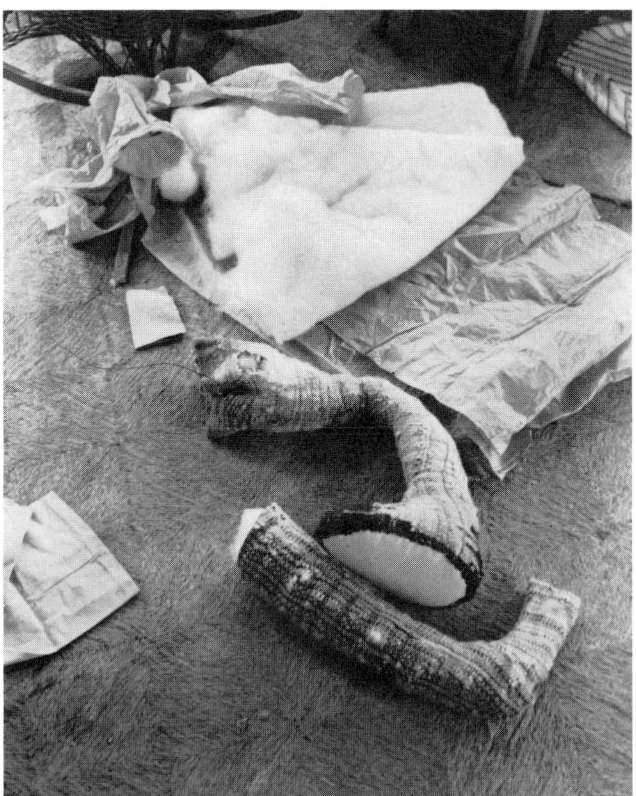

Parts of an animal are made from double-woven tubes formed and stuffed with Dacron batting. Dorothy Zeidman Lipski.

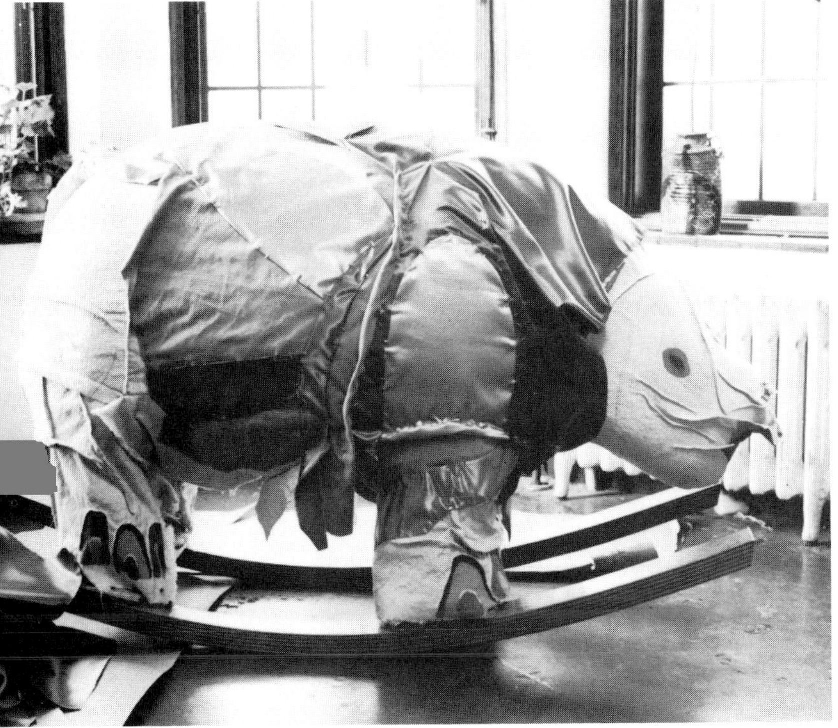

ROCKING RHINO. Dorothy Zeidman Lipski. 4′ high, 5′ wide. In progress photo shows the colored fabrics pinned in place. The understructure is hand-carved Styrofoam; it is covered with Fiberglas cloth and epoxy resin and then two layers of Dacron batting. The color changes of the fabric are used to accent the body proportions.

Photos, courtesy, artist

Sally Dillon prepares for an exhibition. Scale is an important aspect of soft sculpture. The stuffing and preparation may necessitate stringing a piece from a ceiling or rafter to get the feel of it; to make sure it works. Says Ms. Dillon, "The size of my sculpture varies with my mood. Somedays my thoughts are turned inward and the sculptures are small and precious. Somedays I relate well to other people and the sculptures are my size and handleable. Other days I feel aggressive and happy and the sculptures burst the confines of the room and envelop me."

Photos, artist

Sculptures on exhibit. Sally Dillon. They vary in size from tiny to monumental.

TOTEM (in progress). Gloria Bornstein. Rubber tubing is worked in wickerwork and twining techniques. A superstructure is strung across the ceiling from hooks in the molding.

Close-up of the rubber tubing.
Photos, Lee Sims

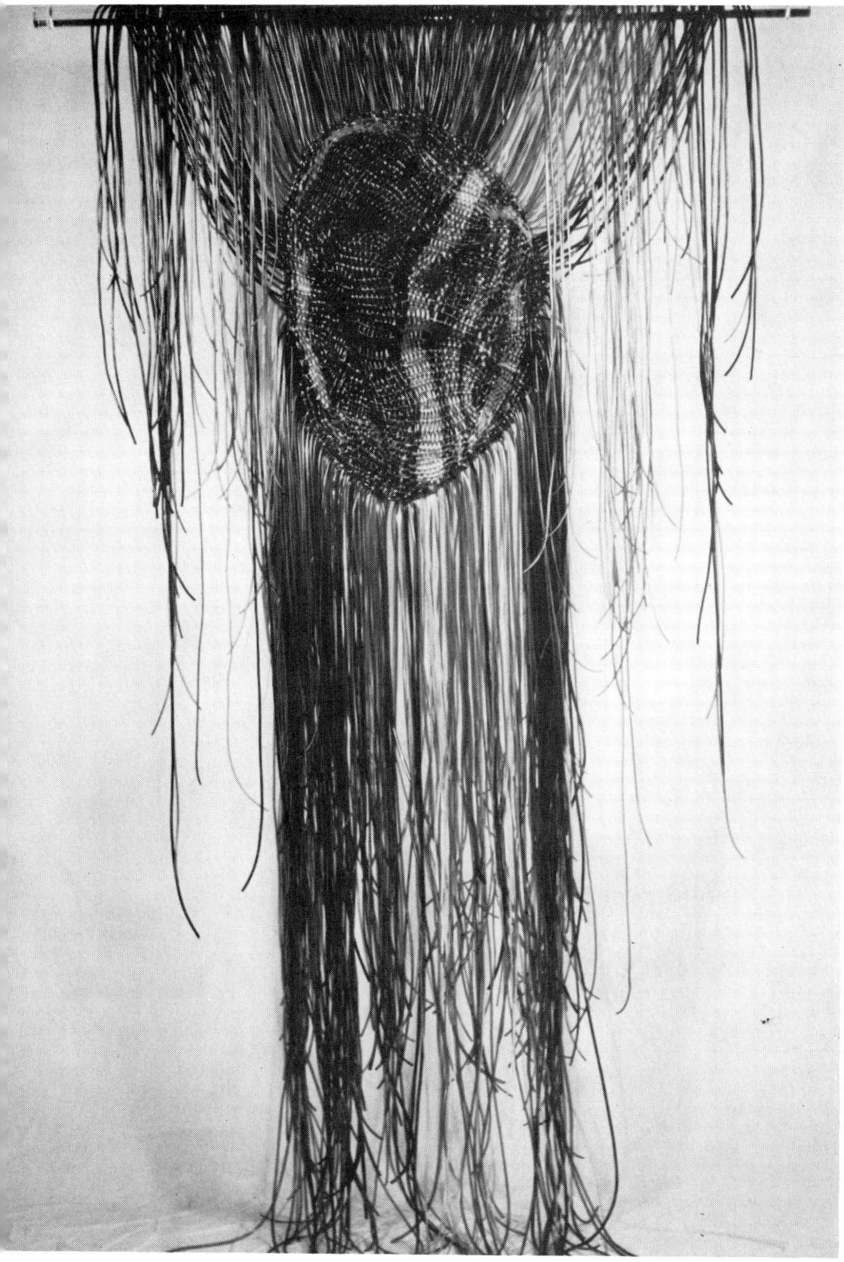

TOTEM. Gloria Bornstein. Finished piece, front view.
Below: other side.
Photos, Chuck Rowe

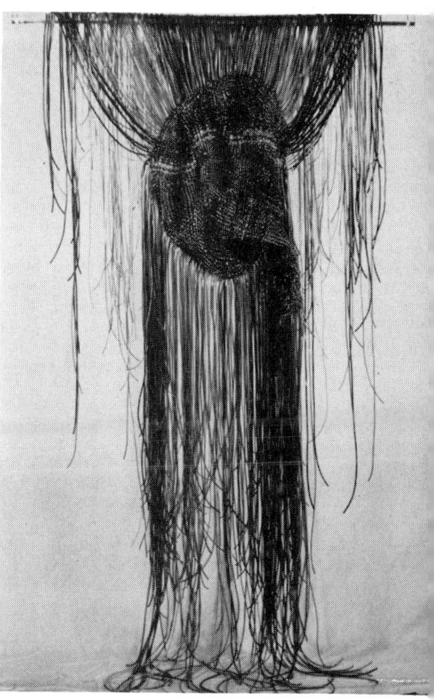

CEREMONIAL FEATHER MASK.
Awar, New Guinea.

PROCESSION, New Guinea.

INSPIRATION . . . IS WHERE YOU SEE IT

Every artist does not have access to the vast facilities of large museums and photographic libraries throughout the country. Nor does everyone think of using these facilities as inspirations for materials, combinations of materials, forms, and techniques. Therefore, photos from primitive art and from nature that have, or could have, inspired some of the objects illustrated are included. These are offered to inspire form and ideas for combining materials for soft sculpture.

The majority of examples from primitive cultures combine soft materials, such as rope, leather, fabrics, with one another and with hard materials. Others are not necessarily soft, but they could easily

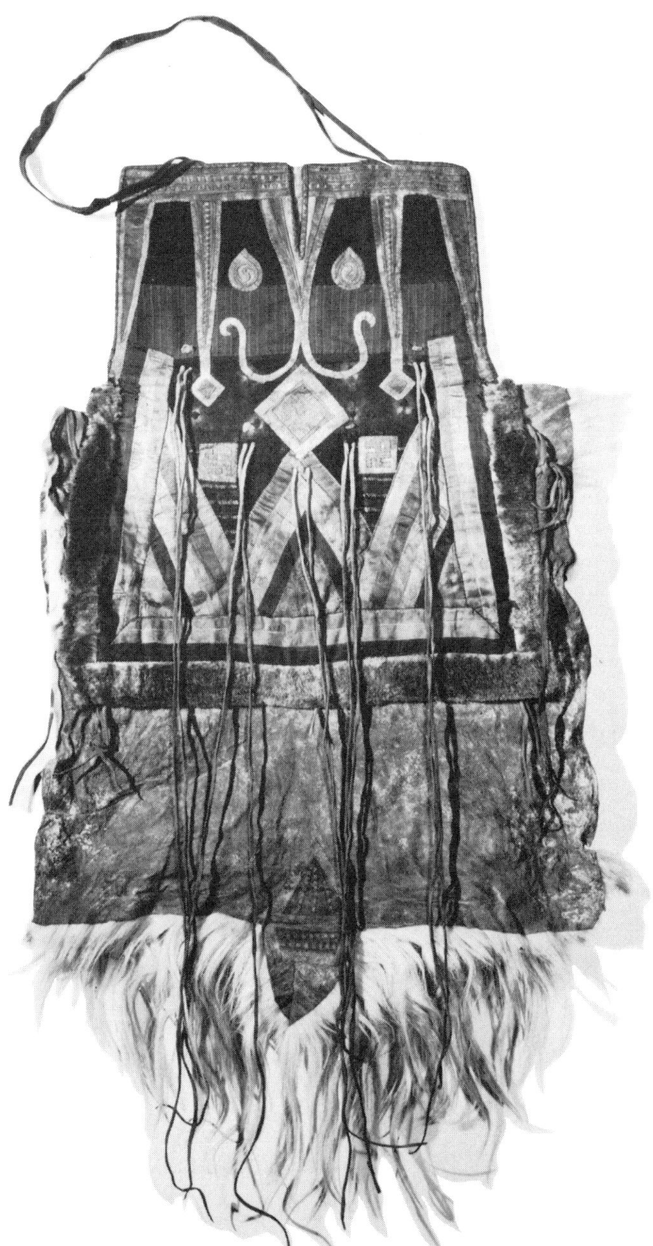

DANCE APRON. Leather, wool, silk, fur.

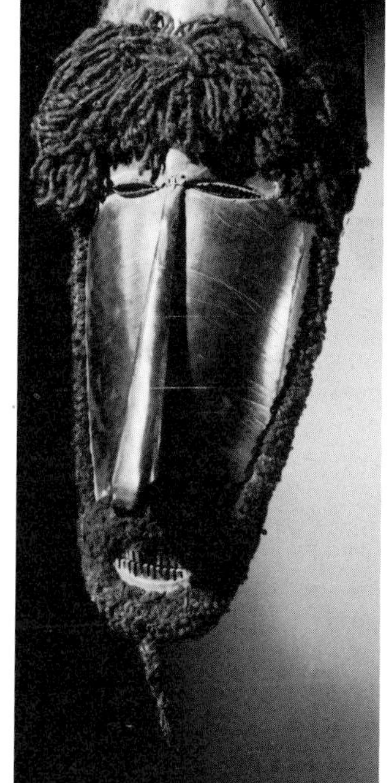

TURTLE SHELL MASK. Tortoiseshell with leather and fiber.
All photos, courtesy, Field Museum of Natural History, Chicago

be interpreted into soft materials. For example, the Benin bronze figure might inspire a stuffed fabric with rope around it; or an idea for a body covering accomplished with macramé or weaving. The Man and Woman by Michi Ouchi (page118)have certain resemblances to this bronze piece.

The photos of man-made and natural objects illustrate images that can inspire soft sculpture, or details of sculptures, by their design, pattern, appendages, and so forth.

The procedure usually involves studying the object, collating the idea it gives you. Each viewer adds his own set of experiences and

DRUM. Cock Island, Polynesia.

SKULL. Marquesas, Polynesia.

ideas to what he sees, so that six artists could interpret the same photo into several different finished sculptures using stuffed fabrics, weaving, knotting, knitting, or liquid latex. You are free to use one or more materials and techniques. Certainly think of adapting one line or shape in an individual photo and team it with parts from other photos to take off in your own creative directions.

Once you train yourself to adapt all or parts of the visual images you see around you, and to look for ideas in everyday objects that are readily available for visual digestion, you will readily recognize their form and design potentials.

FEATHER FINGER RINGS. Marquesas, Polynesia.

BRONZE HEAD. Benin, Africa. 16th century.

CEREMONIAL COURT HAT. Worn by Manchu princess. Peking, China.

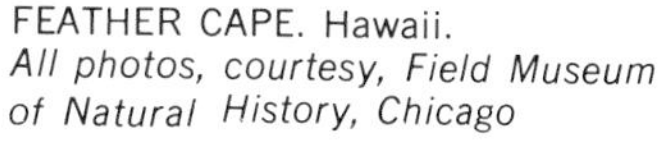

FEATHER CAPE. Hawaii.
All photos, courtesy, Field Museum of Natural History, Chicago

A NATIVE'S PACK IN TUNISIA.

ROPE AROUND A HOLDING DEVICE.

BALED BARBED WIRE.

POLYURETHANE FOAM.

BROKEN COCONUT.

A CATERPILLAR'S DISCARDED SKIN.

CACTUS.

THE HEAD OF A PARROT.

THE FIN AND SCALES OF A FISH.

seeds and typical
burial walk.

3

Relief Soft Art

THE RELIEF DIMENSION IN SOFT ART IS AN INTRIGUING OFFSHOOT of the combination of fabric collage and traditional quilting techniques. The result is usually a brilliantly colored work rich in shimmering textured fabrics that exploit the changes of light and shadow on the surfaces. Satins, silks, rayons, velvets, wet-look synthetics, shantungs, and moiré satins are favored materials because of their color and light-bouncing qualities. To people who are interested in traditional quilting, its application to new art forms is another surprise showing the ability of the innovative mind to apply old techniques to contemporary statements.

There are two basic approaches to designing for relief soft art:

1. The artist conceives a design and then appliqués different materials to one another. In this method he may work much like the collage artist but he usually sews the pieces of cloth rather than gluing them.

2. The artist uses a piece of predesigned fabric and works the padded forms into the design. The fabric may be a commercially printed pattern or it may be one the artist has designed himself by batik, tie dye, silk screen, block printing, and so forth.

In both methods the surfaces may be enriched with other materials such as ribbons, scraps of fur or leather, beads, and stitched details.

The construction is usually related to any of the three basic quilting techniques, but often the artist isn't aware that he is employing quilting methods; he simply does whatever will yield the effect he wishes to convey.

COVERING MY TRACES. Anne Raymo. 1972. 64″ high, 48″ wide. Machine appliqué and quilting with satin fabrics.
Courtesy, Terry Dintenfass, Inc., New York

PRIEST'S SMALL YELLOW SILK HAT. Tibetan. 20th century; collected in 1936. China, Jansu Province, Labrang.
Courtesy, Field Museum of Natural History, Chicago

Quilting techniques used for soft relief art may involve three layers of cloth: a top layer, a middle layer of a thick material used for the padding, and a bottom layer as a lining. If the stitching and padding are not orderly, an additional lining may be used for a fourth layer.

There are three types of quilting: 1) *English quilting* involves the three layers of cloth, as above, all the same size, which are held together by sewing. The sewing may follow the fabric pattern as opposed to: 2) *Italian quilting,* which involves stitches that run in parallel lines. Italian quilting also differs from English quilting in that only two layers of fabric are sewn together; the padded layer is omitted, then only the back layer is slit between the parallel lines and stuffing is pushed in; the slit layer is then sewn up by hand. The result is a quilt with both flat and stuffed layers. 3) *Trapunto* is another Italian version of quilting using two layers but the design is not restricted to parallel lines. Therefore, the trapunto method is more versatile for the contemporary artist.

UNTITLED (detail). Anna M. Sunnergren. Silk and velveteen with Dacron stuffing. Wall hanging using the quilting technique with machine stitching.

Courtesy, artist

But today's artist often develops his own technique. He may make a "pocket" in two layers of fabric and stuff this shape as shown in the demonstration on page 34. A completely padded extra shape may be incorporated onto the surface of the work. This may be made much as a throw pillow for a couch and then stitched to the background.

Another technique is to bond the fabric to a sheet of foam rubber either by gluing or sewing. This gives a soft padded background to which other padded shapes may be sewn.

Modern sewing machines are a boon to the artist because a variety of linear qualities can easily be achieved by changing the type of stitch: satin, zigzag, buttonhole, overcast, and so forth. Anne Raymo uses her machine to write calligraphy directly on the fabric in colored thread. Hand stitching is also included in many of the works. (See page 181 for embroidery stitches.)

Further imagery can be applied with textile paints and waterproof felt-tip pens, if desired.

Quilt in progress. The design is placed against the soft backing, the padding, and a lining fabric so all three layers are stitched together simultaneously.

Soft relief forms can be created in a design by making a pocketlike portion where the relief padding is to appear. Sew an extra piece of lining onto the back of the design but only stitch three sides.

Stuff the resulting "pocket" with a soft material such as polyester, Dacron, until it is as thick as you like.

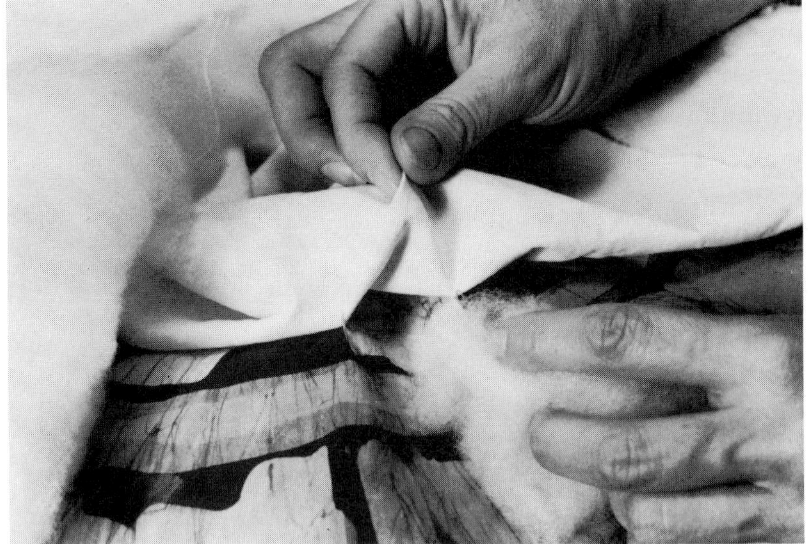

Then complete the stitching on the fourth side. A "zipper foot" has been placed on the machine to permit the stitching to be as close to the shape as possible.

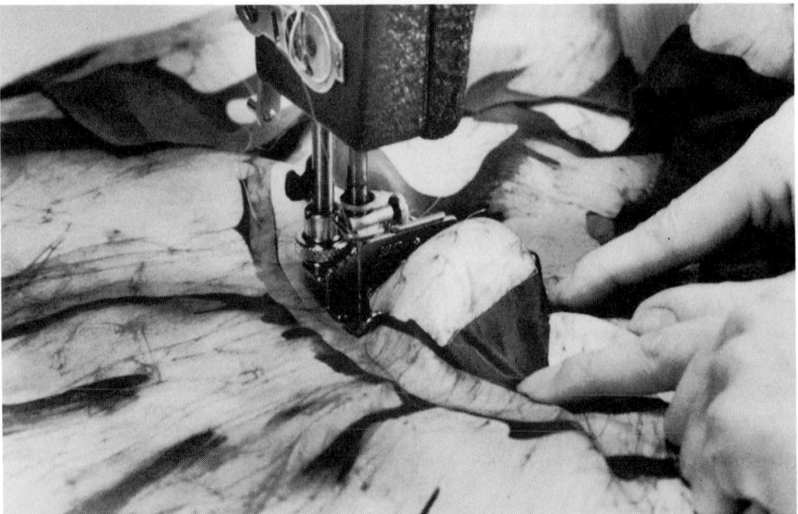

SATIN LIPSTICKS. Coral Onopa. 1973. 20″ high, 16″ wide. Relief designs include stuffed shapes made, as on opposite page, against a straight stitched quilted type background. Colors are vivid in shiny satin fabrics.
Courtesy, artist

WATER FAUCET. Coral Onopa. 1973. 14″ high, 11″ wide. Gray and white satin are stitched to a foam-rubber pad for the soft backing; other shapes stand out as relief dimensions.
Courtesy, artist

Opposite page:
THE COVER. Mary Lou Higgins. 1972. 44″ high, 26″ wide. Quilted satin wall hanging with block-printed design.

Photo, Ed Higgins

HOMAGE TO KLIMT. Marilyn Howard. 1972. 72″ high, 25″ wide. A fabric assemblage including satin bonded to foam rubber, cotton, satin, velvet, silk, beading, ribbon, Dacron filling, fur fabric border, buttons, and self-cording.

Photo, Rupert Garcia

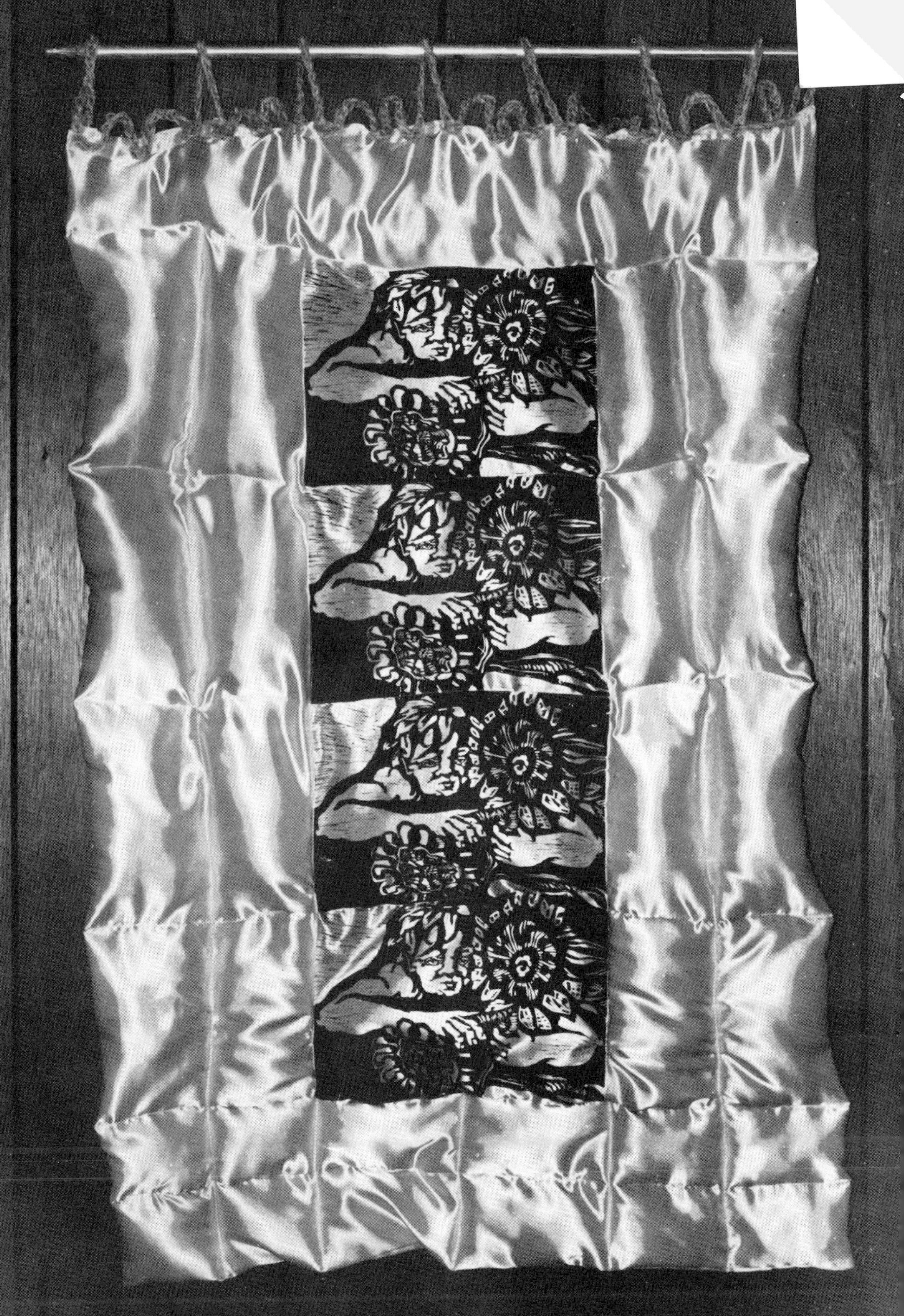

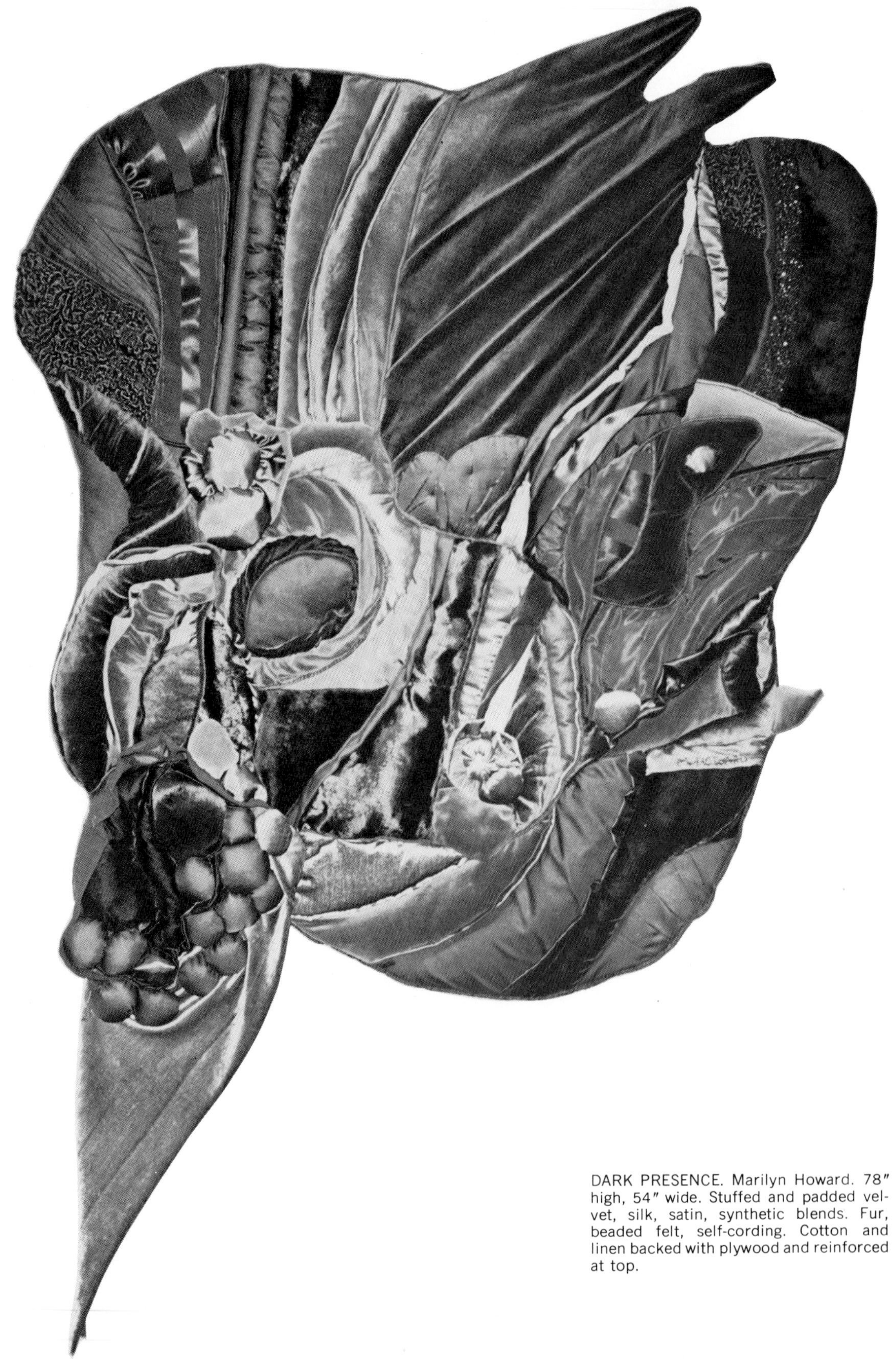

DARK PRESENCE. Marilyn Howard. 78″ high, 54″ wide. Stuffed and padded velvet, silk, satin, synthetic blends. Fur, beaded felt, self-cording. Cotton and linen backed with plywood and reinforced at top.

WOODLAND SPIRIT. Marilyn Howard. 85″ high, 43″ wide. Fabrics stuffed and padded with Dacron, as above. Fabric-covered buttons added.

WINTER HEDGEROWS. Marilyn Howard. 44″ high, 45″ wide. Same as above but with leather and antique lace.

Photos, courtesy, artist

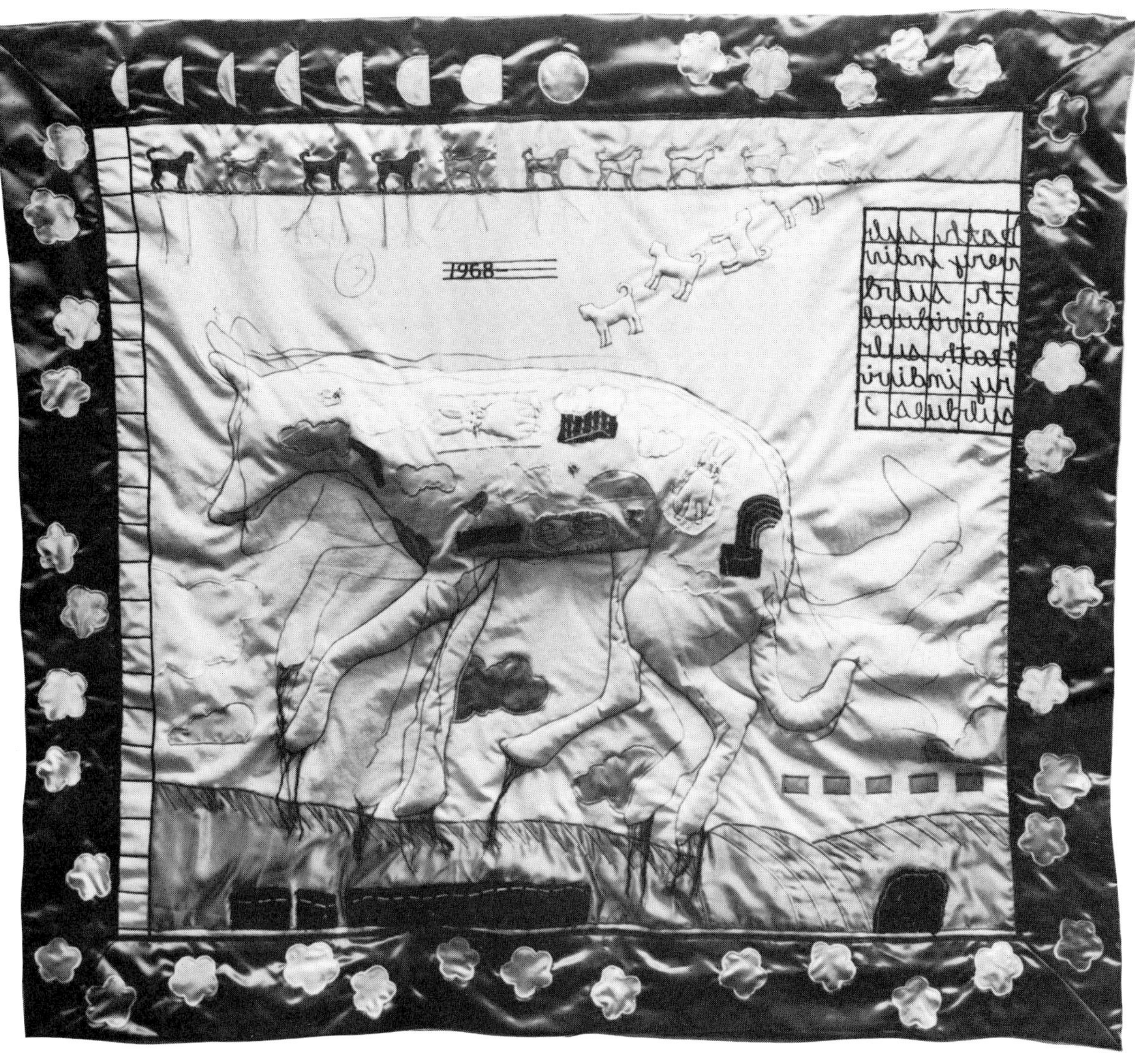

SHROUD. Anne Raymo. 1970. 53″ high, 60″ wide. Fabric collage with padding, appliqué, machine stitching. *Courtesy, Terry Dintenfass, Inc., New York*

Opposite page:
JUNGLE WATERHOLE. John Mulder. 1972. 38″ high, 28″ wide. Batik on silk with animals stuffed in the trapunto technique to create a high-relief contrast with the flat background.

Opposite page:
UNTITLED. M. Joan Lintault. 81″ high, 44″ wide. The trapunto method is used for an entire wall hanging of cotton polyester stuffed with Dacron.
Courtesy, artist

ON THE INSIDE LOOKING OUT. E. Krause. 1972. 3″ square. The shade and window reveal a landscape that is reversed on the other side and retitled ON THE OUTSIDE LOOKING IN.
Photographed at the American Craftsman Gallery, Chicago

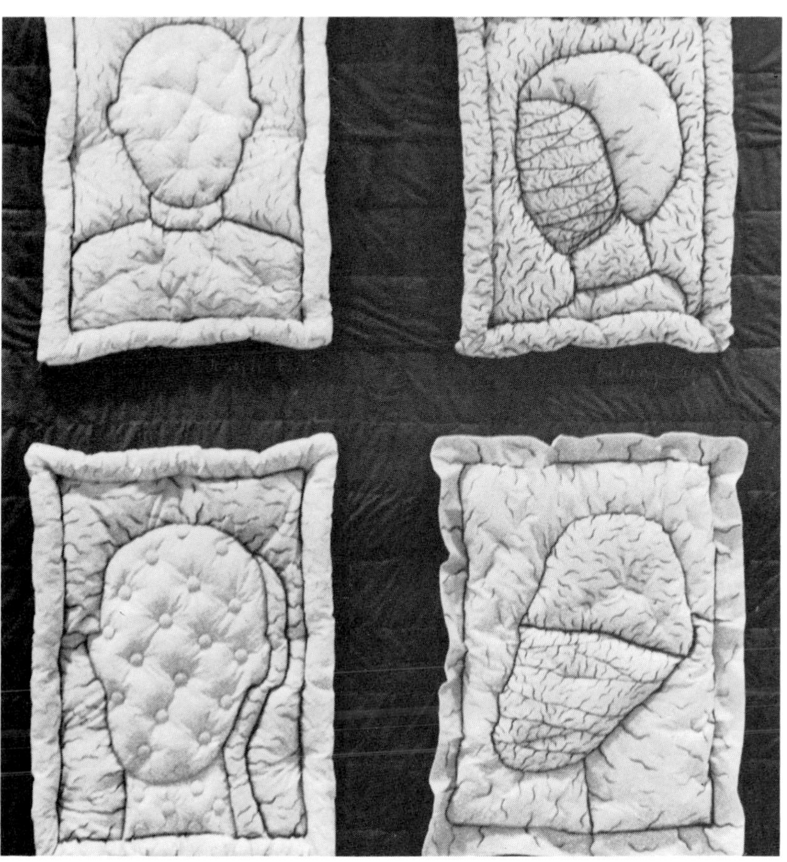

PORTRAITS (detail). Julia Schmitt. 1972. Four of approximately sixteen small portraits hung on a quilted fabric that simulates a brick wall. Some titles are "Bandaged MS," "Hitchcock Bandaged," and "Squeeze My Muscle," which actually has a squeaky toy in the padded arm. Watercolor on muslin.
Photographed at the Art Institute of Chicago

Opposite page:
SOFT DOORS. Barbara Immel. 1972. 6′ high, 20″ wide each door. White cotton with vinyl windows.
Photographed at the American Craftsman Gallery, Chicago

UNTITLED. Marilyn Grelle Duval. 1972. 32″ high, 53″ wide. White cotton partially painted with yellow dyes for a different effect. Stitching, quilting, and added stuffed forms.
Photographed at the American Craftsman Gallery, Chicago

TRAPUNTO DOLL. Elsa Brown. 1971. About 25″ high. The same quilting and trapunto techniques can be applied to three-dimensional forms.
Courtesy, artist

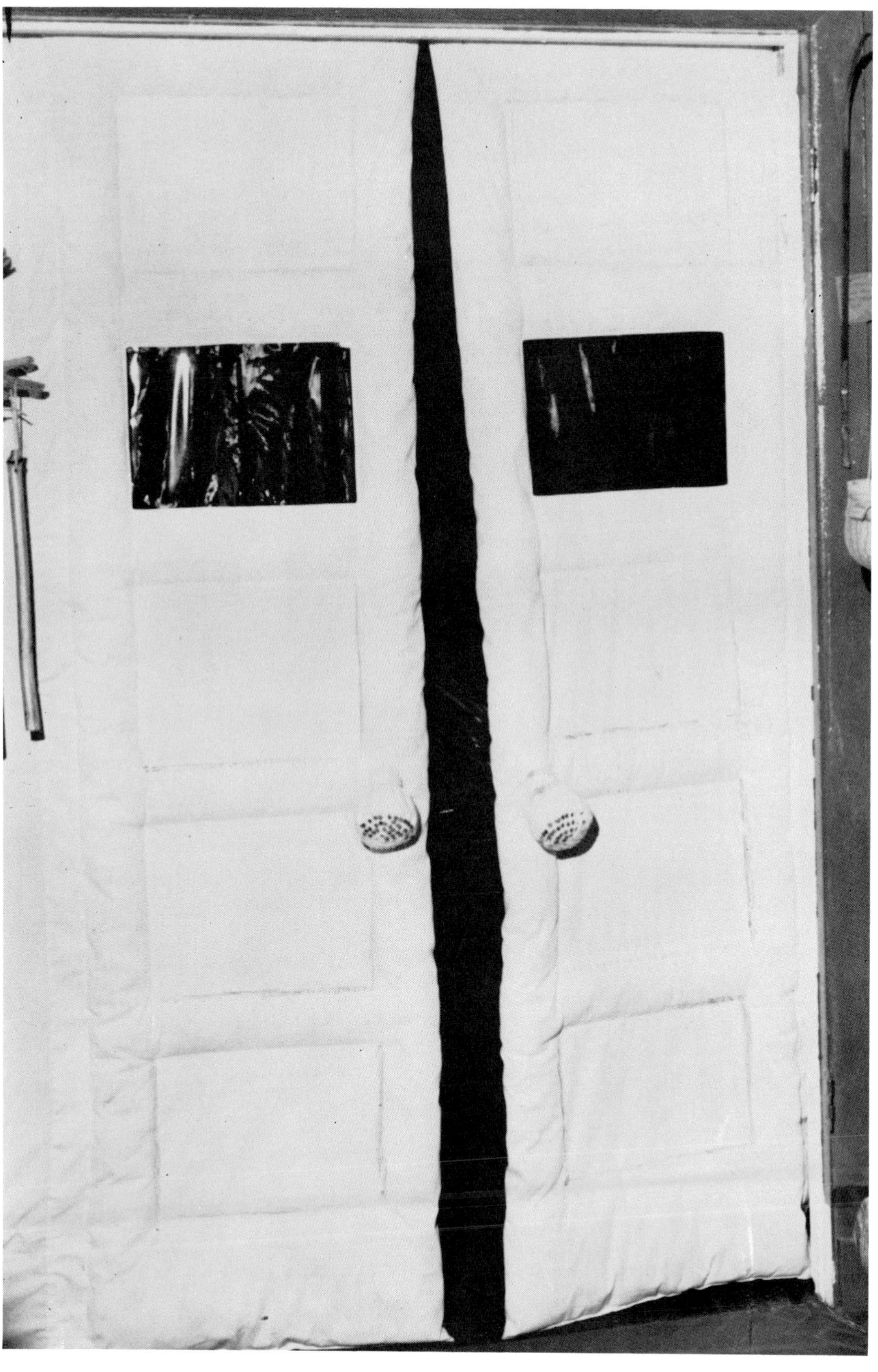

4

Stuffed Fabrics

THE NEW STATEMENTS AND VITALITY OF SOFT SCULPTURE ARE exhibited in the tremendous variations of form, material, and ideas offered by stuffed fabrics. The concepts, as in any other type of sculpture, are limited only by boundaries imposed by the nature of the materials. Yet, the survey of soft sculpture shown in this chapter predicts that there are few limits and the prevailing attitude is that "anything goes."

The act of stuffing is like modeling and carving; it is both an additive and subtractive sculptural process. You can create forms and assemble them; if they are not right or don't work, you can make them shorter, thinner, or remove them altogether. Alterations and revisions are relatively simple.

The variety of materials available, the textures, colors, and patterns, help make the artist's palette more versatile in this medium than in many others. Compare the act of manipulating fabrics and stuffing them to stone or wood carving and the commitment with each stroke of the chisel; or to metal and welding with the torch. They are so different from that which can be done with fabrics. In addition, a soft sculpture can be ever changing; it may be purposely designed so it can be manipulated to alter its form . . . to the chagrin of museums that have a hands-off policy about exhibits.

The real tactile quality is an essential property of soft art. Sculptors incorporate items that will create a surprise for the viewer when he touches it. It might be an unexpected texture that suggests cold or heat, a buzzer or bell, or even a kinetic movement within set off by touch. If a texture or a form doesn't work the way the artist wants it

A TRIAD OF ROSE'S CAST-OFFS. Tom Schantz. 47″ high, 27″ wide. Stuffed fabrics, feathers, macramé.

Photo, Steve Heiland

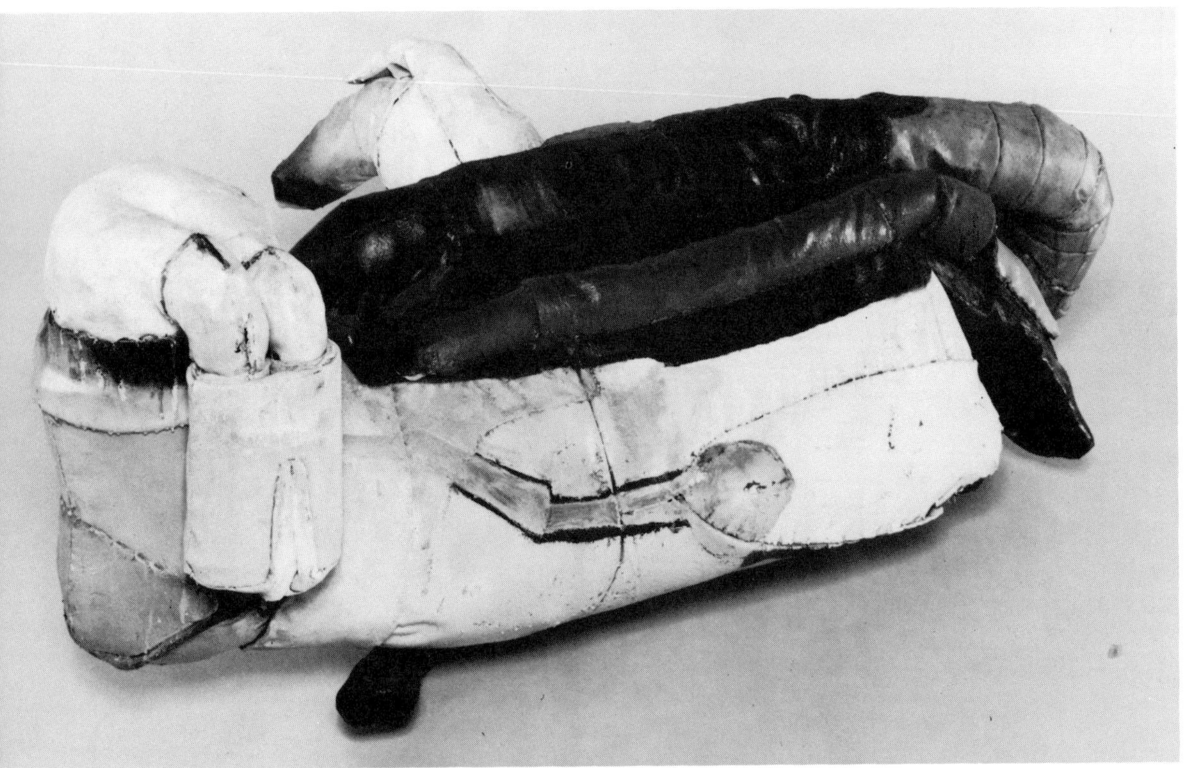

LANDSCAPE. Jean Linder. 1965. 72″ long, 54″ high, 29″ deep. Stuffed painted canvas and polyester resin.
Courtesy, University Art Museum, Berkeley

to, he can continually try fabrics of different weights and other qualities until he is pleased with the result.

The examples in this book illustrate the forms that soft sculptures are taking; one should also note the wide variety of materials that are used, including natural and synthetic cloth and their combinations. Furs, fake furs, and vinyls are sturdy for large objects and a favorite of Barbara Manger whose sculptures hang, loll, drape, and drip about the gallery in an ecstatic use of environmental space. The concept of sculptures hanging from the ceiling in the center of a room, surrounded by others that permeate the space cube and force you to look up, down, everywhere, is all part of the movement.

Many artists, inspired by Oldenburg's ideas of creating objects

into art, have branched out in other directions. Often they create the fabric design that their idea requires. This is especially true in the work of Kathleen Knippel and Suzanne Mancini, who use batik (wax resist process) to simulate life-size objects for a picnic, model or actual size automobile, or to re-create an old-fashioned sewing machine in soft materials. Other artists may use textile paints or silk screen to emulate a real object. Or they may create the illusion of an object by stitching fabrics and details with needle and thread.

Sally Dillon, a young sculptress, sums up a pervasive feeling among those who work in these materials when she asks, "Why soft? Because it is comfortable, warm, playful, unpredictable, funny, and living."

GIANT SOFT DRUM SET. Claes Oldenburg. 1967. 72″ high, 84″ wide, 48″ deep. 125 pieces made of different stuffed fabrics and vinyls.
Collection, Kimiko and John Powers, Aspen, Colorado
Photo, courtesy, Cleveland Museum of Art

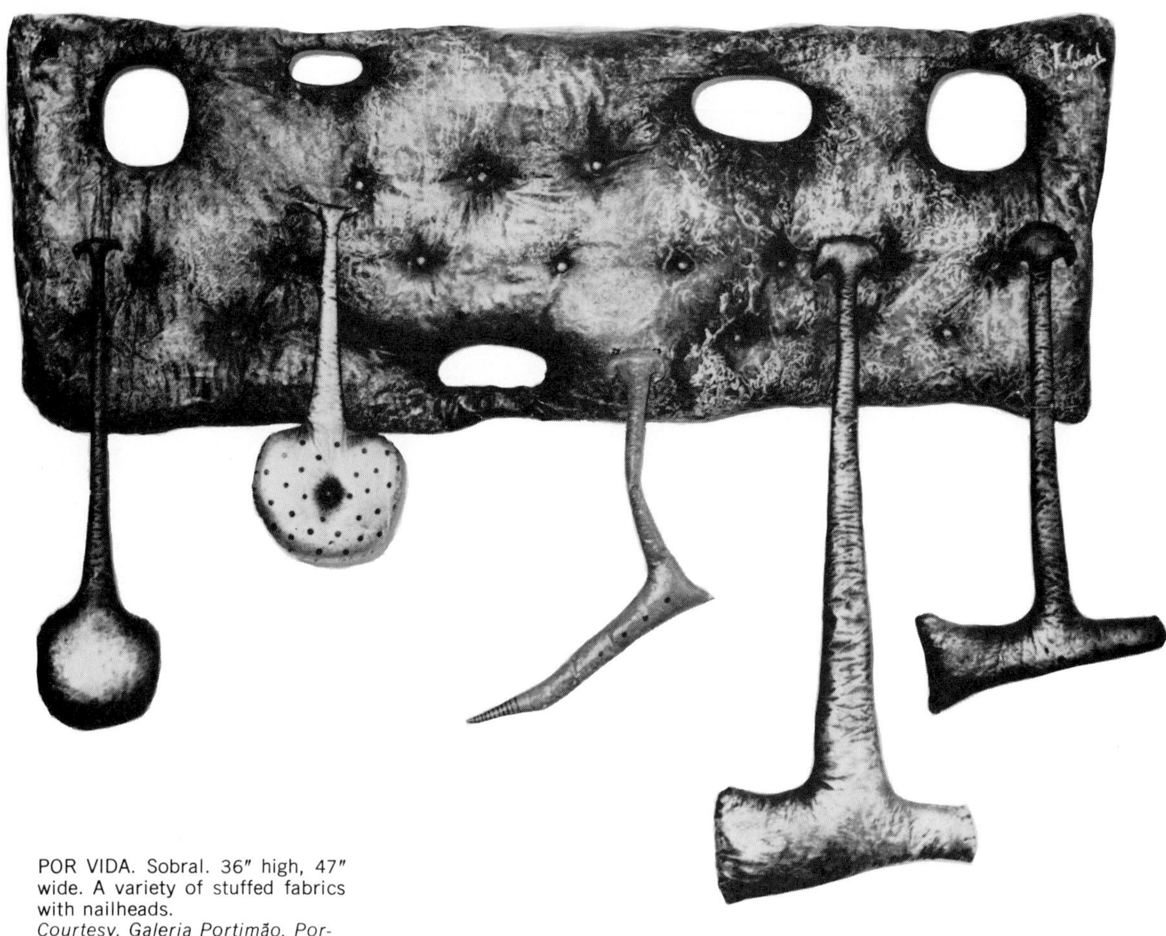

POR VIDA. Sobral. 36″ high, 47″ wide. A variety of stuffed fabrics with nailheads.
Courtesy, Galeria Portimão, Portugal

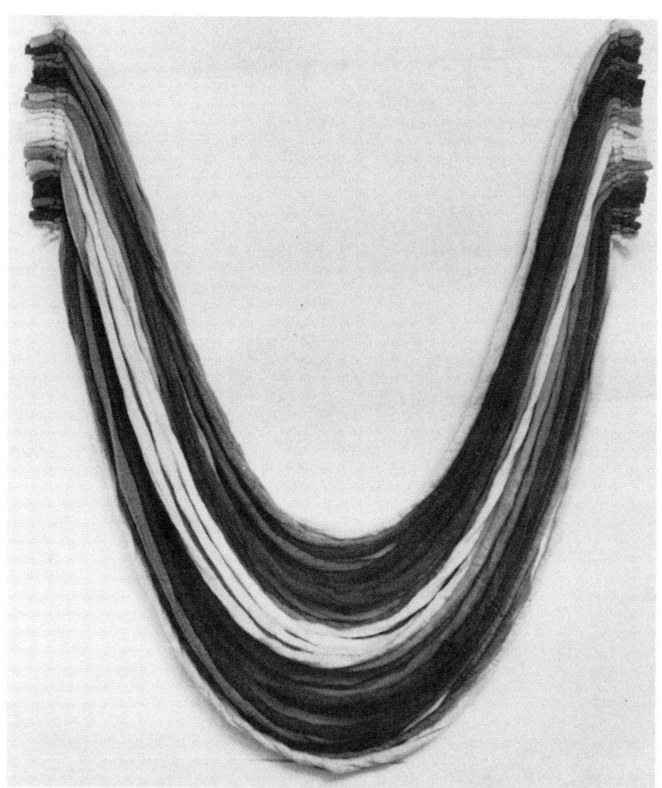

UPSIDE-DOWN RAINBOW. Sara Holt. 1972. Wool.
Courtesy, Galerie Boutique Germain, Paris

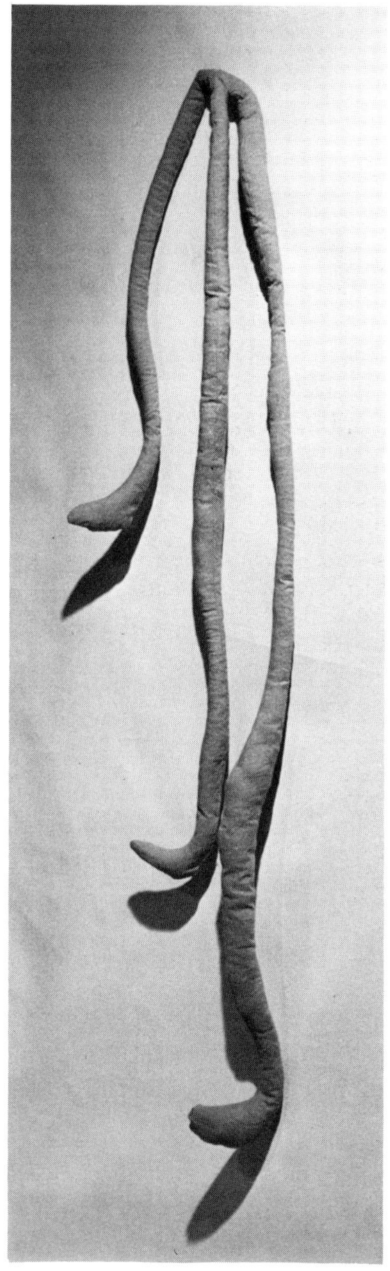

SKINNY PROCESSED. Gillian Bradshaw-Smith. 1972. 66″ high, 13″ wide. Natural linen stuffed.
Courtesy, artist

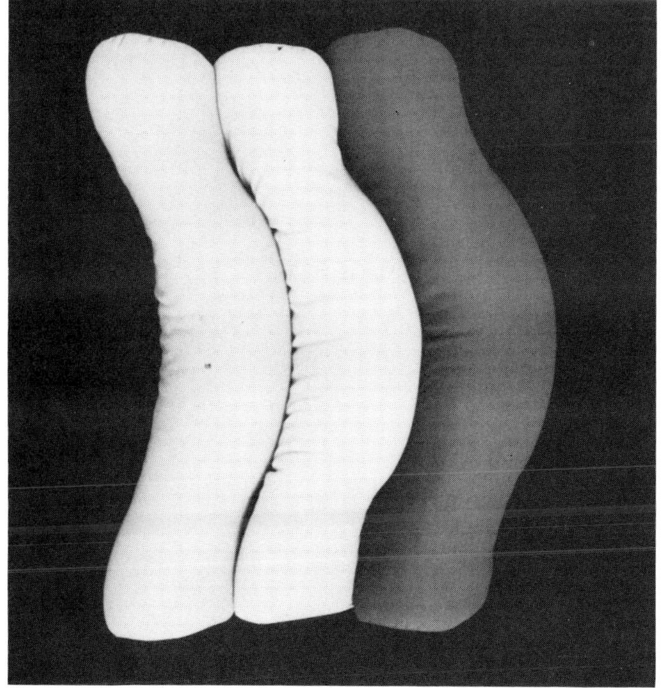

ELEMENTS. Pierre-Martin Jacot. 1972. 39″ high. Stuffed jersey in turquoise, green, fuchsia, and black.
Courtesy, Galerie Boutique Germain, Paris

POLLY AND ESTHER DOUBLEKNIT. Priscilla Sage. 1972. 11″ high, 4″ wide. Double-knit polyester fabrics stuffed with polyester. Large shapes are red, magenta, and orange. Connecting elements are many colors of different natural and synthetic fibers.

Photo, Perry Struse

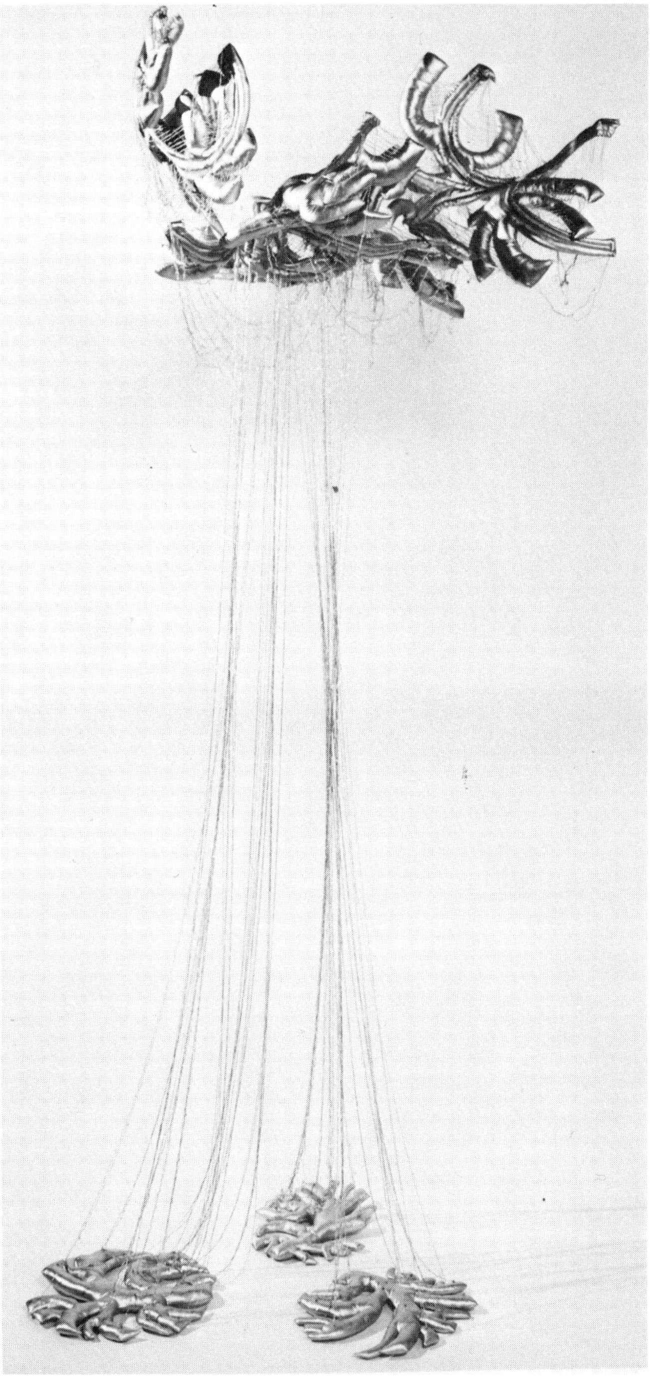

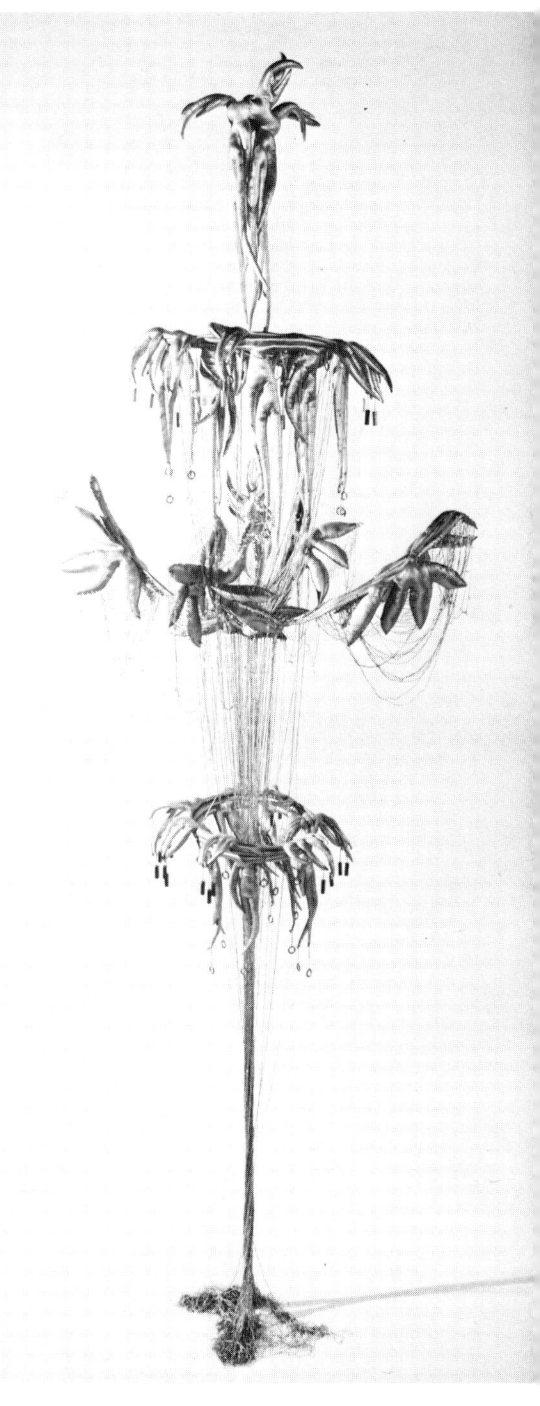

Two pieces by Priscilla Sage of gold double-knit fabrics and fibers. *Left:* FOOTED GOLD. 1971. 10″ high.
Right: GOLD. 1972. 13″ high.
Photos, Perry Struse

Opposite page:
OZYMANDIAS. Gillian Bradshaw-Smith. 1972. Same materials as on opposite page. A greater illusion of folds, wrinkles, and puckers than exists in the real fabric is created with drawing. "Pieces are sometimes reminiscent of strange beasts of the past or beasts yet to be."
Courtesy, artist

BERNINI COLUMN. Gillian Bradshaw-Smith. 1971. 62″ high, 40″ wide, 47″ deep. Linen canvas sewn to shape over a wood box construction. The linen is stuffed with polystyrene pellets and drawn on with ink and sewn with threads to emphasize the linear elements.
Courtesy, artist

SEAFORM III—THE TAKEOVER. Kay Gonzalez. 1972. 48″ long. Quilted, stuffed fabric, dyed shredded sisal, crocheted tentacles. Yellows, purples, and whites.

Courtesy, artist

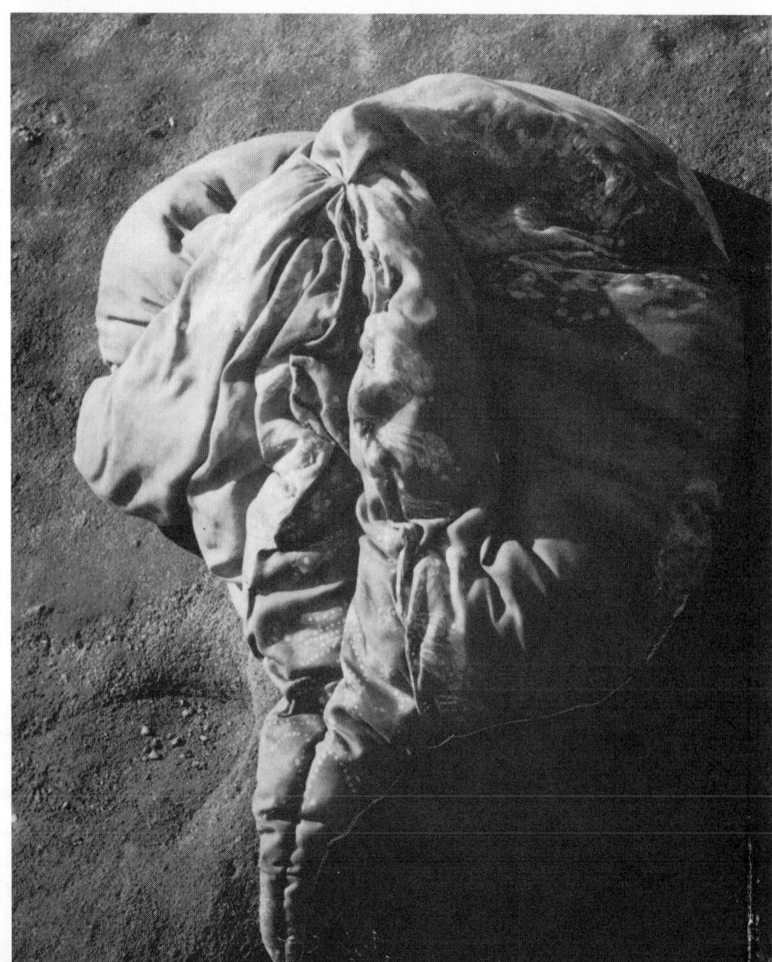

SEAFORM II—PEACE AND TRANQUILITY. Kay Gonzalez. 1972. 40″ diameter. Batiked rayon stitched, gathered, folded, and stuffed. Blues and greens.

Courtesy, artist

SEA ANEMONES. Sally Dillon. 1972. 18″ high, 36″ wide, 18″ deep. Roughly textured solid color fabrics with striped smooth fabrics.
Courtesy, artist

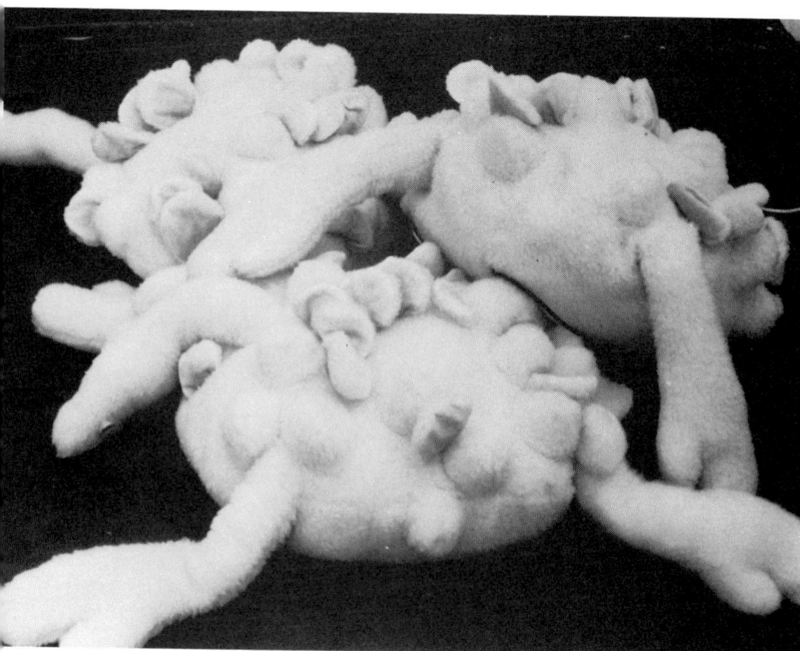

SHEILA, WANDA AND MONA. Glory MacDonald. 1972. 12″ high, 66″ deep. Lambskin. Motors and squeaky toys are placed inside so when the piece is electrically activated it undulates and squeaks.
Photographed at the American Craftsman Gallery, Chicago

UNTITLED. Gayle Luchessa. 1972. 20″ high, 6′ wide. Recycled sheer drapery material and dyed canvas, stuffed, wrapped, and sewn.

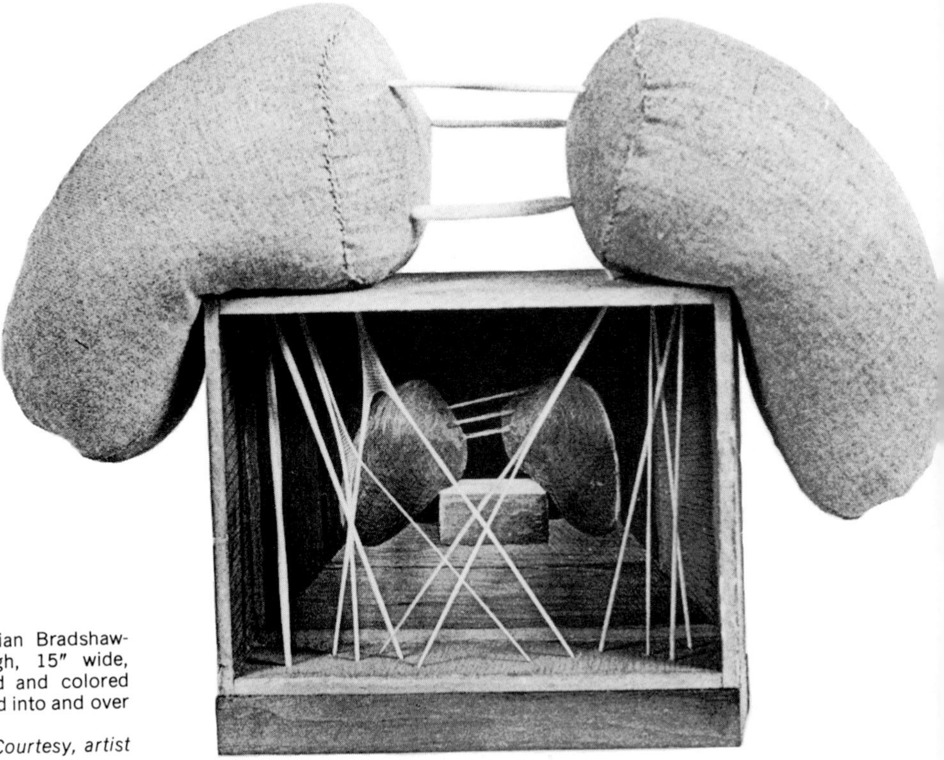

DOUBLE-DOUBLE. Gillian Bradshaw-Smith. 1972. 12″ high, 15″ wide, 4″ deep. Linen stuffed and colored with gouache assembled into and over a wood box.
Courtesy, artist

UM SOL POR UN CHÃO. Sobral. 1972. 59″ wide, 39″ deep.
Courtesy, Galeria Portimão, Portugal

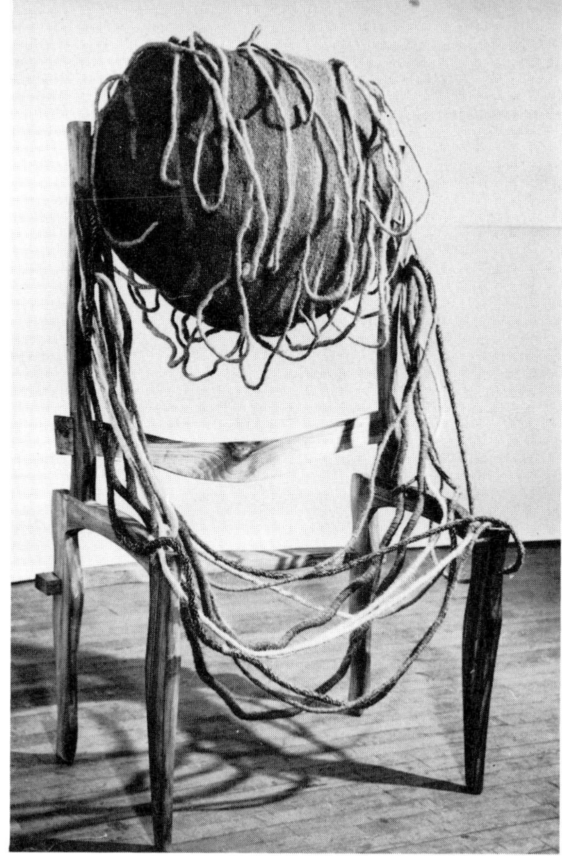

CHAIR. Ritzi and Peter Jacobi. Goat hair woven into fabric and stuffed; also wrapping and wood. *Collection, The Power Gallery of Contemporary Art, University of Sydney, Australia. Courtesy, artists*

TOTEM. Jeanne Boardman Knorr. 7′ high, 10″ wide, 2″ deep. Padded velvet, wrapped tassels, feathers; supported by metal.
Courtesy, artist

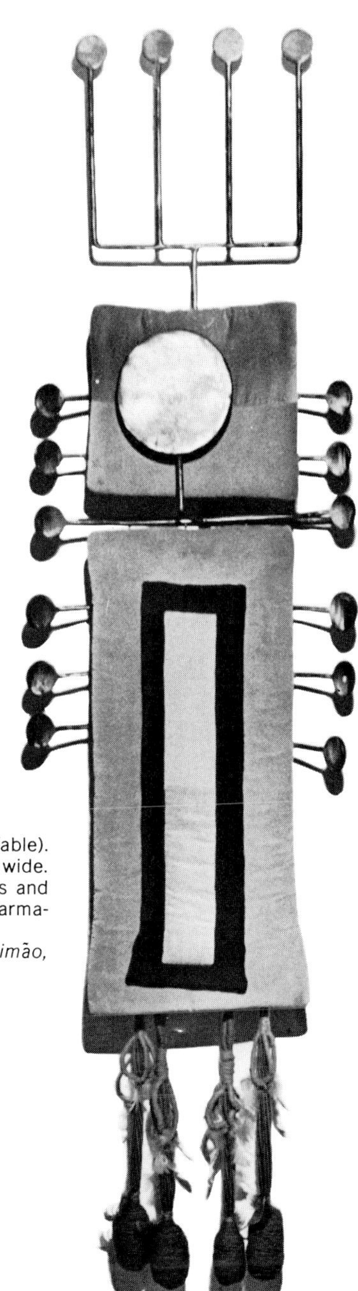

TOCADOR (Dressing Table). Sobral. 1972. 69″ high, 45″ wide. Stuffed fabrics with drawings and paint over wood frames and armatures.
Courtesy, Galeria Portimão, Portugal

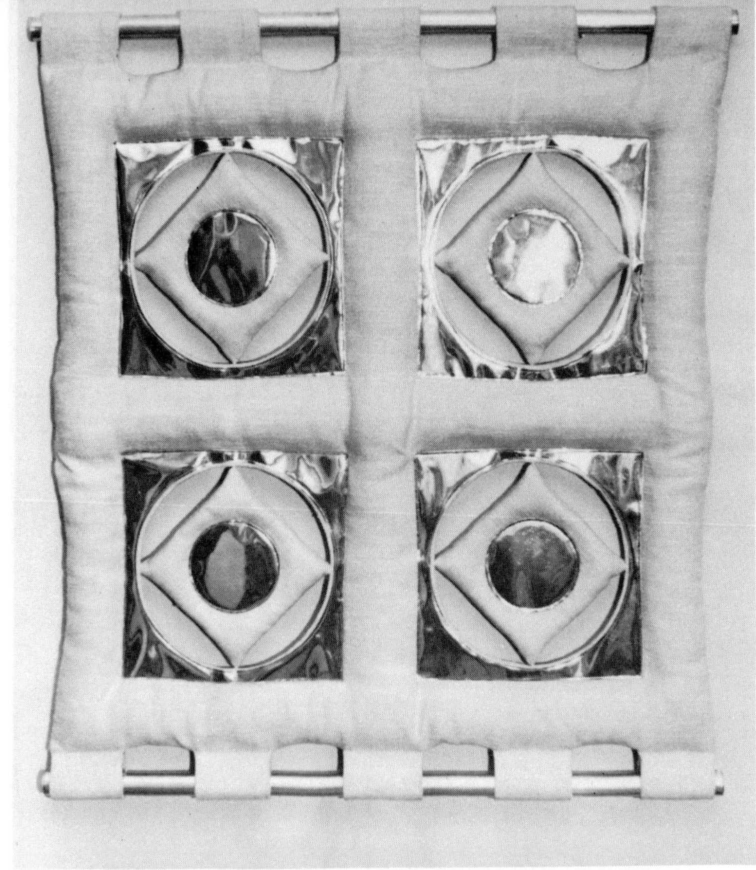

PILLOW PANEL. Pat Malarcher. 36″ square. Stuffed linen with Mylar.
Courtesy, artist

FABRIC MANIPULATIONS. College student work. 36″ high. Stuffed striped cotton. Parts may be moved in relation to one another.
Collection, Bob Falwell, DeKalb, Illinois

MA BELL. Kay M. Aronson. 1972. Approximately 40″ high, 18″ wide. Silk, satin, velveteen. Some stitchery. Wire, plastic, and beads.
Photographed at the Richmond Art Center, Richmond, California

UNTITLED. Jan Wagstaff. 1971. 60″ high, 27″ wide. Velvet, satin, ribbons, with cotton hand screened and painted, lined with Pellon and lightly stuffed.

INDIAN RITUAL OBJECT. Jeanne Boardman Knorr. 1972. 6′ high, 12″ wide, 12″ deep. Padded forms are covered entirely with feathers and wrapped yarns and hung on a metal frame.

Courtesy, artist

SHAMAN. Jeanne Boardman Knorr. 1972. 5½′ high, 3′ wide, 1′ deep. Padded wools with wrapped yarns and feathers on a metal stand.

Courtesy, artist

BUTTERFLY. Naomi Kahan. 1972. 36″ high, 27″ wide. Dyed natural linen quilted and stuffed with Dacron. The linen has been fringed; metal objects hang from the leather.

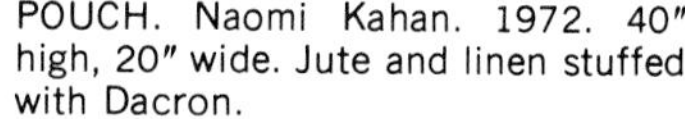

POUCH. Naomi Kahan. 1972. 40″ high, 20″ wide. Jute and linen stuffed with Dacron.

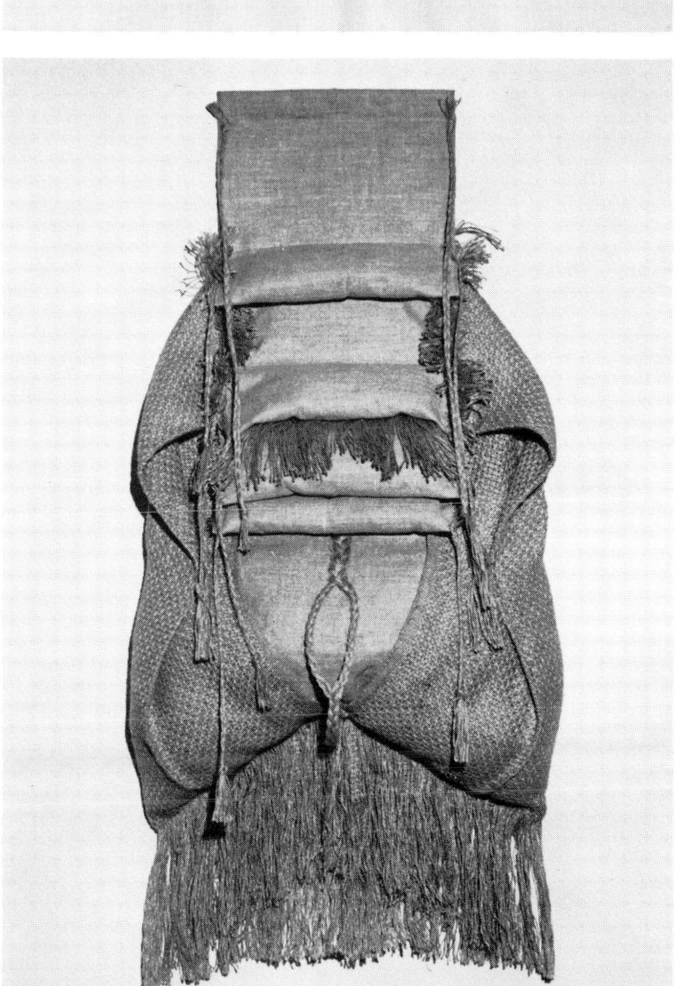

HERITAGE. Naomi Kahan. 1972. 48″ high, 14″ wide. Linen, stuffed with Dacron, fringed, and hung with beads.
All photos, courtesy, artist

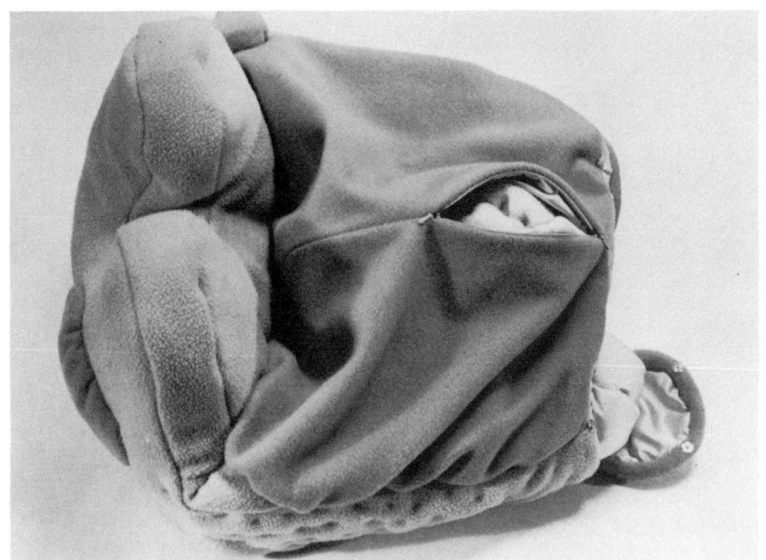

The following pieces are by Judith Roston Freilich. 1973. They are made of wools, satins, and velvets. When the pieces are shut, they present a solid, but soft, visual impression. Literally scores of hidden long and short zippers and snaps can be opened to disclose innumerable oddly shaped stuffed satin and wool balls that can be arranged, bounced, and transferred to new hiding places. All the pockets and pouches are lined with contrasting pastel color satin.

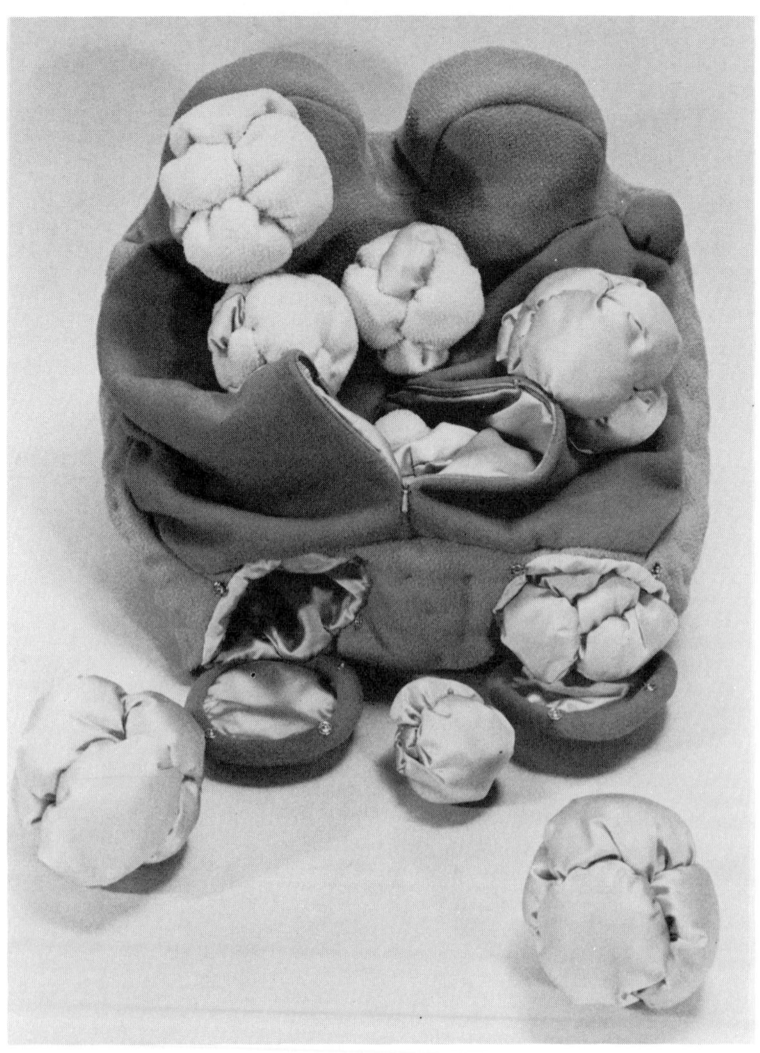

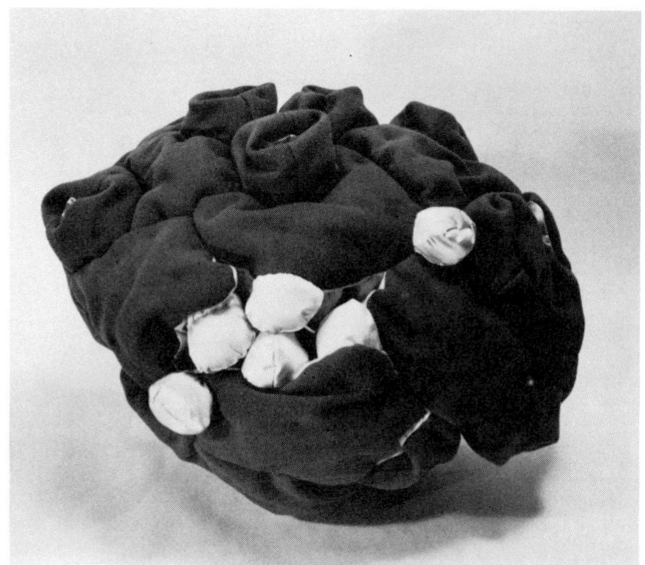

Also by Judith Roston Freilich. Piece shown slightly open is approximately 12″ high, 20″ wide, 20″ deep. *Below left:* Open.

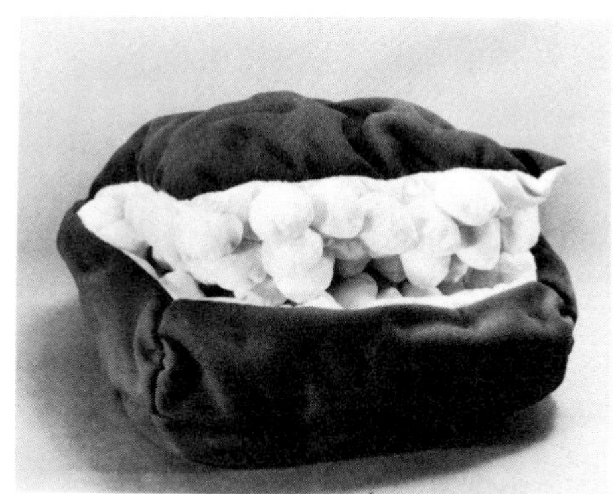

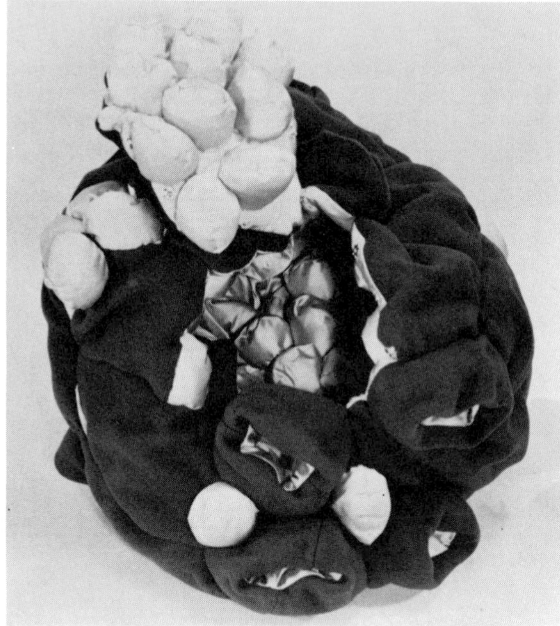

Wool and satin. 20″ overall diameter. Magenta wool soft box environment, 18″ high, 21″ wide, 25″ deep, holds white satin and magenta velvet ball-like projections. Additional forms are contained in the bottom and reached through a short zippered opening.

GROUP. Barbara Manger. 1972. 12 parts, each 4′ long. Vinyls and furs.
Courtesy, artist

NOW THAT'S POLLUTION. Misty Potter. 1972. Three pieces ranging in size from 14″ x 18″ to 2′ x 7′. Fake fur, sewn and stuffed.

UNION 76. Misty Potter. Various sizes ranging from 18″ x 14″ to 2′ x 3′. Vinyl, sewn and stuffed and attached to garden hose to simulate puddles.
Photos, courtesy, artist

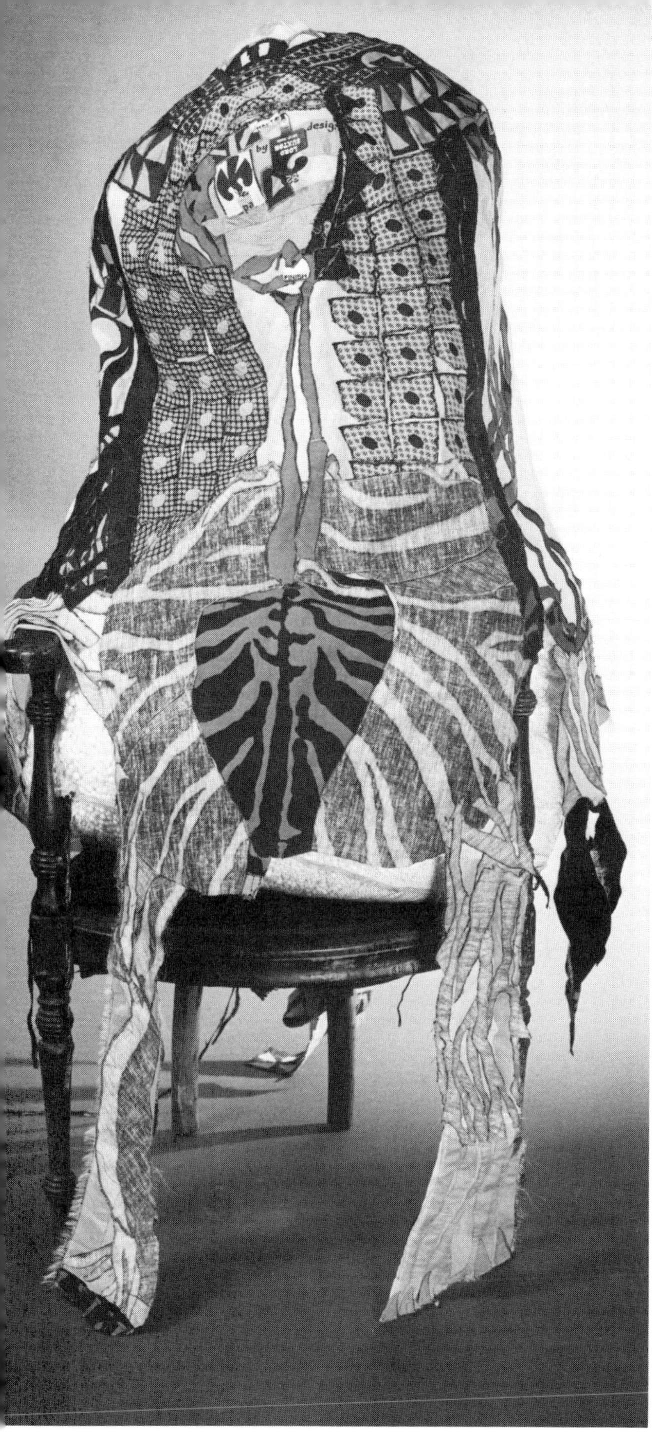

THE CHAIR WOMAN. Nell Booker Sonnemann. 1972. 4½′ high. A plastic bag stuffed with foam pellets is covered with assorted fabrics appliquéd. *Left:* Front view. *Below:* Right and left side views.

Photo, Charlie Brown

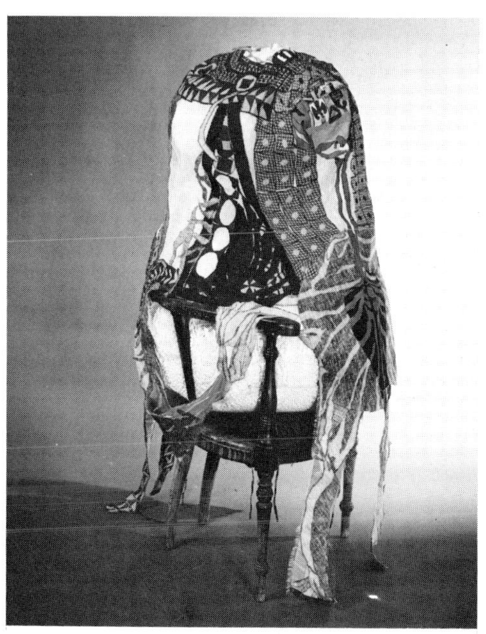

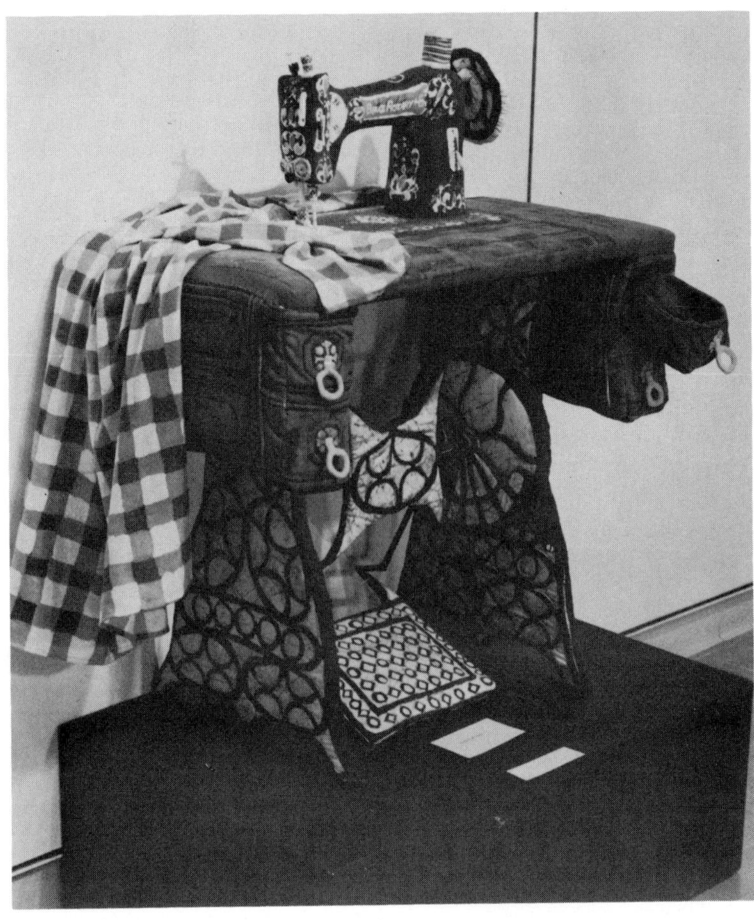

STUFFED SEWING MACHINE. Kathleen Knippel. 1973. Actual size. Cotton fabric batiked and stuffed.
Courtesy, artist

BATIK

Opposite page:
FLAG MOTIF (in progress). Kathleen Knippel. 1973. 6′ high. Finished piece will consist of eight stuffed tubes. Cotton fabric batiked.
Courtesy, artist

The batik process is ideal for creating special designs on cloth that can be used for unique soft sculptures. Batik, an ancient Javanese art that means "wax writing," involves painting melted wax on cloth made of natural fibers such as cotton, silk, or linen, and then plunging the fabric into a dyebath, or painting the dye onto the fabric. Areas covered with wax resist the dye and remain white; uncovered areas accept the dye. You can create two-color batik fabrics with one wax brushing and one dyebath. For multiple colors, you wax parts of each color to hold them before redyeing. As many as fifteen to twenty, or more, dyebaths may be used.

For overall designs, yardage can be dyed. For special design projects such as the sewing machine (above), the pattern parts are cut first. The design is drawn on according to a preliminary sketch, then each color area is waxed and dyed as necessary. Such a project requires careful planning.

Batik requires four basic procedures:

1. Prepare the fabric and plan the design.
2. Wax the areas that will remain white.
3. Dye (rewax for additional colors).
4. Remove the wax.

To batik you will have to gather the necessary fabrics, dyes, and waxes in addition to the items shown on the following pages:

FABRICS: Use a fabric made of natural fibers such as cotton, muslin, linen, or silk. (Do *not* use synthetics or permanent press materials as they will not take the dye satisfactorily.) It is *essential* that you wash all fabrics in hot, sudsy water, rinse and dry them before applying the wax. This removes the factory starches and sizing, which also prevent the dye from penetrating the fabric.

WAX is the resist material. Use paraffin wax, available in grocery stores (the same used for sealing Mason jars at canning time), or a combination of half paraffin wax and half beeswax (from a craft shop or bee farm). You will need about a half pound of wax for 1½ square yards of fabric. The wax is melted in the top of a double boiler on a kitchen stove or on a hot plate. Wax can be placed directly in an electric fry pan set at 225° to keep the wax at an even temperature. The wax is spread onto the cloth with a small paintbrush. It is hot enough when it appears translucent on the fabric. If it appears opaque, it does not penetrate between the fibers and will not resist dye satisfactorily.

DYES: Waxed fabrics must be dyed in cool water so the wax will not melt. A recently developed cold water dye, called fiber reactive, is marketed especially for batik by craft and hobby shops (or from the suppliers listed in the Appendix). It is relatively colorfast and dyes in cool water about 90° to 100° F., which is below the melting point of wax.

Household dyes such as Putnam, Rit, Tintex, and Cushings are available at supermarkets and drugstores. These may be used, but because they are "hot water dyes" they yield maximum color brilliance and fastness in simmering water at about 140°. To use these household dyes for batik, you must alter the directions: Dissolve the package in a cup of very hot water, then add this to enough cool water in the dye tub so the dyebath will cover the fabric. Keep the water at 90° to 100°, or just comfortable to your hands, to get the best possible results.

For additional exploration into batik, see *Contemporary Batik and Tie-Dye* by Dona Z. Meilach (in this same Crown's Arts and Crafts series). Once you are familiar with the technique, and the results, you'll discover scores of ways to apply the materials to soft sculpture.

Materials:
Frame, thumbtacks, pencil, paintbrushes, piece of washed 100 percent cotton fabric, wax with pan and heating device, plastic or enamel vessel for dyeing, paper towels, iron, dyes, salt, thermometer, and stirring spoons.

Spread the fabric flat and lightly draw the design with pencil, pen, or charcoal. You can place a sketch beneath the fabric and trace it. You can also wax directly on the fabric without a sketch. Circles are easily made with different size plates and glasses. For other repeat shapes, cut a cardboard template and trace around. Fabric must be prewashed to remove all sizing; it must not be synthetic or have a permanent or soil-resistant finish.

Tack the fabric to a frame so it is taut. If the cloth is bigger than the frame, wax one portion, then move the material over to continue the waxing. Apply the first waxing to all areas you want to remain white. The wax will resist the dye, all unwaxed areas will dye your first color. Wax must be applied hot enough so it is translucent and not opaque. If opaque areas occur, turn the fabric over and wax the same area from the back, also.

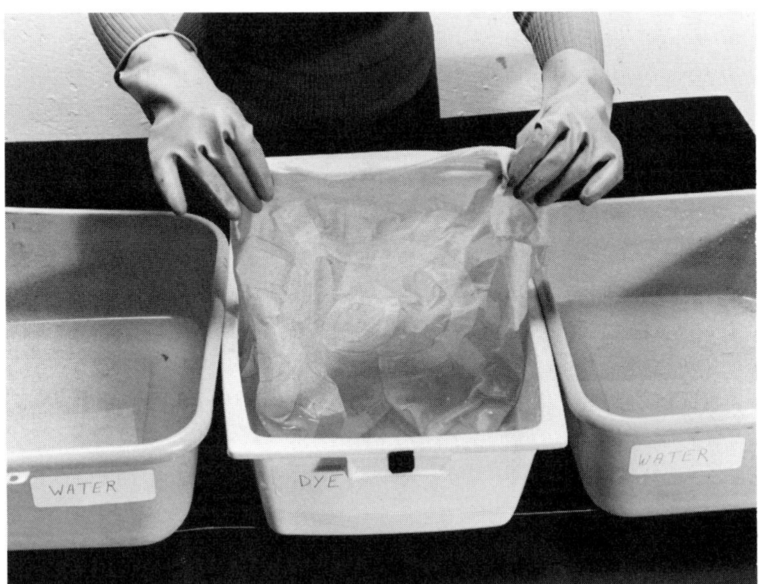

Fabrics should be soaked or wetted out for a few minutes; then immersed in the dyebath for the time required for the specific dye being used. Use large enough dye vessels to prevent unnecessary cracking of the wax coats during the first dyebaths. After dyeing, rinse in cool water and dry.

Rewax and cover all portions you wish to retain the first color. Then dye a second color. Dry. Rewax and redye for as many colors as desired. During the final dyebath, usually with the darkest color, and when crackle is desired, crush the wax, allowing the dye to penetrate between the cracks. For greater crackle, use more paraffin wax than beeswax. Place the wax fabric in the freezer for a few hours; wax will crack sharper when it is cold and brittle.

The wax is removed by placing the fabric between layers of newspaper and paper toweling. Iron over the top layer of paper with a hot iron. This pulls the wax out of the fabric and into the papers. Change the papers frequently. The heat of the iron is usually sufficient to set colors. Any residual wax can be removed by dipping fabric in a solution of 1 part paint thinner to 5 parts warm water with a couple of teaspoons of laundry detergent added. It can also be dipped in cleaning fluid or it can be cleaned commercially.

Opposite page:
ASSEMBLY LINE CAR QUILT. Suzanne Mancini. 1973. 72″ high. Batik on raw silk quilted. Border of tire treads with small stuffed wheels around edge. Cars shown are a Volkswagen station wagon, Chevrolet truck, Jaguar, Volkswagen bus, Lotus. This is a quilted wall hanging adaptation of the patterns and methods used to create the stuffed cars opposite.
Courtesy, Kathleen Knippel

SUNDIAL CAMPER. Kathleen Knippel. 1973. Approximately 20″ long. Batik on cotton.

VOLKSWAGEN. Kathleen Knippel and Suzanne Mancini. 1973. Approximately 18″ long. Stuffed batik on cotton.
Courtesy, artists

CAN OF WORMS (Portrait). Joyce Stack. 1973. A stuffed "can" of Teflon fabric with a quilted zip-off lid reveals a batch of colorful stuffed batik worms. The side of the can, made of cotton, is batiked with a portrait.

SOFT REFRIGERATOR. Karlen Allard. 1972. 5′ high. The vinyl material covers layers of laminated foam with cotton batting around it. A wood base and some wood framing is used. Refrigerator's contents are hand-decorated fabrics with embroidery and appliqué.

Courtesy, artist

PICNIC BATIK. Suzanne Mancini. 1973. Actual size of pieces including a gingham tablecloth, paper plates, hot dogs, and so forth . . . all batiked.

Courtesy, artist

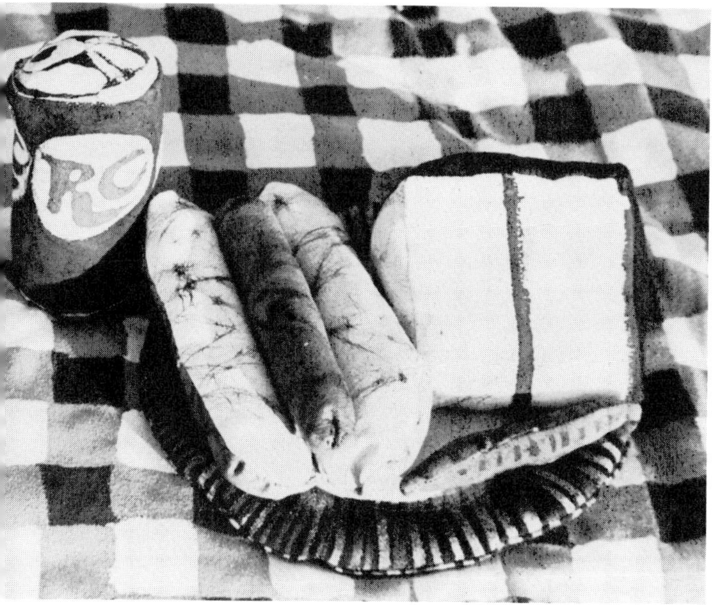

Left: Detail of hot dogs, bun, cake, plate, and cola. *Below:* Thermos, lunch box and sandwich, cake and banana of batiked cotton. Suzanne Mancini.

Courtesy, artist

CITY ENVIRONMENT. Stephen Blumrich. 1972. Stuffed batik on cotton including a church, houses, rain, lightning, rain cloud, and, in the distance, the sun.

UNTITLED. Lynn Hanzel. 1972. Stuffed batiked fabric is used to illustrate people coming out of a stuffed batik space module.
Photographed at the Richmond Art Center, Richmond, California

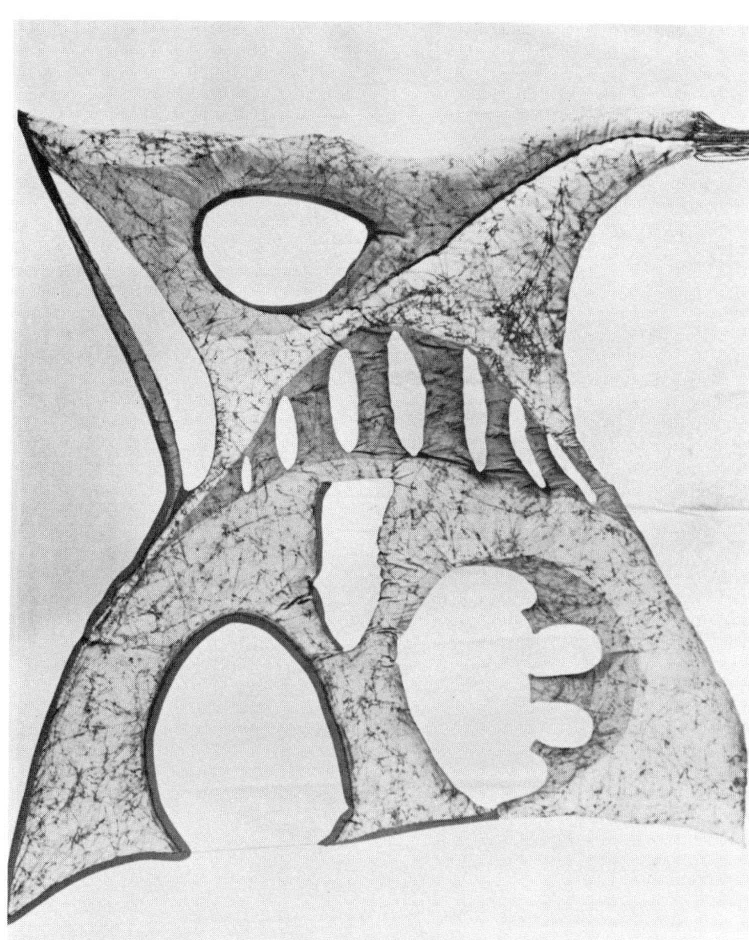

PISCES. Rita Shumaker. Batik.
Courtesy, artist

UNTITLED. Rita Shumaker. 1972. 9½' high, 54″ wide. Tie-dyed fabric shaped and stuffed.
Photo, Chuck Simmons

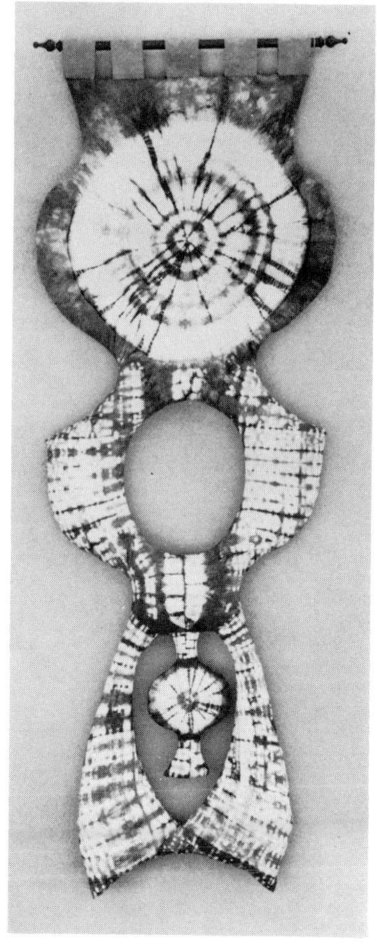

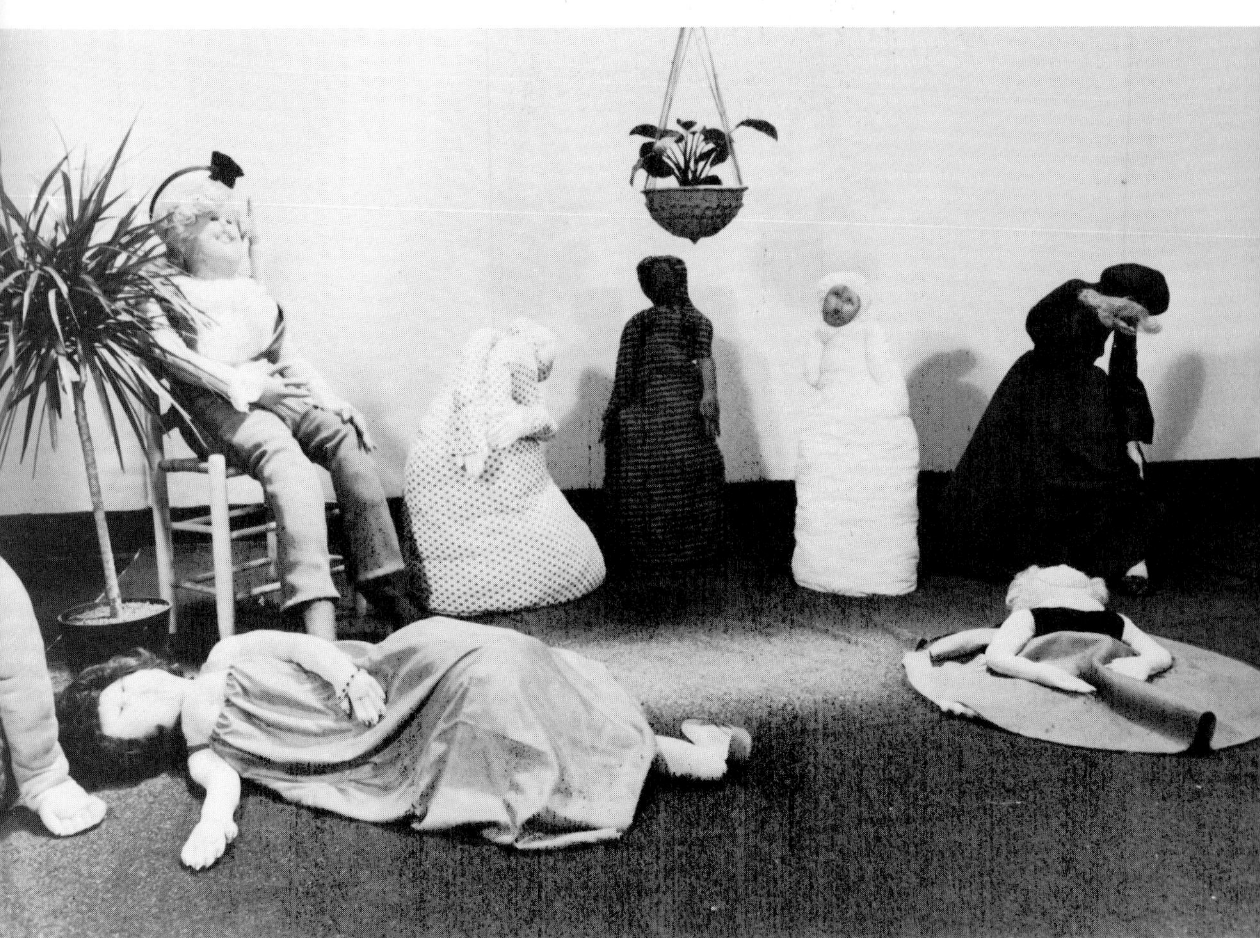

A room setting of soft-sculptured figures by Kay-Karol Mapp on exhibit at the American Craftsman Gallery, Chicago.

In Chapter 2, photos were shown to stimulate ideas for creating soft sculpture based on recognizable objects. The following examples will emphasize the use of such images as sources for inspiration. They are presented in three groups so you can see, first, the many interpretations of human form. A second group illustrates interpretations of flowers and vegetables, and the third group consists of animals created from stuffed cloth over a simple wood armature by Dahlov Ipcar.

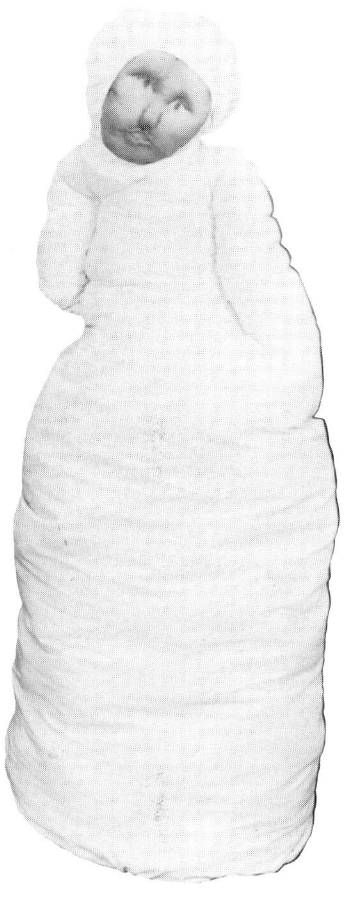

FIGURE. Kay-Karol Mapp. 1972. 38″ high. White muslin with a nylon stocking for a face.

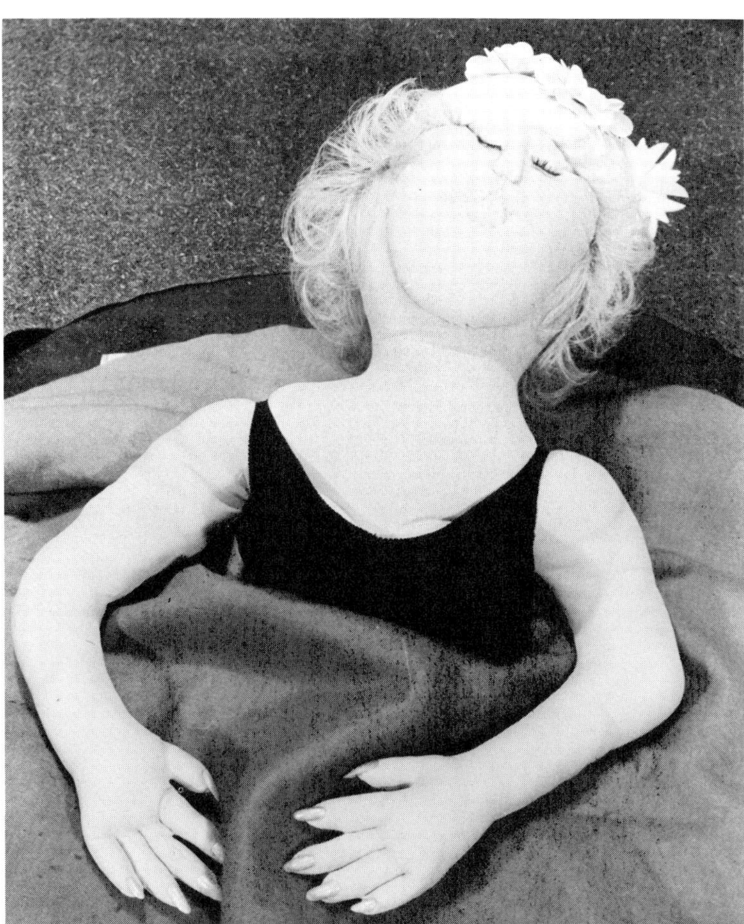

BATHING BEAUTY. Kay-Karol Mapp. 1972. 36″ diameter. Felt skirt, white muslin body, nylon face, unplied yarn for hair.

ROSIE. Mary Gould Quinn. 1971. 38″ high, 50″ long. Fiberglas, upholstery cotton, nylon and silk fabrics.
Courtesy, Wenger Gallery, San Francisco

Left: UNCLE SAM. William King. 1972. 82″ high, 28″ wide. *Below:* OBSERVER. William King. 1972. 33″ high. Both are painted canvas. *Courtesy, Terry Dintenfass, Inc., New York*

THE LANDLADY. Mary Sprague. 1972. 4′ high, 3′ wide. Assemblage of stuffed fabrics and found materials. *Courtesy, artist*

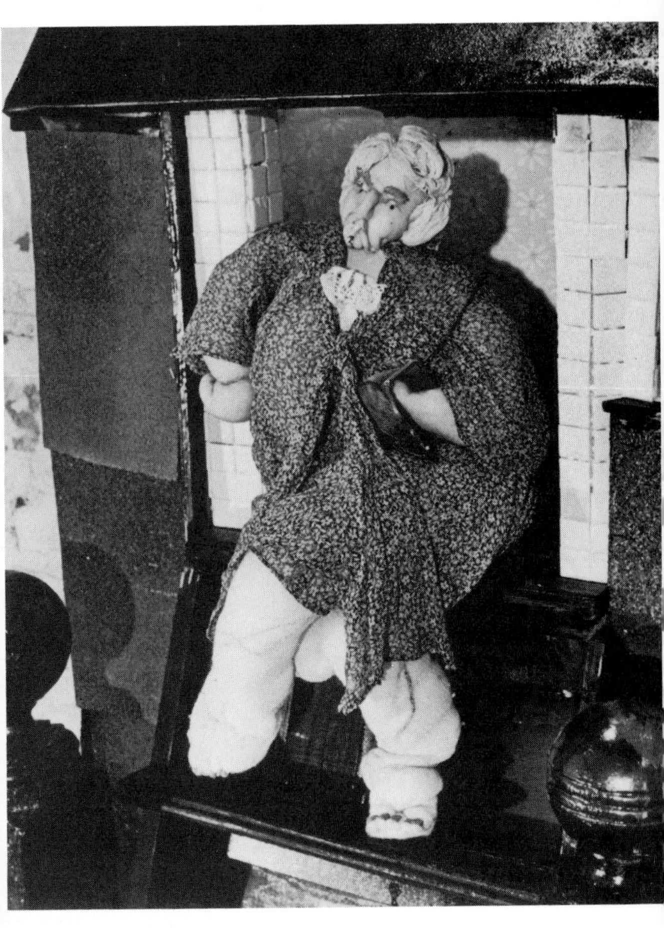

THERE'S NOT MUCH LEFT OF RUSSELL. Mary Sprague. 1972. 24″ high. Cloth, sticks, bones. *Courtesy, artist*

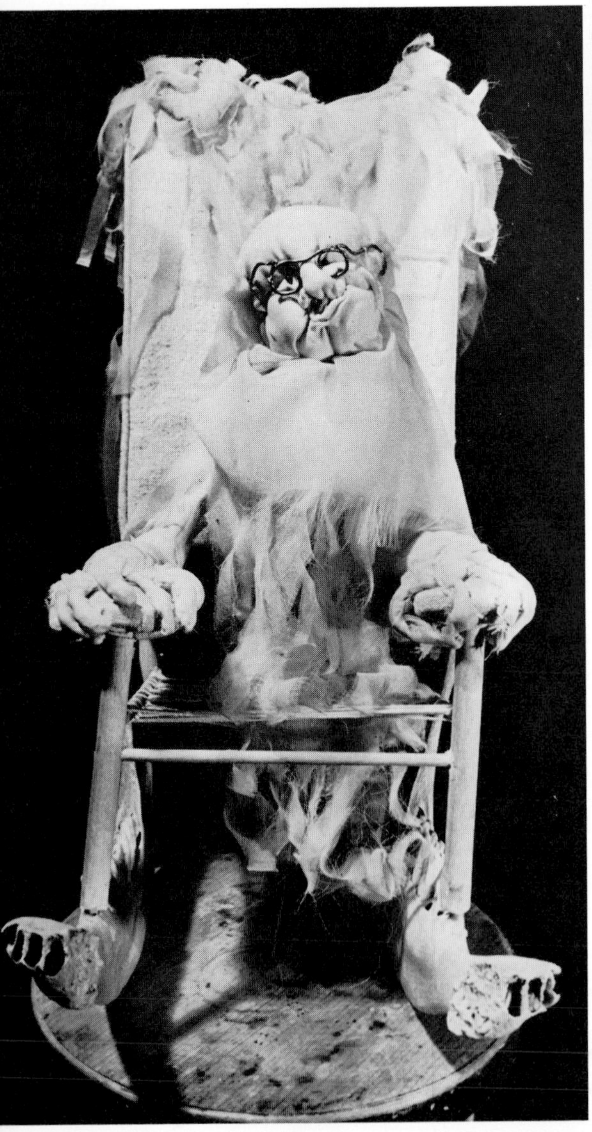

SKIN FOR A STRIPED PERSON. Nicola. 1972. Plastic over stretched canvas. Loose parts of body are soft so that a person can put his feet and arms through and thereby become the "stuffing" for the sculpture. *Courtesy, Galerie Boutique Germain, Paris*

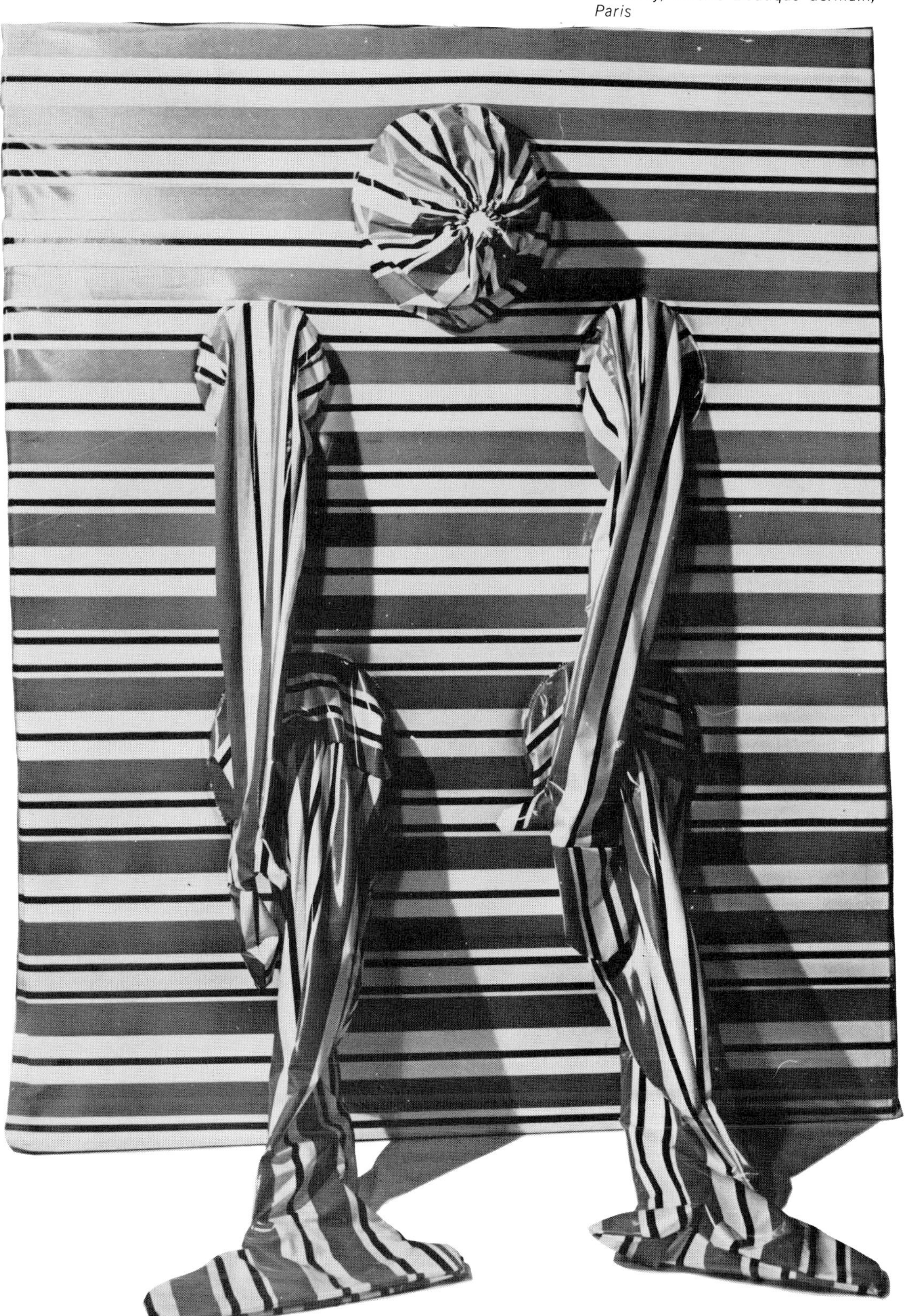

UNTITLED. Lani Hayes. 1972. *Below:* 16″ high, 10″ wide, 6″ deep. *Right:* 16″ high, 12″ wide, 3″ deep. Upholstery fabrics, laces, and cottons. Faces are hand drawn.
Photographed at the American Craftsman Gallery, Chicago

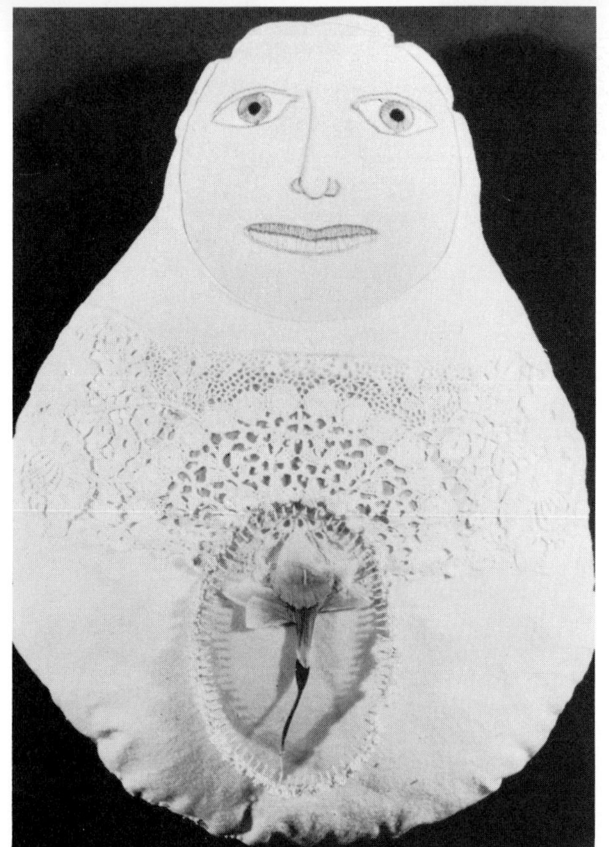

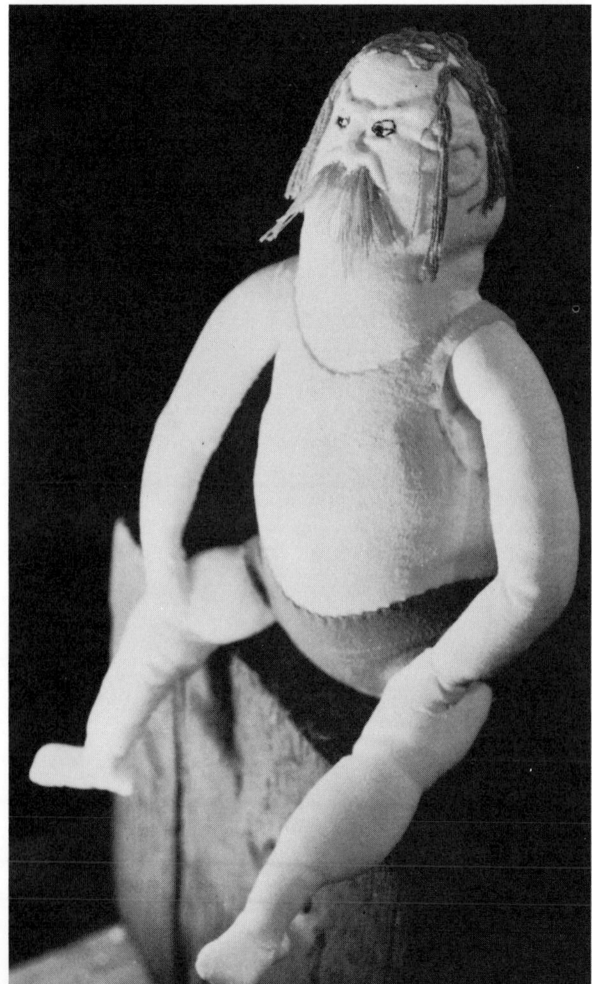

DOLL. Linda Downey. 1971. Stuffed fabrics with yarn hair.
Courtesy, artist

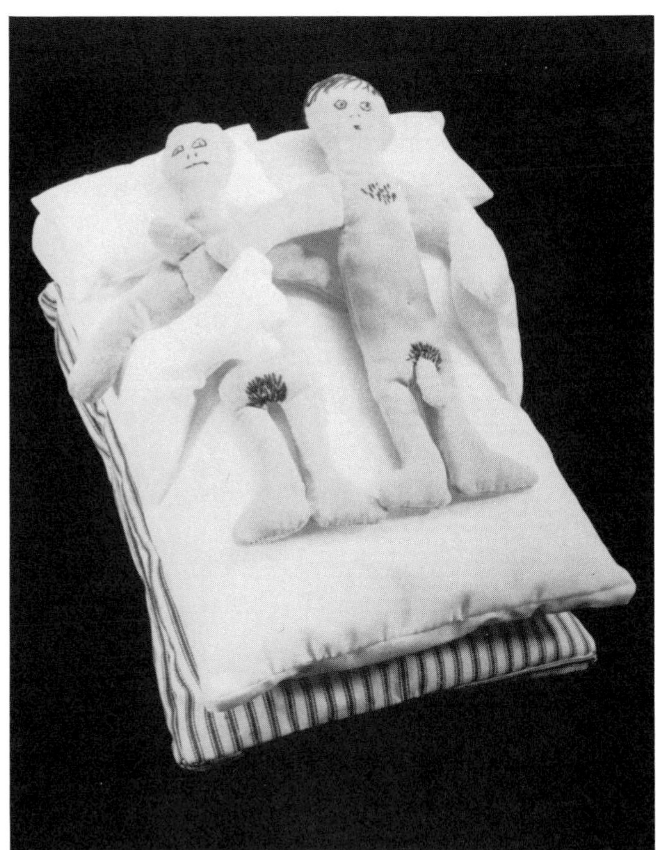

SOMETIMES YOUR BED WON'T LET YOU GET UP IN THE MORNING. Benita Cullinan. 1972. 14″ wide, 18″ deep. Pink velveteen figures on white cotton mattress, mattress ticking, and stitchery.

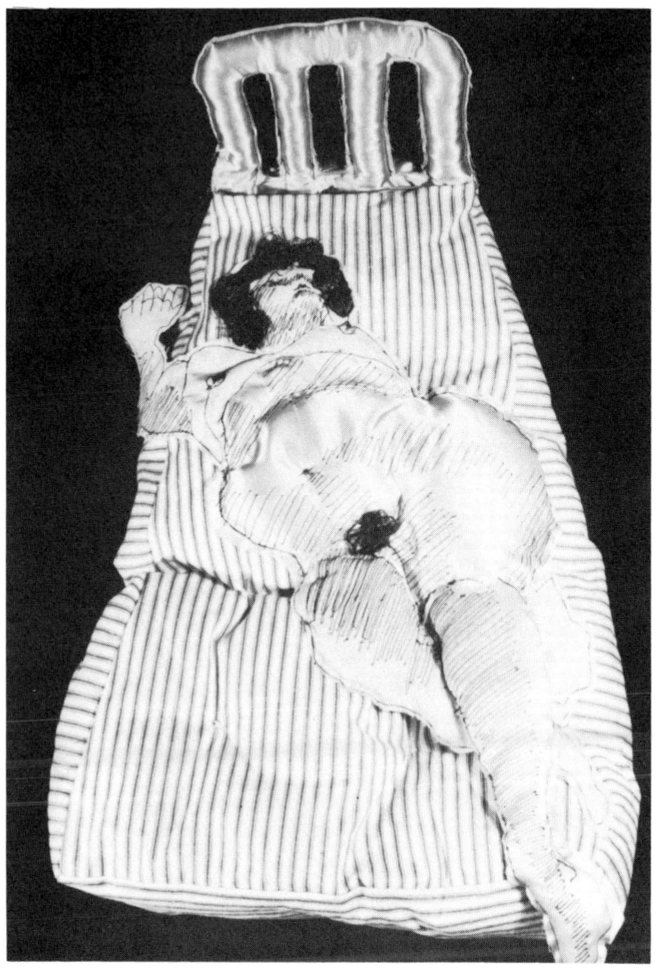

NUDE ON A BRASS BED. Maggie Nicholson. 1972. 20″ wide, 28″ deep. Mattress ticking, gold and peach satin with dark red nylon for hair. Black thread, machine stitched, creates the effect of line drawing.

Courtesy, artist

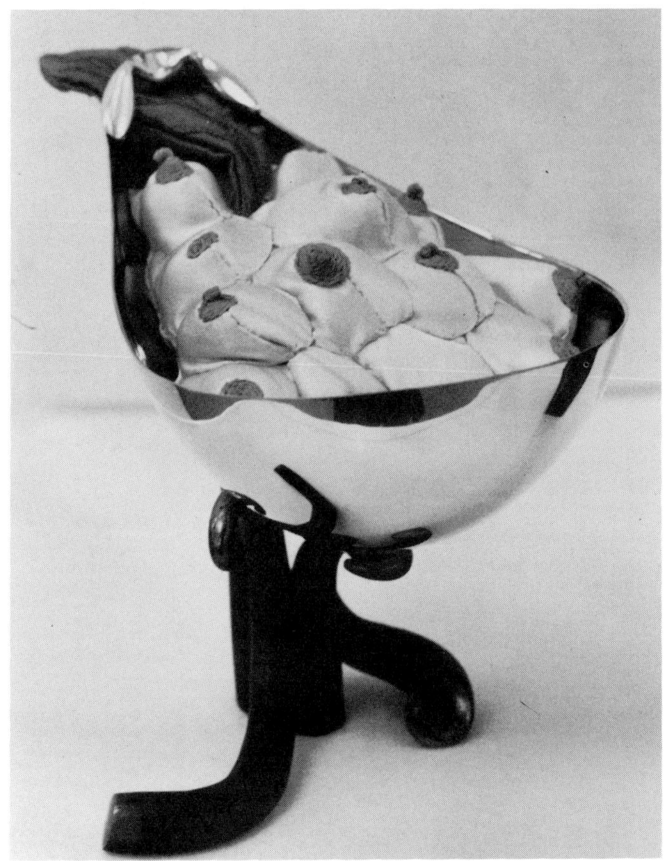

LADY GOBLET WITH ASPARAGUS TIP BREASTS. Ruth Clausen Girard. 12″ high, 10″ wide. Pink satin with stitchery in a silver dish.
Photographed at the Richmond Art Center, Richmond, California

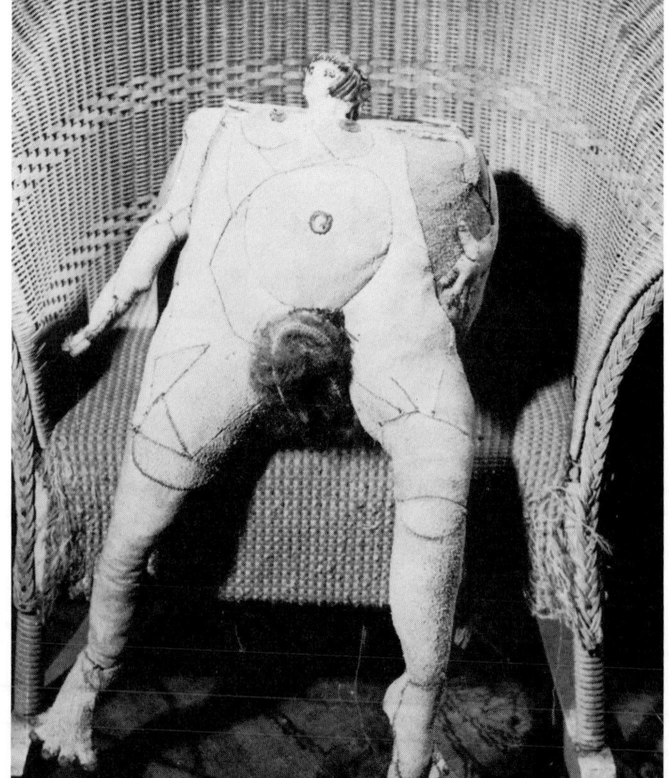

VOLUPTUOUS MARGARET. Anne Kingsbury. 1970. 30″ high. Suede and feathers.
Courtesy, artist

ASPARAGUS. David O'dell. 1972. Each "stalk" is 12′ long and made of raw canvas stuffed with mattress padding, which gives a firm, but flowing effect.

Courtesy, artist

MOLAR ON A COB. Benita Cullinan. 1972. 18″ high, 24″ wide, 16″ deep. Cast replicas of the artist's lost molar become the kernels for the corn made of stitched and stuffed fabrics placed on a soft platter.

UNTITLED. Jan Wagstaff. 1971. 39″ high, 30″ wide. Tapestry and appliqué over a board. Fabrics are velvet, satin, and handspun natural and dyed wool.

FABRIC SCULPTURE #1. Jan Wagstaff. 50″ high, 8″ wide. Satin, and velvet stuffed with kapok.

EXTENDED BULB SCULPTURE. Jan Wagstaff. 1971. 62″ high, 17″ wide. Velvet and satin with kapok stuffing.

NOSFERATU. Susana Rolando. Jute, tufting, and knotting. *Courtesy, artist*

THREE WITCHES. Park Chambers. 36″ high. Sisal and wool. *Courtesy, artist and Deson-Zaks Gallery, Chicago*

FUJI'S VW STATION WAGON. Kathleen Knippel. Batik stuffed. *Courtesy, artist*

CENTAUR. Dahlov Ipcar. Cloth sculpture. *Courtesy, artist*

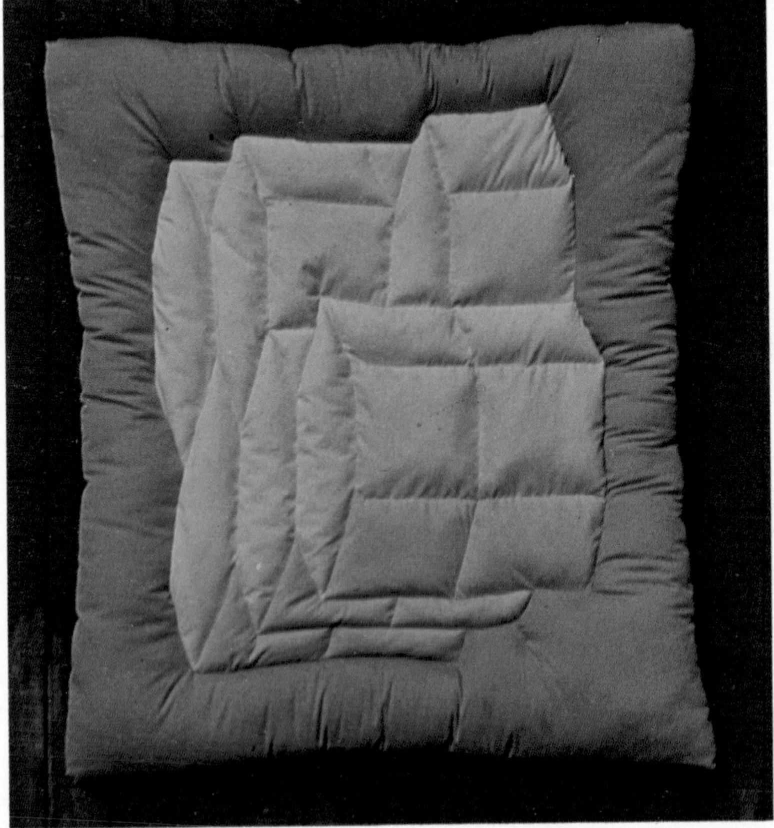

UNTITLED. Joan Lintault. 44″ high, 38″ wide. Cotton wall hanging using the trapunto technique and stuffed with Dacron. *Courtesy, artist*

FEATHER BODY ADORNMENTS. Susan Seligman. Feathers are combined with shells, buttons, and macramé.

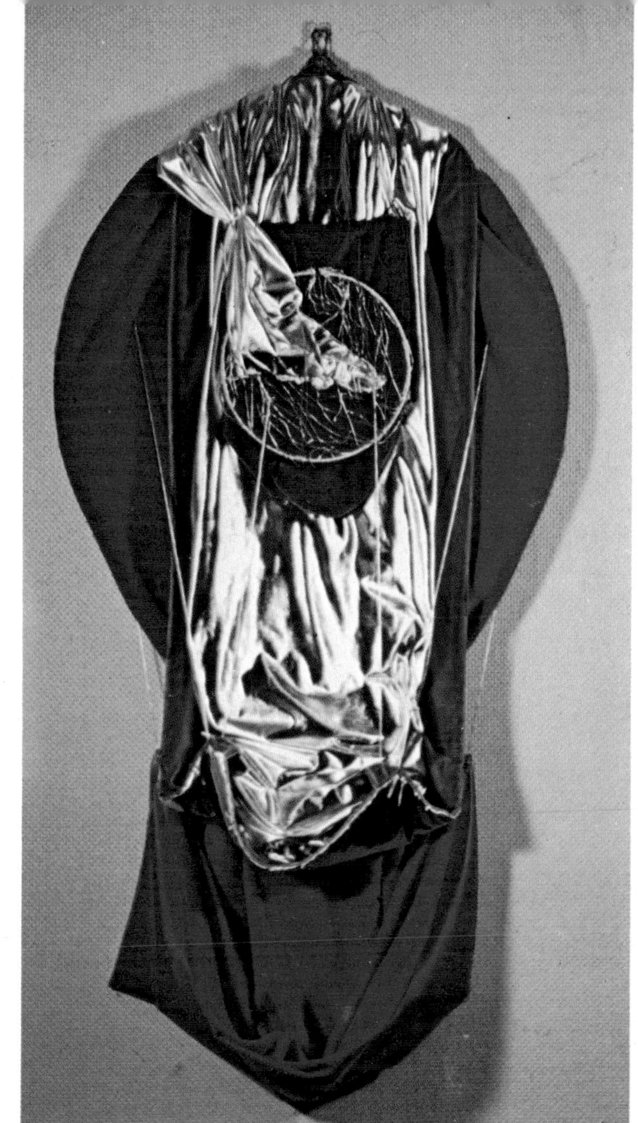

ROYALTY SERIES: THE PRINCESS. Jeanne Boardman Knorr, 5′ high, 3½′ wide, 4″ deep. Metallic fabrics and threads with velvet on a metal frame. *Courtesy, artist*

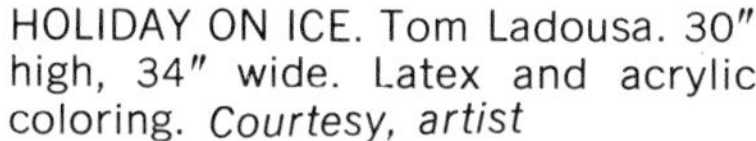

HOLIDAY ON ICE. Tom Ladousa. 30″ high, 34″ wide. Latex and acrylic coloring. *Courtesy, artist*

UNTITLED. Dolores Pacileo. Synthetic and natural fiber construction. *Collection, Beaunit Corp., New York. Courtesy, artist*

KNOTTING VENTURED—KNOTTING GAINED. Joan Michaels Paque. Hand-dyed sisal. Hollow coil sculpture. *Photo, Henry Paque*

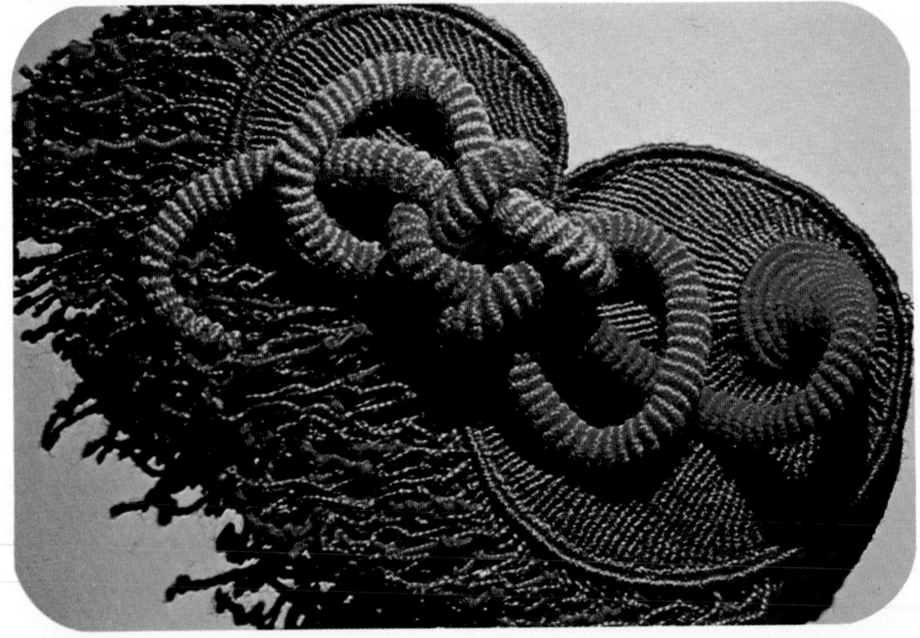

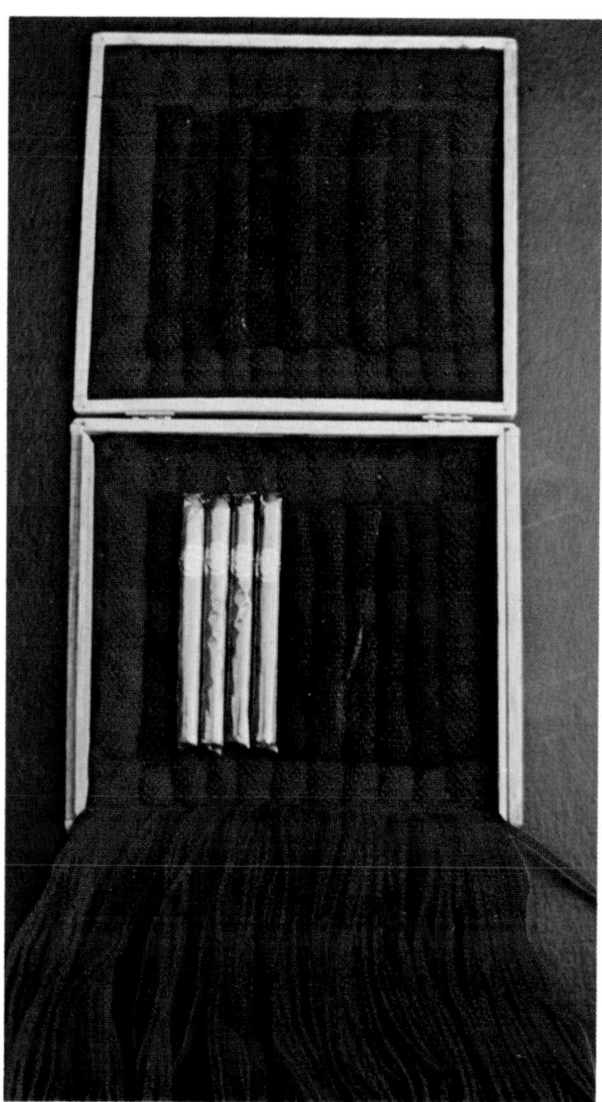

HUMIDOR. Elizabeth Kuhs. Woven and stuffed shapes in a box. Courtesy, artist

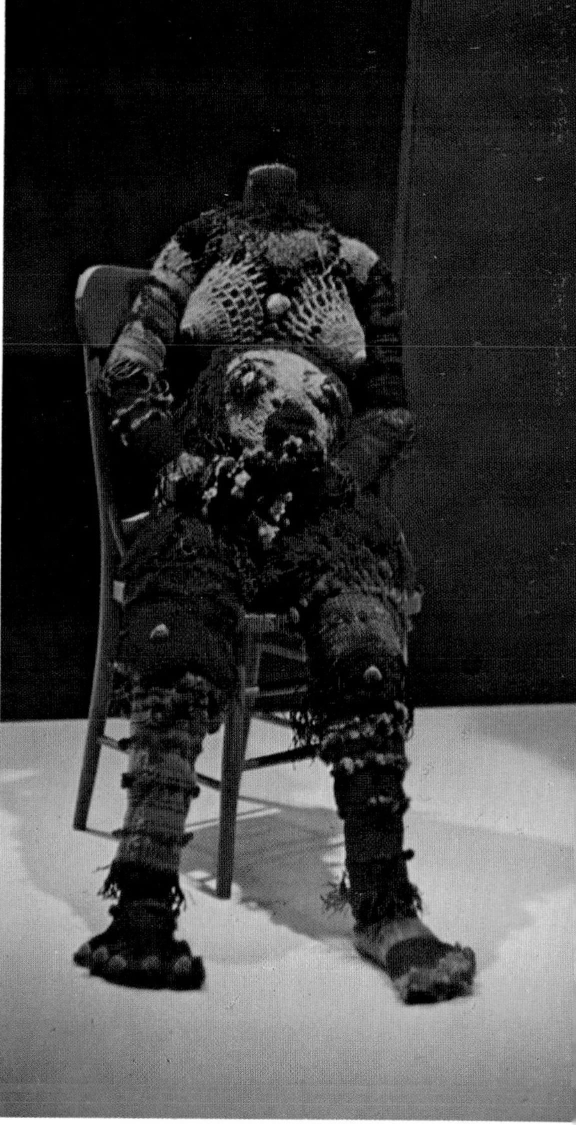

ROSIE. Gwynne Lott. Stuffed tapestry. *Courtesy, artist*

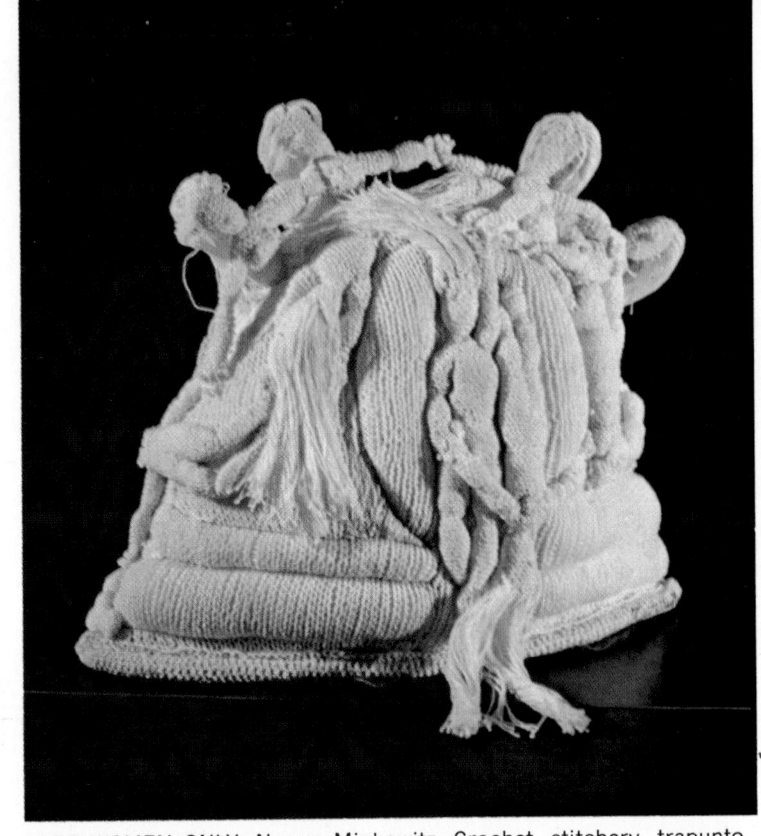

FOR WOMEN ONLY. Norma Minkowitz. Crochet, stitchery, trapunto, and hooking. *Courtesy, artist*

ANIMAL FARM. David Riegel. Stuffed and stitched animals. *Courtesy, artist*

INSIDE OUTSIDE MOVEMENT VI. Kenneth Weedman. 45″ high, 35″ wide, 23″ deep. Acrylic sheet. *Courtesy, artist*

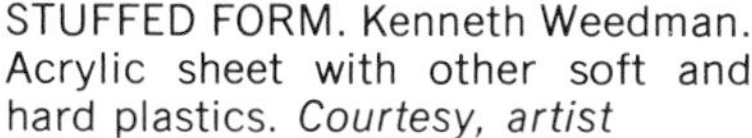

STUFFED FORM. Kenneth Weedman. Acrylic sheet with other soft and hard plastics. *Courtesy, artist*

WOVEN WIRE. Linda Ulvestad Fisher. Woven wires and fibers cascade from a stretched soft backing. *Courtesy, artist*

ENDOMETRIUM. Park Chambers. 30″ high, 6′ diameter. *Courtesy, artist and Deson-Zaks Gallery, Chicago*

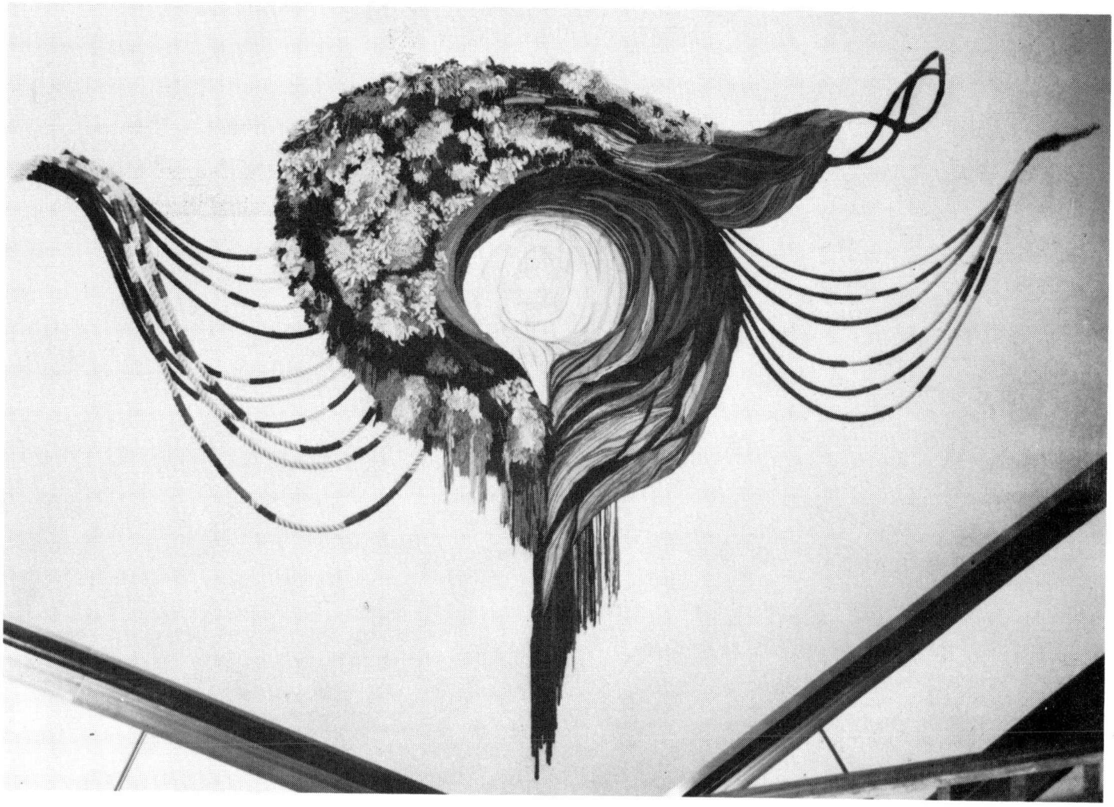

CHRYSALIS. Janet Kuemmerlein. 1972. 12′ high, 20′ wide. Fabrics and yarns were constructed in sections, then sewn together to a heavy backing with stuffing placed where desired.
Collection, Linscott, Haylett, Kansas City, Missouri, courtesy, artist

VENUS'S FLYTRAP. Becky Kirian. 1972. 28″ high, 12″ wide at bottom. Handwoven fabrics, rug hooking and sewing. Mohair and other fabrics.

Above and opposite page: Stuffed cloth sculptures by Dahlov Ipcar.

Above: ST. GEORGE AND THE DRAGON. 1972. 15″ high, 36″ wide for group.

Opposite page top: BLUE GNU.

Opposite page bottom: HEN AND ROOSTER.

Photos, Tom Jones

5

Fiber Sculptures: Non-woven

FIBER SCULPTURE (detail). Patrick Stokes. 1972. 10′ high. *Photographed at the American Craftsman Gallery, Chicago*

SINCE THE EARLY 1960S AN EXTENSIVE INTERNATIONAL MOVEment has developed using fibers in three-dimensional constructions. An early exposure signaling a new direction for textile arts occurred in 1963: an exhibition of *Woven Forms* at the Museum of Contemporary Crafts in New York. The creative stimulus offered by this show gradually changed the creation and shape of weavings. They moved from the flat two-dimensional statement into relief dimension and three dimensions.

Lenore Tawney was among the first weavers who broke away from the rigidity of the square or rectangle to shapes that extended out in a free-form movement. The surfaces of the hangings were enriched with fibers of varying lengths and some that flowed beyond the edges.

Eventually, craftsmen sought additional techniques compatible with the woven surface that would allow them a greater freedom than those used with the loom: a freedom to explore the potential of fiber structurally and expressively. Soon a whole new vitality burst forth. Macramé became a method and an end in itself that captured unprecedented enthusiasm among craftsmen. The knots themselves provided a structural, expressive, and decorative quality by virtue of repetition. Other techniques that were explored included twining, braiding, plaiting, knitting, crochet, and basketry methods. All are single element techniques that are as ancient as they are new. They are techniques that have appeared in utilitarian fiber objects since the beginning of time. It was only for craftsmen to relearn these techniques and apply them to their contemporary statements.

In early 1970 the show *Fiber as Medium* was organized in Los

UNTITLED. Sheila Hicks. 1971. 30″ diameter. Wrapped mohair.
Photo, Jan Ságl

Angeles. From this, the exhibit *Deliberate Entanglements* was born and traveled to many museums throughout the country. In some instances it was a museum's first nontraditional show. The pieces were termed sculpture, but not of the traditional media. Yet the sizes and aesthetic quality of the works were so outstanding that public awareness began to open up to fiber as a serious art medium.

Materials used for fiber sculptures include a vast assortment of cords and yarns. Jute, sisal, cotton, nylon, and other cords and ropes can be purchased from hardware stores and cordage companies. Yarns can be purchased from any weaving or knitting supplier; many are listed under Sources of Supplies. In addition to readily available

UNTITLED. Sheila Hicks. 1968. 36″ wide, 36″ deep. Wrapped linen.
Photo, Jan Ságl

yarns, craftsmen also use handspun yarn, roving, unplied fibers, raw wool, fur, plastic cords, plastic strips, metallic materials such as wires, aluminum strips—in short, anything that is available and that can be worked into the statement. Some pieces are supported on armatures; others are self-supporting by the combination of the cords and the technique, knotting or wrapping, which makes them stiff and solid.

Directions for macramé, wrapping, braiding, and so forth follow at the end of the chapter. There is no one best way to progress; once you know the techniques, you are free to combine them any way you like.

Opposite page:
Fiber sculptures on exhibit at the Deson-Zaks Gallery, Chicago. Park Chambers. 1972. *Left:* LEATHER LINGAM. *Center:* LIP GLOSS. *Right:* BUSBY.
"Busby," Collection, Dr. and Mrs. Porter, San Francisco

BOA. Park Chambers. 1972. 40" high. Sisal and wool.
Courtesy, artist

PARAVANT. Ritzi and Peter Jacobi. 1970. 5′ high, 10′ wide, 16″ deep. Wood and wrapped fibers. On exhibition at the Biennale Venice, Pavillion Romania.
Courtesy, artist

MACRAMÉ TEXTURED WALLS. Françoise Grossen. 1969. Earth-colored hand-dyed jute is used for extensive wall treatments in the lobby of the Hyatt Regency O'Hare Hotel, Chicago.
Courtesy, Hyatt Regency O'Hare, Chicago

ABAKAN. Magdalena Abakanowicz. 1971. On exhibition at the show *The Fabric Forms of Magdalena Abakanowicz*, Pasadena Art Museum, California.

Photo, Richard Gross

UNTITLED. Mary Ann Glantz. 1972. 18″ high, 10′ wide. Jute and polypropylene. Macramé and twining. Three fragmented parts are related to one another. The horizontal openings symbolize mouths ready to give and receive whatever comes along.

Photographed at Fabrications '72, Detroit

OCCULT IMAGES. Joan Sterrenburg. 1973. 44″ high, 18″ wide, 6″ deep. *Above:* Black and beige cotton and linen using hitching and twining and combined with wheel-thrown ceramic forms. *Right:* 44″ high, 17″ wide, 6″ deep. Clove hitching with a white ceramic earthenware wheel-thrown form. Black raffia.

Detail showing the ceramic forms created with holes that allow the fibers to be strung through for macramé.

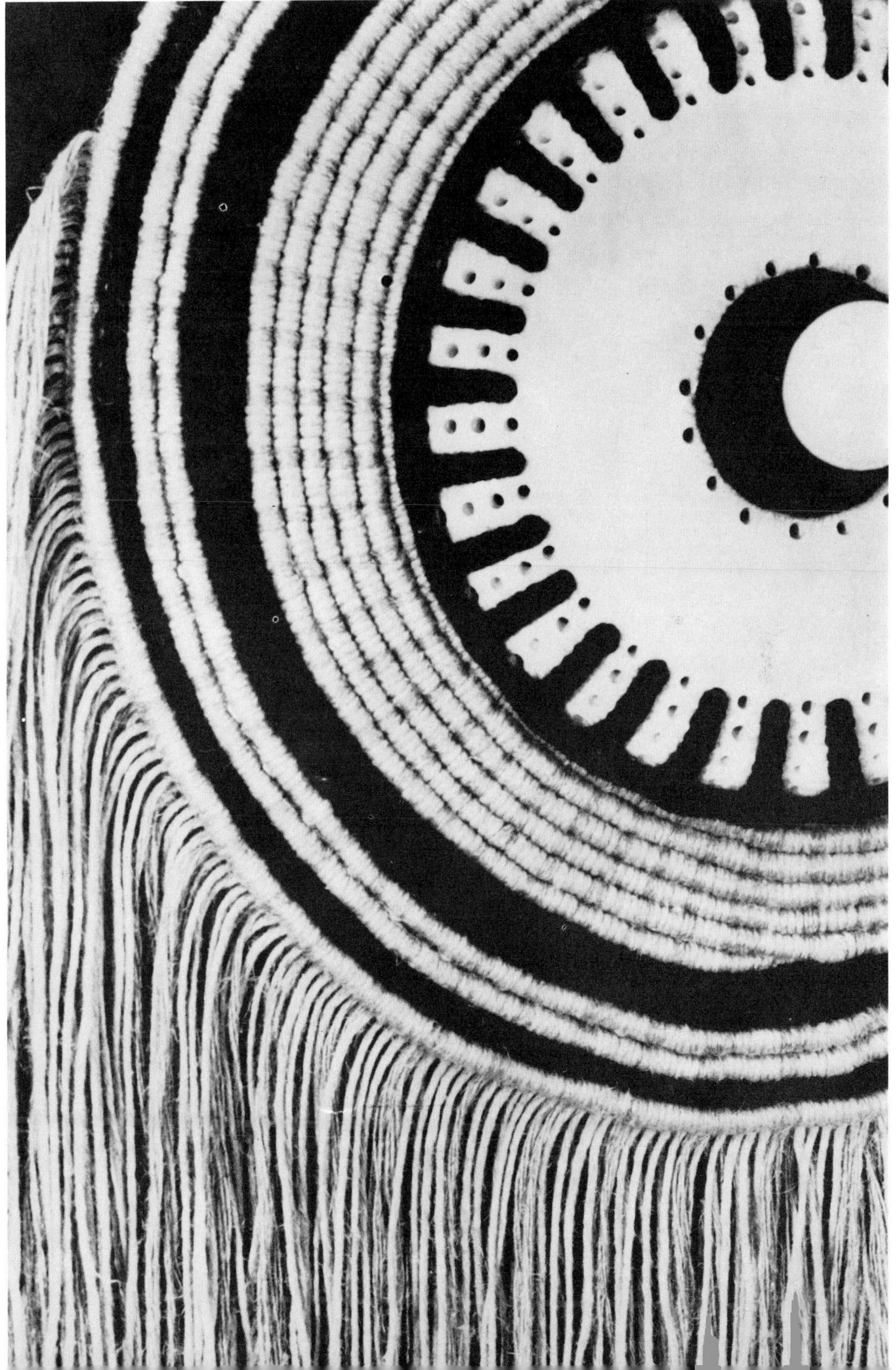

NET OF FIREFLIES. Park Chambers. 8′ high. Sisal and wool. *Collection, Mr. and Mrs. J. Reinish, New York Courtesy, artist*

FETISH OBJECT. Jeanne Boardman Knorr. 1973. 2½′ high, 14″ wide, 6″ deep. Wool yarn wrapped over metal and ornamented with feathers. *Below:* Back view.
Courtesy, artist

VIGOUREAU. Patrick Stokes. 1972. 36″ high, 8″ diameter. Dyed hemp wrapped around the coils of an automobile spring and placed within. *Below:* Detail. *Photographed at the American Craftsman Gallery, Chicago*

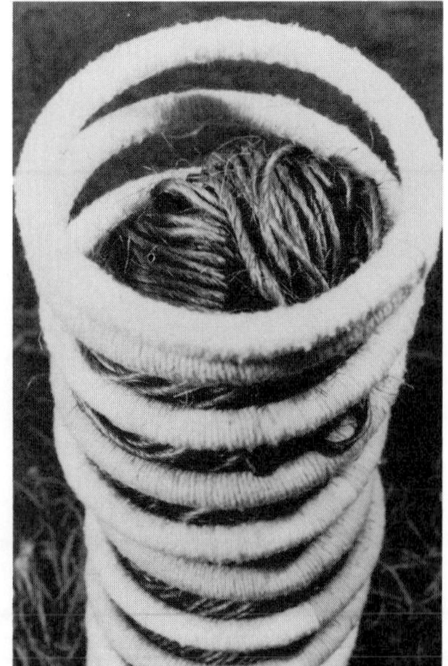

SOFTWARE ARRANGEMENT #1. Susan Sabin. 1972. 7′ high, 2½′ square. (Two views.) Wood, nylon, and mohair.

Photos, Lee Milner

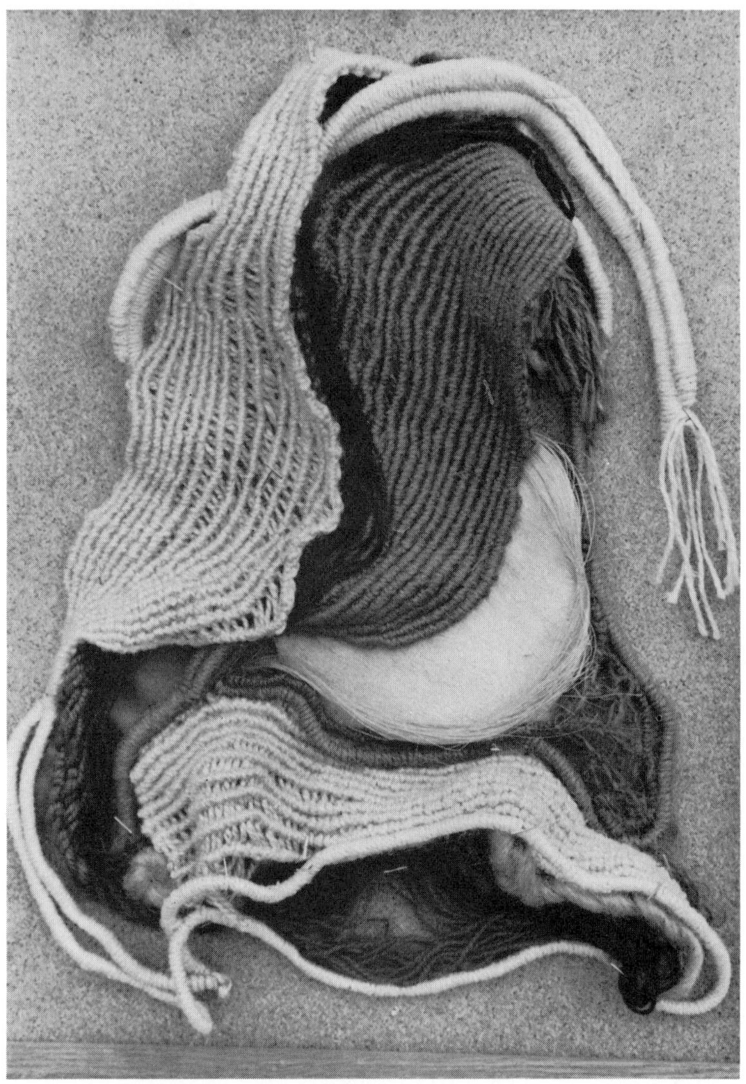

Approximately 15″ x 20″. Maquette for the wall was made to scale and mounted on a board.

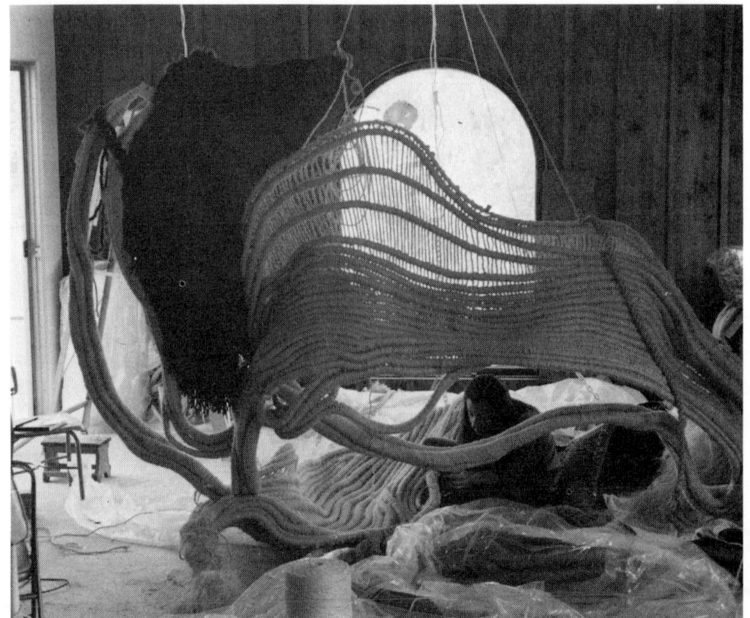

Work in progress in the artist's living room from which all furniture has been removed. The work is strung to hooks and pulleys set in beams in the ceiling. Techniques include knotting, latch hooking for the leather strips, and general assembly techniques. The piece had to be fireproofed to conform to building codes (see Appendix).

Photo, Virginia Black

FIBER SCULPTURE WALL. Libby Platus. 1972. 12′ high, 10′ wide, 2′ deep. Sisal, cowhide, and leather. An environmental wall created as part of the architectural planning of the Irvine Corp., Big Canyon Country Club, Newport Beach, California. *Photo, Jack Koeler*

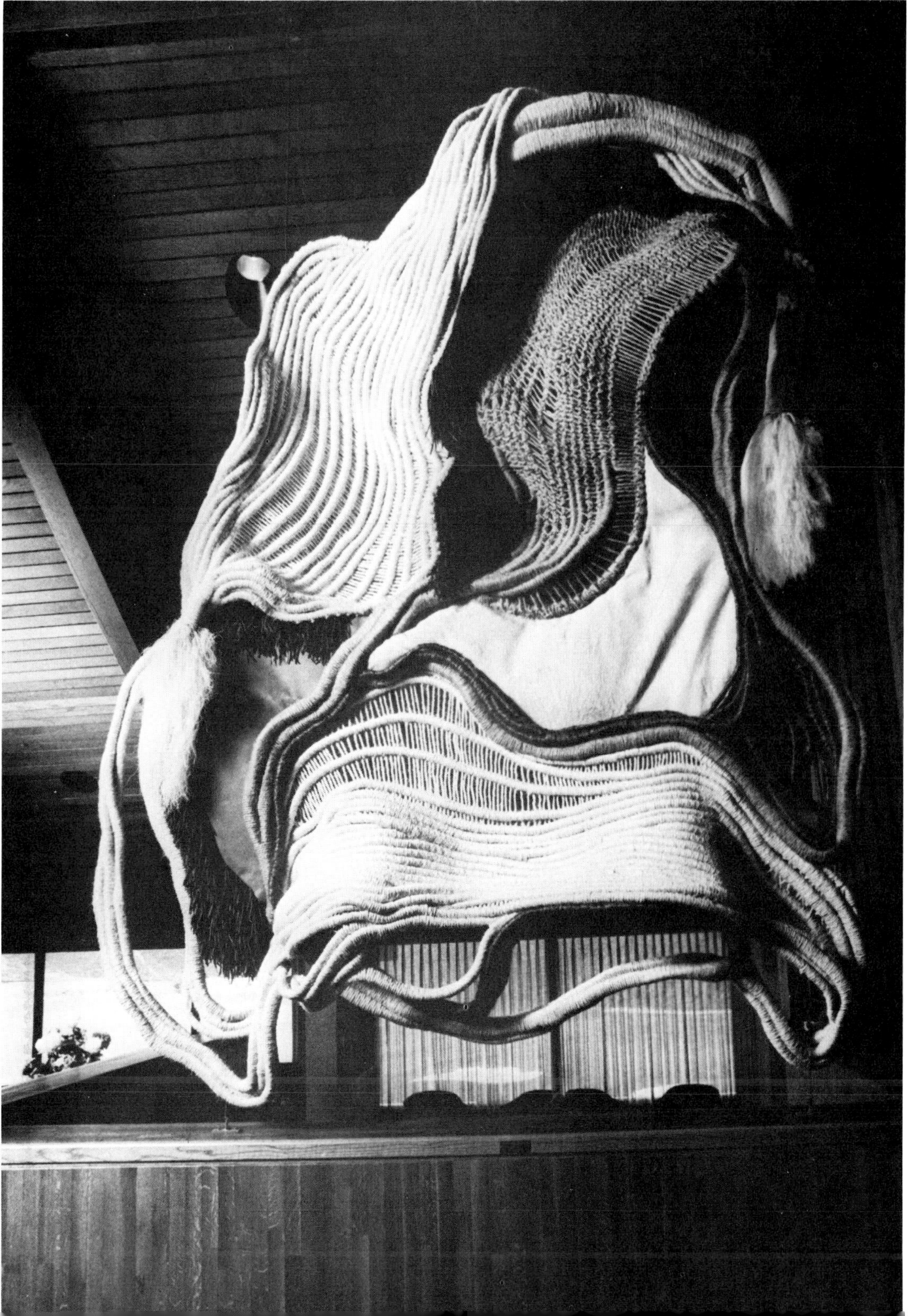

Opposite page:
ERETZ STAU. Libby Platus. 1973. 7½′ high, 6′ wide, 1′ deep. Fiber sculpture wall installed at the Carolando Hotel, Orlando, Florida.
Photos, Phil Shuper

Back view of *Eretz Stau.*

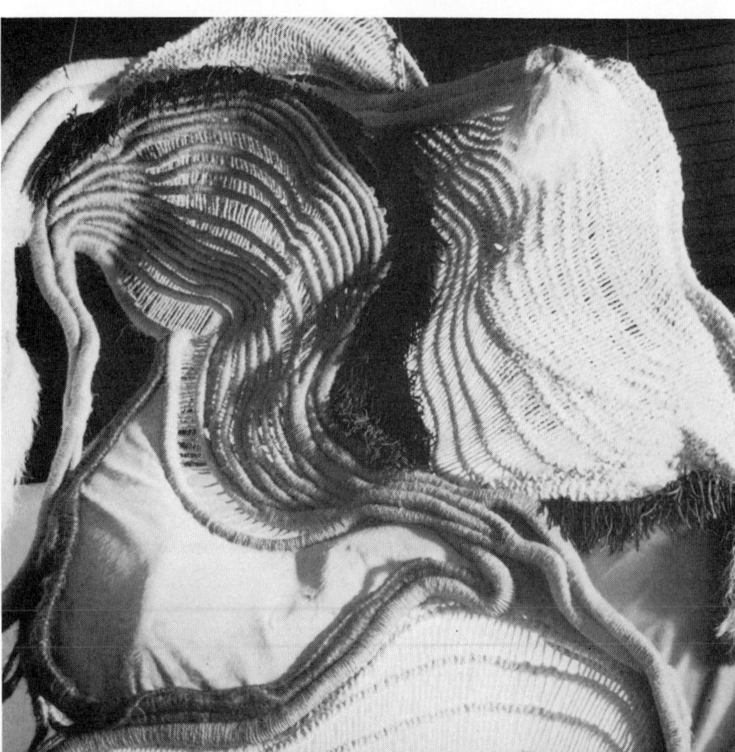

Front view of *Eretz Stau.*

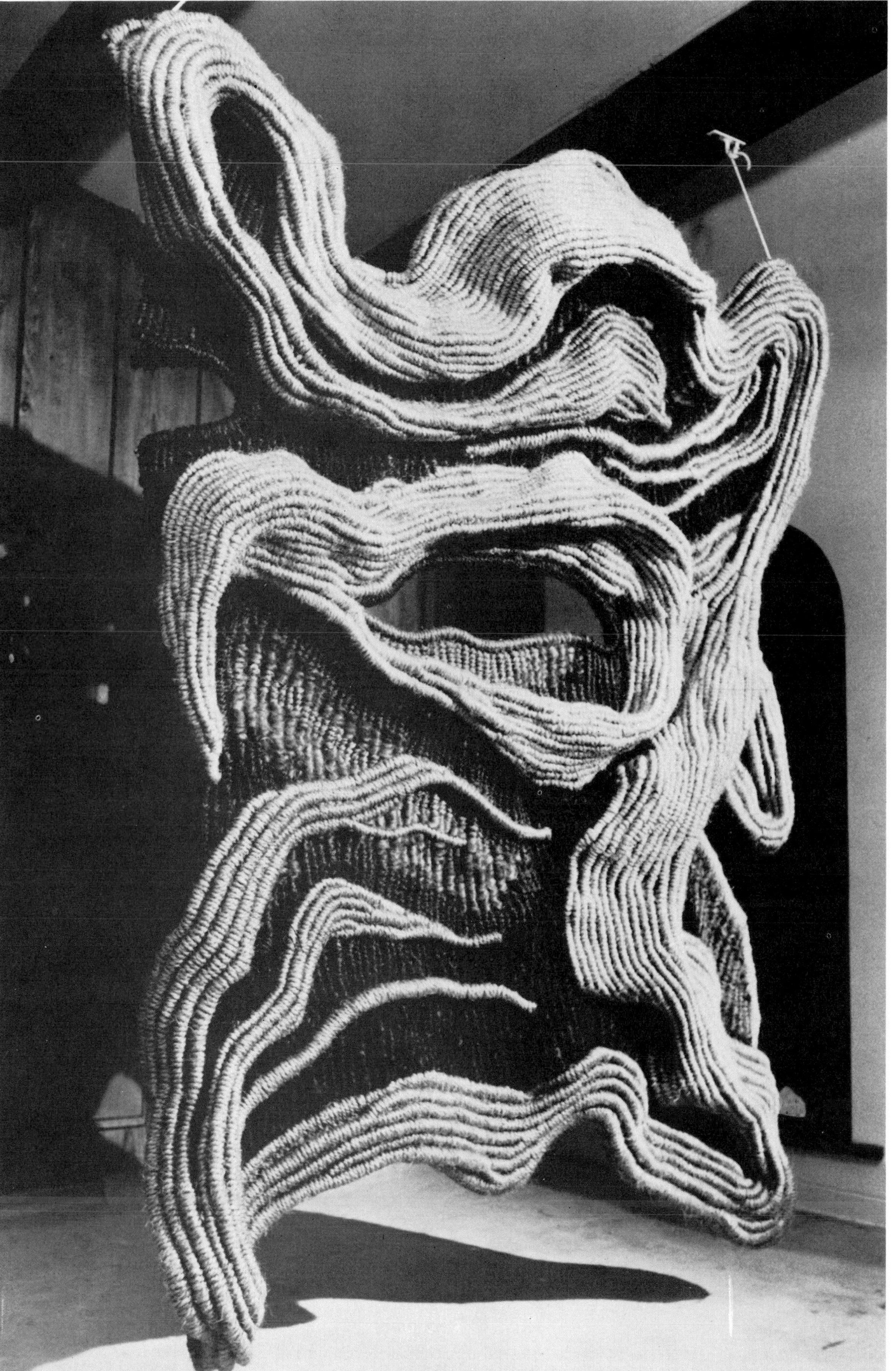

MACRA METAMORPHOSIS. Aurelia Muñoz. 1972. Pearl white cotton rope. Clove hitching with the front and back of the knot for different motifs.
Collection, Miguel Adria, Barcelona, Spain

MOTHERBALL #2. Sharon Giacomo. 4½′ high, 4′ 2″ wide. Thick jute. Shaped entirely with clove hitching; no stuffing added.
Courtesy, artist

WITH RESPECT TO ALL THOSE WHO HAVEN'T. J. Leroy Steele. 1972. 7′ high, 18″ wide. White cotton cord (mason line). Handwoven split tapestry panels at the back portion are offset by square knotted and wrapped endings at the back and front.

USELESS TOTEM. Yves-Armand Millecam. 1972. 51″ high. Wool in browns, grays, and blues.
Courtesy, Galerie Boutique Germain, Paris

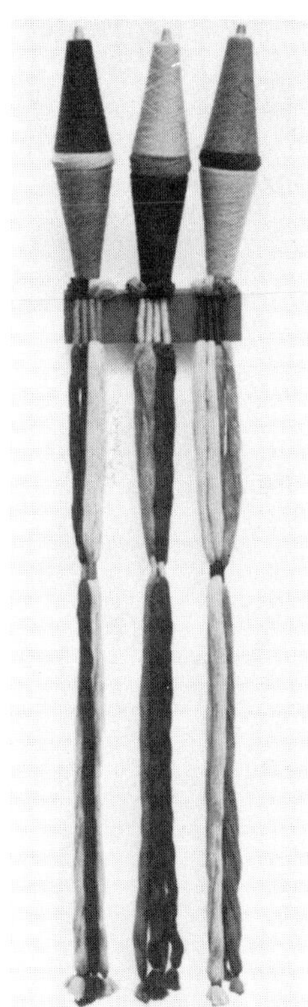

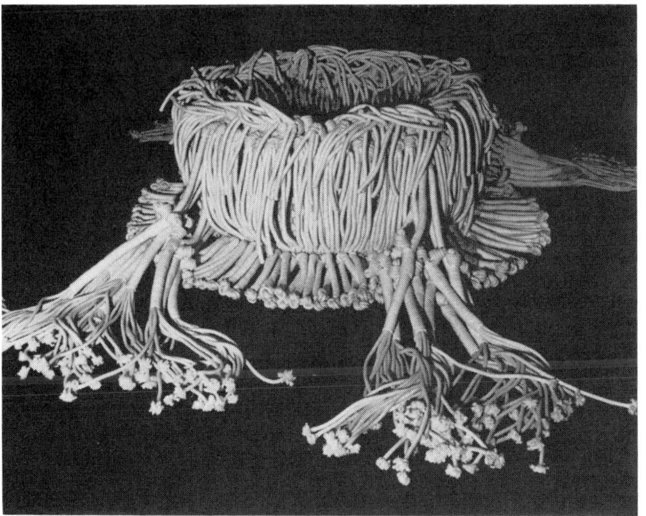

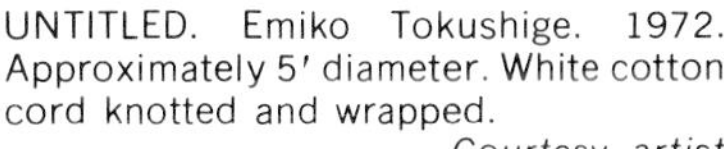

UNTITLED. Emiko Tokushige. 1972. Approximately 5′ diameter. White cotton cord knotted and wrapped.
Courtesy, artist

HANG ON. David Holbourne. 30″ high, 36″ diameter. Sisal rope in shades of yellow.

Courtesy, artist

TEASEL WEED. Martha Ronfeldt. 1972. 19″ high, 15″ wide at bottom. Knotting and rug hooking.

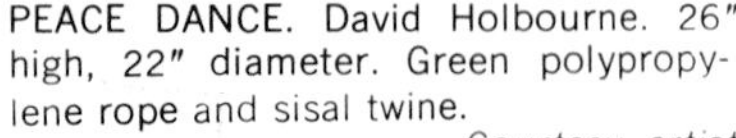

PEACE DANCE. David Holbourne. 26″ high, 22″ diameter. Green polypropylene rope and sisal twine.

Courtesy, artist

Left: MEANDROUS FORM #1. Michelle Lester. 1972. 7½′ high. Wool yarn wrapped around cotton cords.

Right: BLUE DACTYLOID. Michelle Lester. 10′ high. Rayon yarns wrapped around nylon, wool, and cotton cords.
Courtesy, artist

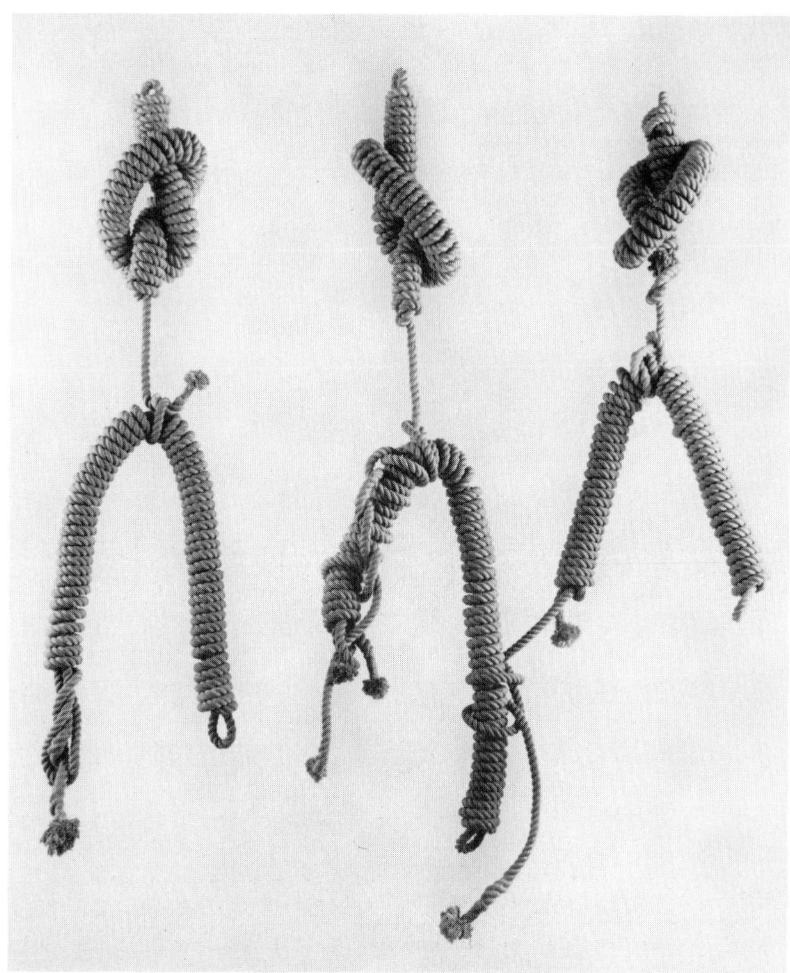

DANSEUR. Michelle Lester. 4′ high, 4′ wide grouping. Cotton rope.
Courtesy, artist

T. W.'S FLY SWAT. Gary Trentham. 12″ long. Natural linen knotted and wrapped.

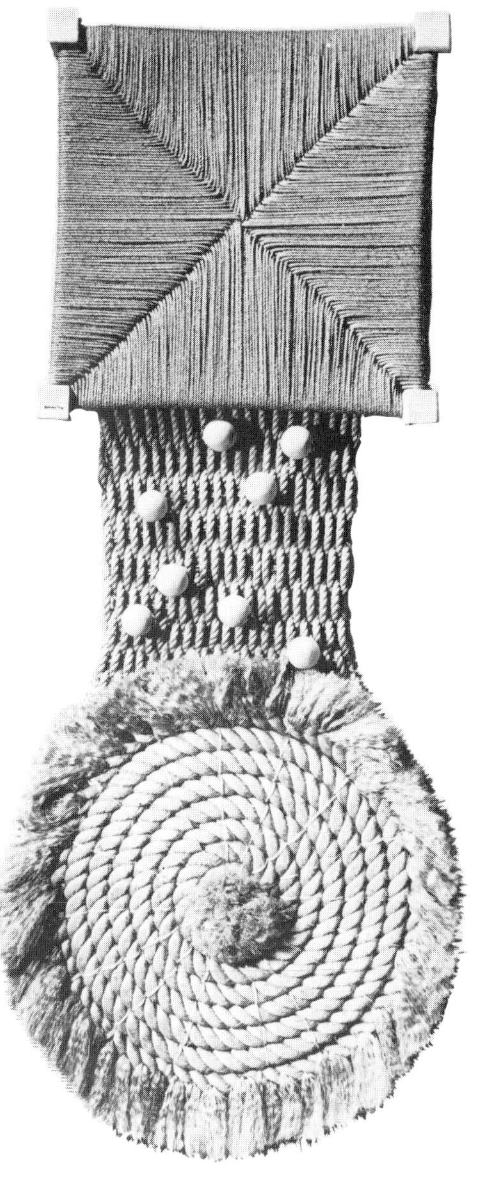

UNTITLED. Rolando Lopez Dirube. 1970. 10′ high, 3½″ diameter nylon rope.
Courtesy, artist

THE OCEAN EAGLE. Rolando Lopez Dirube. 1970. 10′ high. Ropes and parts washed ashore from a capsized ship.
Courtesy, artist

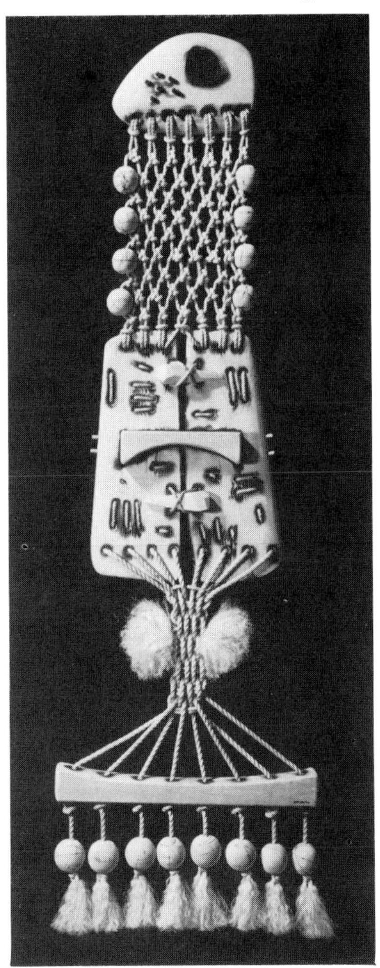

GEOSHAPE I. Nancy J. Howell-Koehler. 48″ diameter. Sisal and jute on duck canvas.
Courtesy, artist

FORM IN PLAIN AIR. Aurelia Muñoz. 1971. 63″ high, 23″ diameter. Sisal cord macrame.

Courtesy, artist

BANYAN. Sheila Hicks. 1971. Wrapping.
Photographed at the Museum of Contemporary Art, Chicago

OF VIRGIN BIRTH. Eugene Eby. 1972. 17″ high, 15″ diameter. Knotting and wrapping.

UNTITLED. Sharon Kouris. Wrapped fibers are worked to create graduated sizes, widths, and changing colors.
Photographed at the Art Institute of Chicago

MAN AND WOMAN. Michi Ouchi. 1972. Man: 60″ high, 36″ wide. Woman: 50″ high, 36″ wide. Hand-dyed jute twine knotted and woven with tie-dyed cotton broadcloth quilted.

Opposite page:
Detail showing the knotting and weaving; observe that panels of the clove hitching hang away from the woven surface.

Courtesy, artist

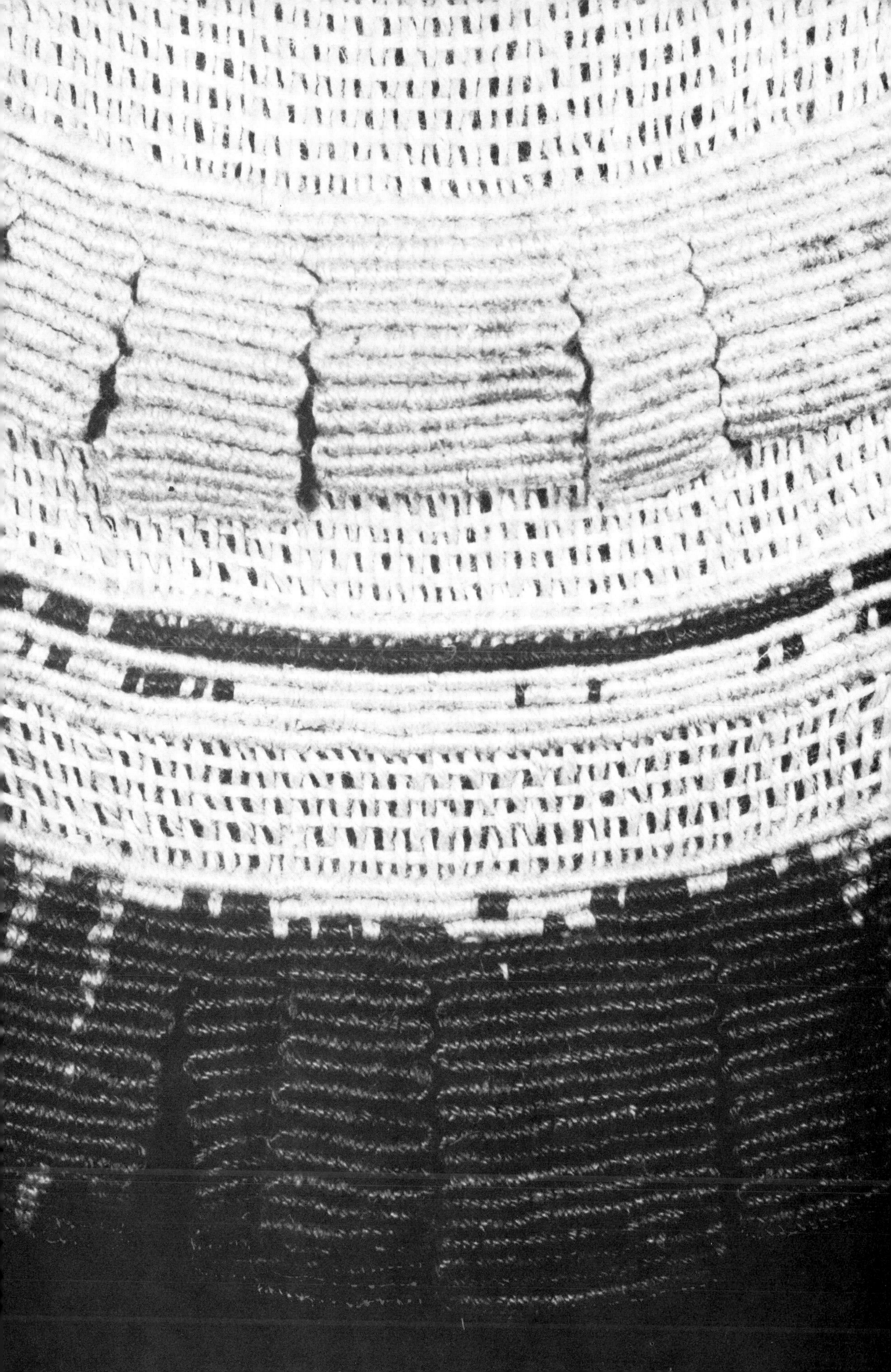

WATERFALL. Loera K. Stewart. 1968. 48″ high, 12″ wide, 4″ deep. Jute knotted and looped.
Collection, Jules Cogan, Chicago Photo, Don Williams

HEADDRESS. Leora K. Stewart. 1968. 24″ high, 9″ wide, 5″ deep. Jute knotted and looped. Inspired by headdress and hair arrangements of Egyptian works. Each side is different.
Collection, Donald Sheffield, New York

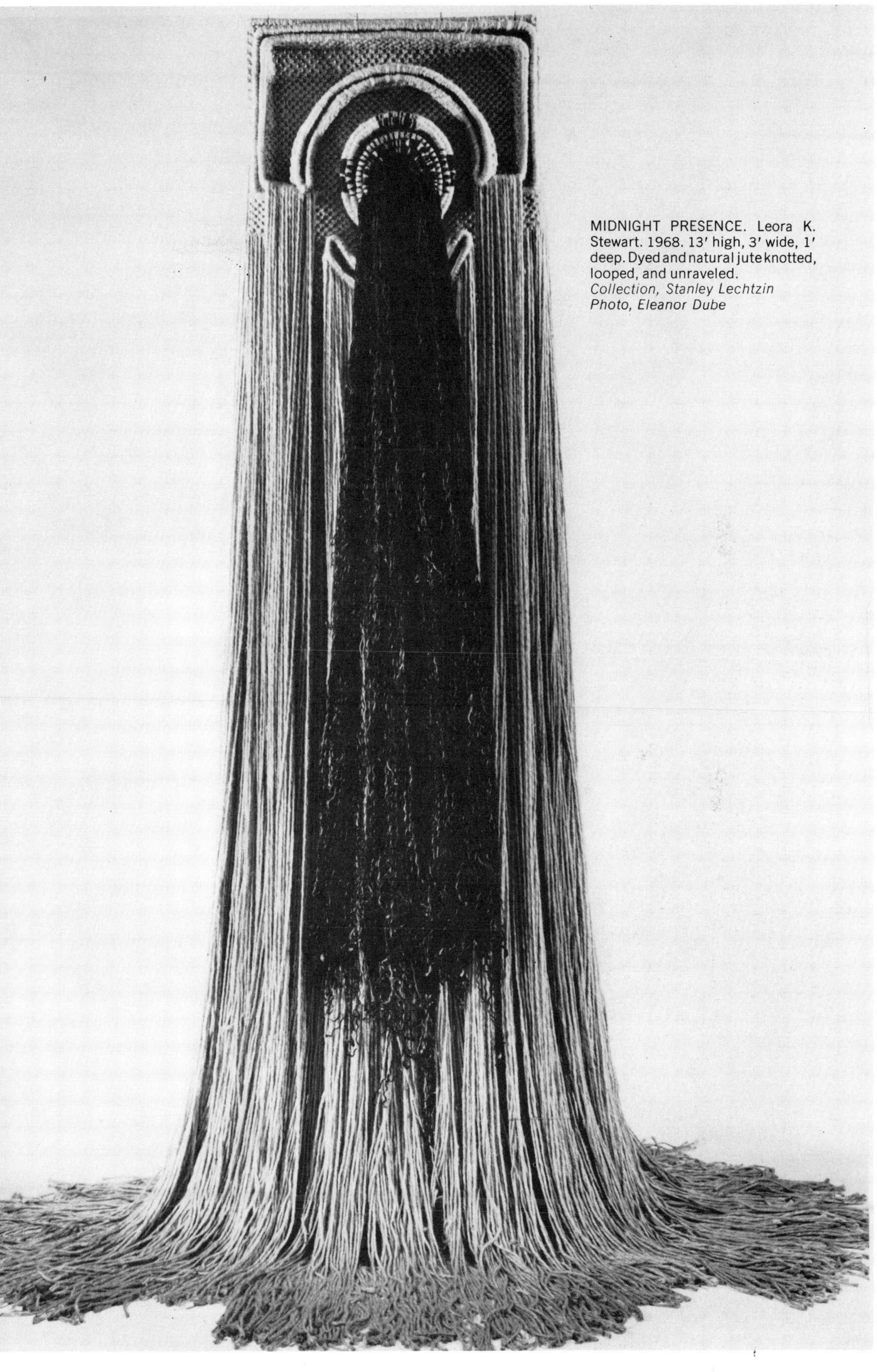

MIDNIGHT PRESENCE. Leora K. Stewart. 1968. 13′ high, 3′ wide, 1′ deep. Dyed and natural jute knotted, looped, and unraveled.
Collection, Stanley Lechtzin
Photo, Eleanor Dube

NON-WOVEN FIBER TECHNIQUES

Non-woven fiber techniques are usually very simple, single element procedures. It is their repetition and combination that gives them strength and impact in an aesthetic statement. Knots, braids, twists, wrapping, and basket-coiling methods were all used by primitive man and usually are learned by young children in Scout groups and primary art classes. The examples substantiate the use of these simple methods as a modern art form. When combined with the elements of design using form, structure, repetition, texture, color, and so forth, a work of art results.

Macramé

Basic macramé includes a progression of two knots used in multiple arrangements; the clove hitch and the square knot. Beginners usually work on a soft foam or cardboard surface that will accept pins. With experience, you can knot the cords while they hang freely from rods or armatures.

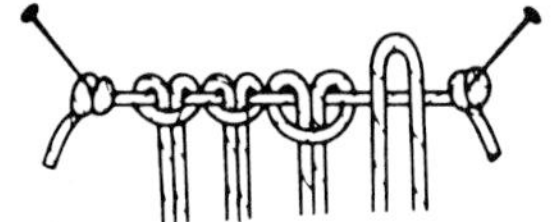

1. Knotting cords are mounted onto another cord, bar, twig, or other object with a Lark's Head. Double the cord and place it over the mounting cord. Fold it over the mounting cord and bring the two loose cords through from front to back.

Clove hitch

2. The Clove Hitch can be tied in any direction: horizontally, diagonally, and vertically. It is one of the basic macramé knots. Each strand of the knotting cords is tied individually over an anchor cord. The angle of the anchor cord determines the angle of the finished bar of clove hitches.

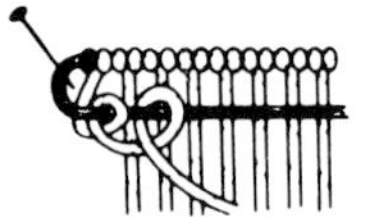

Left to right: Pin the left-hand cord to your working surface. Bring it horizontally *over* all the vertical cords and hold it taut. This becomes the anchor cord. With the next cord make a loop over, around, and under the anchor cord. Make a second loop over, to the right of the knot, to the back and under the anchor cord. This completes the clove hitch.

Continue tying *each cord individually* over the same anchor cord. Push each knot close to the anchor cord and the preceding knot to form an even ridge of knots.

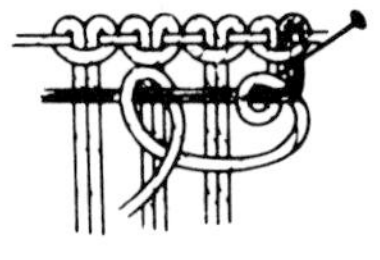

3. *Clove hitch right to left:* To carry the knotting back: Pin the anchor at the right side and reverse the knot procedure. Loop the first strand over, around, and behind the anchor cord. Make a

second loop with the same strand to the left of the first, over, around, and under the anchor.

4. *Diagonal clove hitching:* Macramé patterns are made by changing the direction of the clove-hitch bars. This is done by holding the anchor cord in the direction you wish the bar to take and continuing to clove hitch. A cord may be picked up anywhere in the knotting and used as an anchor cord for angled, short, and long clove-hitch bars.

The square knot

1. *The square knot,* the second basic macramé knot, is usually tied with four cords. The two inside knotting cords serve as anchor cords for the two outside knotting cords. Square knot patterns appear infinite; they may be tied loosely or tightly; in any multiples.

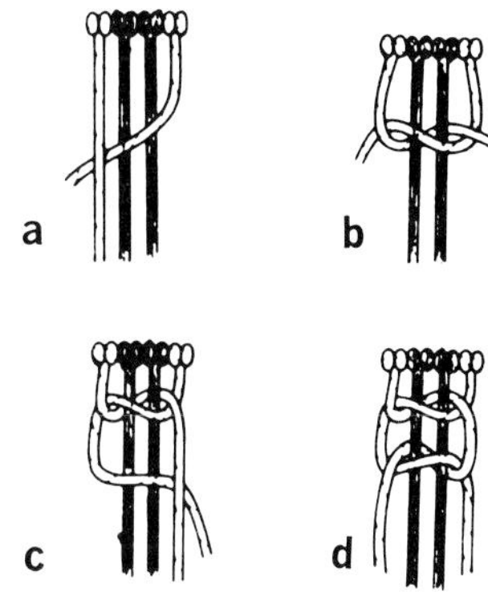

a) Hold the center cords taut. Bring the *right* cord *over* and to the *left* of the two anchor cords; place the *left* cord over the *right.*

b) Bring the left cord *under* the anchors and up through the loop formed by the right cord. This completes only the first half of the square knot.

c) For the second half, reverse the procedure; bring the *left* cord over and to the *right* of the two anchor cords and place the *right* cord over it.

d) Bring the *right* cord *under* the anchors and up through the loop formed by the left cord. Pull the cords tight for the finished knot.

2. *Alternating square knots.* To make patterns and hold the cords together, the alternating square knot progression is indispensable. Work with multiples of four cords. For the first row: Make the square knots using four cords for each knot.

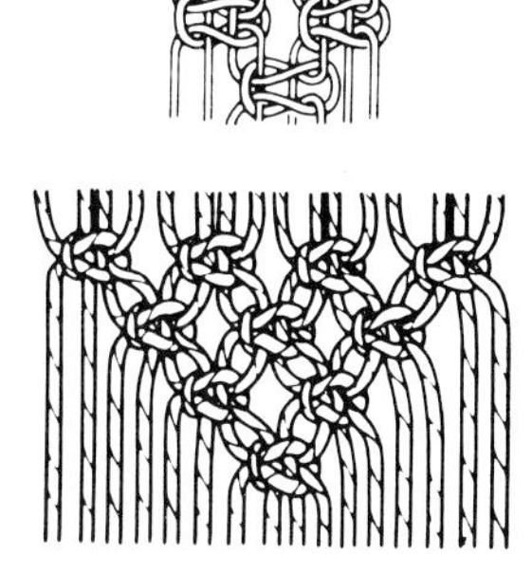

For the second row: Leave two strands at the beginning unknotted and begin to knot with the next multiple of four cords and continue across the row leaving two unknotted cords at the end. For the third row, pick up the two unknotted cords and use again as in the first row.

Different progressions of the alternate square knotting yield a variety of patterns.

3. *To make a circular form:*

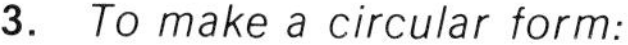

Mount knotting cords with a Lark's Head from a circle of cord, a metal or plastic ring for an immediate progression into a three-dimensional shape. New cords may be added into the work at any point by pinning as shown. As the knotting progresses, work over a round stool or hang from a rope or other device so that you can manipulate the form in three dimensions.

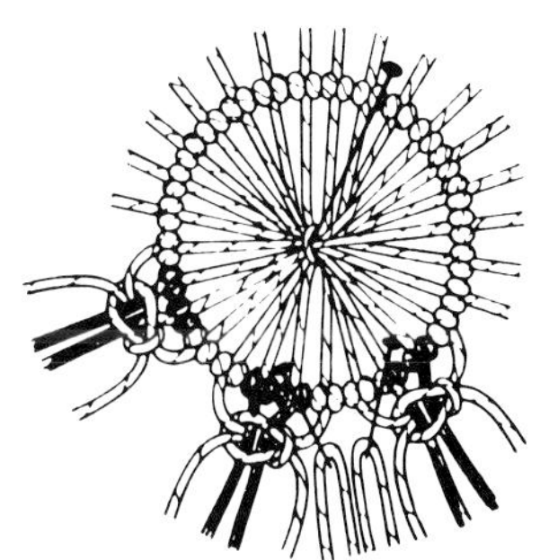

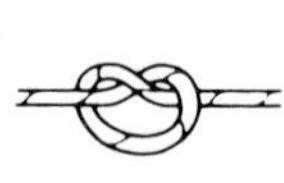

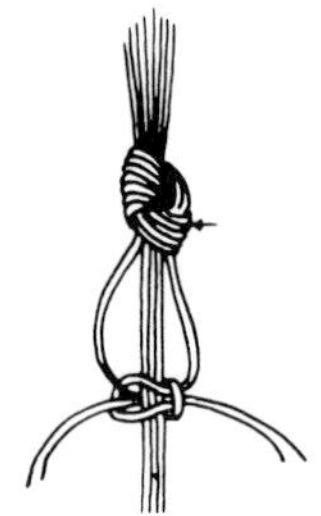

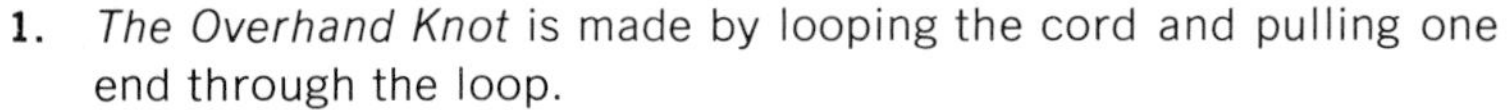

1. *The Overhand Knot* is made by looping the cord and pulling one end through the loop.

The grouped overhand knot is frequently used to work several cords from one starting point and then divide out into a pattern; it may be used instead of the Lark's Head mounting.

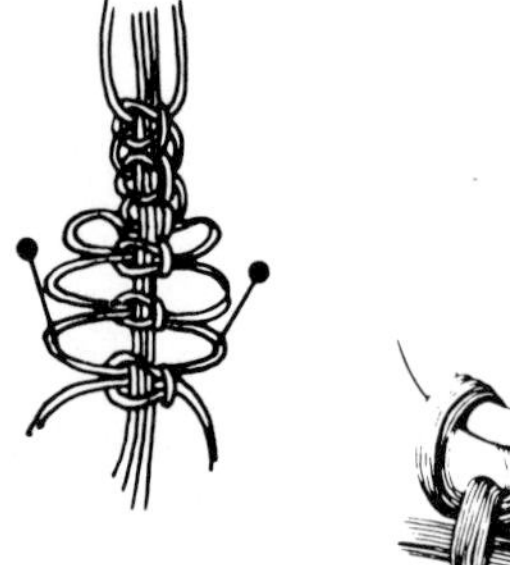

2. *The Butterfly Square Knot* is used to create a motif along a chain of square knots; the resulting loop can also be used for beads. When making the square knot, pin the knotting cords out as far as you want them and then make your knot. When you remove the pins, the loops remain.

3. Cords can also be mounted directly over a hoop or ring with the square knot or with groups of cords tied into a square knot. No Lark's Head mounting is used.

Wrapping

4. Wrapping cords around a core of another cord or other material can be used as a statement in itself or in conjunction with other knotting, weaving, and coiling techniques. There are many ways to wrap and the following will offer suggestions. Usually, it is easier to hold the core cord, or cords, taut by anchoring one or both ends to an object.

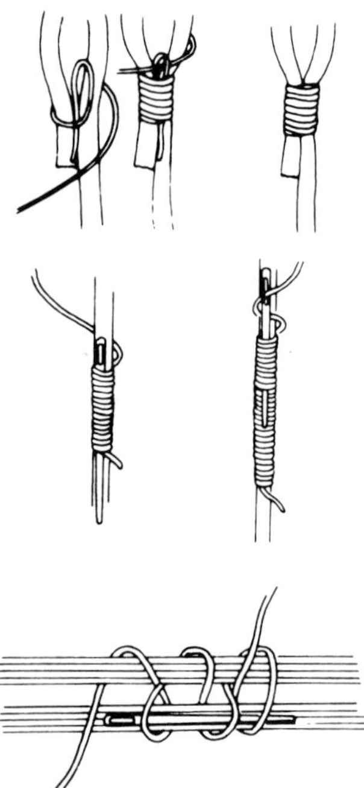

5. *Self-cord wrapping:* Can be used to wrap two or more cords together, or for one cord. Loop the end parallel with the core; make the loop longer than the wrap is to be. Wrap the cord and bring the end through the loop. Pull the opposite end of the looped cord into the wrap to secure it.

1. *Needle wrapping:* This method is convenient when wrapping very long lengths of cord, and when the wrapping cord is small enough to fit through a large eye needle. Wrap the core and wrap the needle along with the core. Near the top, thread the wrapping cord through the needle and pull the needle all the way through the wrap. The cord will then be secure within the wrap.

2. *Figure 8 wrap:* Two groups of cords can be wrapped with a figure 8 progression to result in a doubled appearance to the wrap. Insert the needle into one side of the figure 8 as in the needle wrap, above, thread through, and pull tightly. The entire wrap should be done tightly; the drawing shows the progression loosely.

Basket coiling

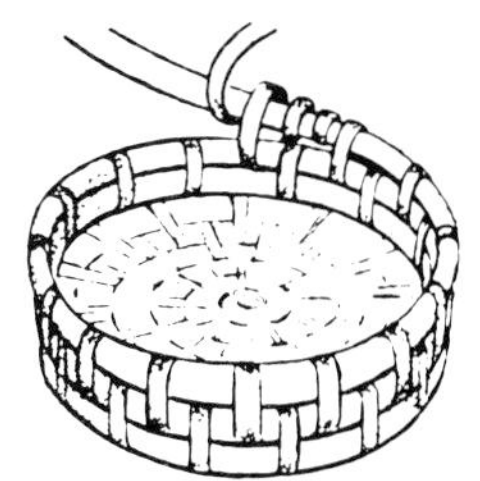

Simple basket-coiling techniques are being employed in many of the sculptural forms. This involves wrapping a core of a thick cord or multiple cords with string or cord and working the wrapping so that one coil is joined to another. Coiling is an ancient technique normally used with grasses such as reed and raffia. But it is also done with cords and yarns in contemporary fiber techniques.

1. Taper the core cord and wrap by hand or with a needle for a short distance.
2. Bend the wrapped cord and bring the wrapping around two coils as shown. When enough coils are worked, the basket is shaped by placing one coil on top of the other instead of next to it. Another stitch used to hold the coils together is the figure 8.
3. Sewing—A core can be wrapped, coiled, and the coils sewn together with clear thread. Or they can be sewn with another color decorative thread to create an obvious design.

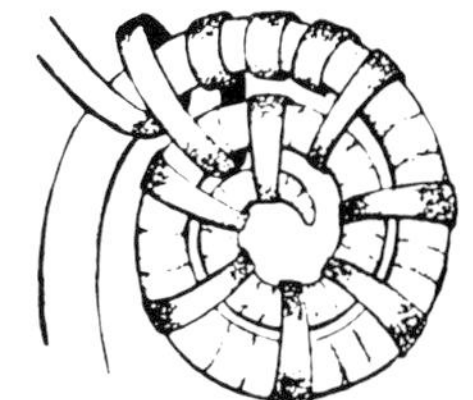

Lazy Squaw

Twining

Twining is actually a weaving technique. but it is also used extensively in basket methods and other nonwoven fiber forms. It consists of working two horizontal weft cords simultaneously over the verticle warp cords. The warps are held taut and the wefts are passed one over and one behind the warp; they are crossed and then worked over the next warp, crossed, and so on. Twining can be used with macramé, braiding, and other techniques.

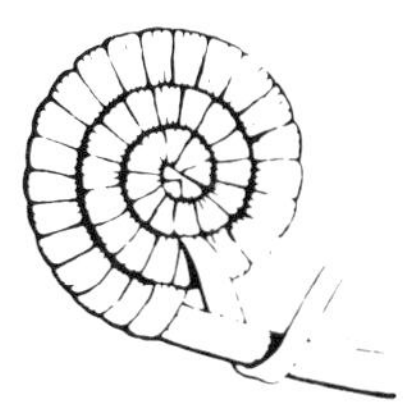

Figure 8

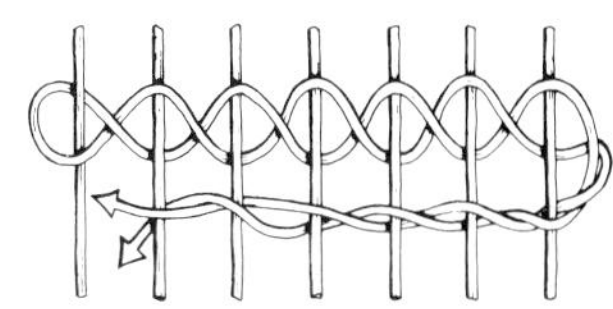

Twining

View of studio of Leora K. Stewart with works in progress.

6
Woven Forms

WOVEN FORMS HAVE BROKEN AWAY FROM CONSERVATIVE APproaches; they have fragmented into a staggering variety of innovative trends and statements. Simultaneously, weaving techniques also have changed. Traditional looms are, and always will be, popular. Many of the pieces or portions of those works illustrated are achieved by working at a loom. However, the weaver has also adapted many off-loom weaving techniques; these have been stimulated by the study of historical weaving methods by primitive peoples who devised and improvised weaving methods based on materials at hand. Such devices as simple frames, circular hoops, branches, and cardboard are all warped and used for weaving. Finger weaving and braiding, Indian braiding, and other techniques have been investigated and adapted to the modern woven work.

The concept of purism, or weaving for weaving's sake and involving no other discipline, is usually a classroom exercise. Once the weaver decides to create with threads, any technique that will further the statement he wishes to make can be employed. The more weaving methods and other adaptations of the threads the weaver learns, the more versatile he can become. Modern off-loom forms frequently combine nonwoven techniques explored in the previous chapters.

Essentially, weaving is considered a two-dimensional art form but by rethinking the surface as a "relief" or "in the round," a transition into the third dimension can be accomplished.

MIDSUMMER NIGHT'S DREAM. Jan Wagstaff. 1971. 96" high, 48" wide. Wool.
Photo, David Cordoni

Creating a successful woven three-dimensional form involves a stronger discipline than simply stuffing a double weave or bending a woven strip around itself; the structure must be convincing as a

NAR. Neda Al-Hilali. 1971. Weaving and knotting.
Photographed at the Contemporary Museum of Art, Chicago

result of its commingling with inner and outer space. To stuff double weave, for the sake of stuffing, is Victorian in attitude, much like the architecture of that time; the outer shell existed only to cover a multitude of evils within and did not necessarily relate to the interior or the exterior.

The problems of constructing large weavings and devices for working them can pose problems and each composition may require an individual solution. One artist suspends wires across the ceiling from hooks set in the moldings all around the room. Two-by-fours, weighted with bricks, hold the warp at the bottom. The vertical threads are then warped from the wires at the ceiling under and around the boards on the floor and the weaving progresses. Ladders are essential.

For a cylindrical form, hoops may be suspended from wires with another set of hoops weighted at the base and then warps strung from

top to bottom hoops. A large cardboard tube could also serve as a "loom" by notching the top and bottom edges and working them vertically. Extra pins or nails could be added for additional warps.

Often large weavings are composed of assembled parts. The piece is planned so it can be made in sections, either on the loom or on an off-loom device, and then the pieces are put together either by weaving or other techniques such as knotting, crochet, and tying, so the threads purposely extend beyond the surface plane to yield texture and dimension.

Many of the following examples are suspended; others are free-standing. Artists find it a challenge to use a basically pliable material and create a form that is, or appears, rigid. Often the techniques of fiber with fiber alone will result in a sturdy, self-supporting form. Armatures are used occasionally; stuffing is used frequently. Although

SCULPTURAL WEAVINGS ON EXHIBITION FROM THE SHOW *DELIBERATE ENTANGLEMENTS,* photographed at the Contemporary Museum of Art, Chicago, November 1972.
Left: ABAKAN. Magdalena Abakanowicz.
Center: BLACK ENVIRONMENT, STRUCTURE '70. Jacoda Buić. Woven sisal, wool, and silk.
Right: LARGE FLOOR SCULPTURE. Claire Zeisler. Twenty independent spheres of varying sizes are covered with sheared wool pile.

WOVEN WALL. Olga de Amaral. 1969. Muted earth tones of wool woven as solid tapestry at the bottom and different width strips. *Courtesy, Hyatt Regency O'Hare, Chicago*

the artist usually has a preconceived idea of the form he wishes the finished piece to take, it is not unusual for him to change his thinking as he progresses; to revise and alter a form; to make it evolve, grow, take shape as he manipulates the materials.

The purpose of this chapter is to illustrate the variety of giant innovative steps weavers have taken in the past few years toward sculptural statements. The methods for weaving are too vast to cover in one chapter; the reader is encouraged to consult the vast number of excellent volumes dealing with loom and off-loom weaving listed in the Bibliography. The following examples are both a chronicle of what is being done and a stimulus for the professional and student to attempt further forays into the use of threads as a vital art form.

YELLOW ORANGE ABAKAN. Magdalena Abakanowicz. 1969.
Courtesy, Hyatt Regency O'Hare, Chicago

FOLIAGE WOVEN WALL. Olga de Amaral. 1969.
Courtesy, Hyatt Regency O'Hare, Chicago

MP #2. Misty Potter. 1972. 6′ high, 5′ wide. Hand-dyed jute woven. *Courtesy, artist*

TOASTER SERIES. Janet R. Taylor. 1972. Toaster, 18″ high, 24″ wide, 12″ deep. Each tapestry, 40″ high, 32″ wide. Woven hand-dyed wool, linen, rayon, machine-spun yarns, and hand-spun roving. *Courtesy, artist*

CINDERELLA. Louise Todd. 1973. 60″ high, 38″ wide. White wool and jute. Weaving and wrapping on a metal frame.

Opposite page:
FOUR BALLERINAS. Ruth Geneslaw. 1972. 61″ high. Tubular weave in white wool and unspun fleece. The tubes are reinforced with metal rods and wires for structural support and stuffed with polyester.
Photo, Michael Smirnoff

THE WRAITH. Max Lenderman. 1972. 8′ high, 40″ wide, 14″ deep. Linen, wool, rayon, roving, and chenille; quadruple woven Rya knotting. Polyester stuffing.
Courtesy, artist

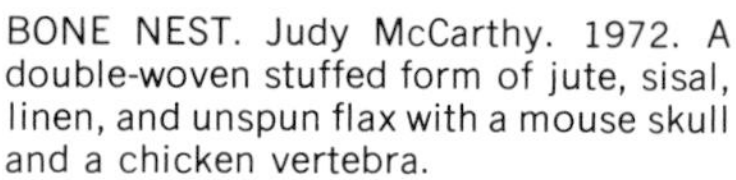

BONE NEST. Judy McCarthy. 1972. A double-woven stuffed form of jute, sisal, linen, and unspun flax with a mouse skull and a chicken vertebra.

Courtesy, artist

THE FLOCCULENT ARTICHOKE HEART. Max Lenderman. 1973. 6′ high, 21″ wide, 9″ deep. Tubular weave of linen, rayon, and linen and rayon blends, with polyester stuffing. Rya knotting on top surface with some wrapping.

Courtesy, artist

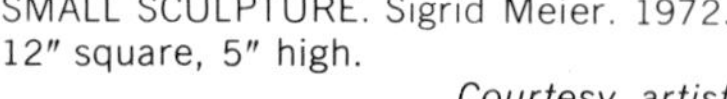

SMALL SCULPTURE. Sigrid Meier. 1972. 12″ square, 5″ high.

Courtesy, artist

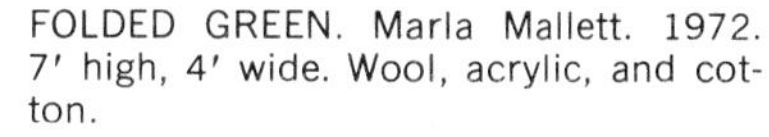

FOLDED GREEN. Marla Mallett. 1972. 7′ high, 4′ wide. Wool, acrylic, and cotton.

Courtesy, artist

UNTITLED. Ritzi and Peter Jacobi. A woven and wrapped form with clear vinyl tubing containing yarn and feathers.

Courtesy, artists

The pieces on these two pages are woven forms by Marla Mallett. Dimensionality is achieved by the manipulation of the fibers in space; the pieces do not contain padding or stuffing.

Below left: DECEMBER RED. 1972. 94″ high, 30″ wide. Wool and acrylic fibers.

Right: SEVEN PARTS IN YELLOW (detail). 1971. Sisal, wool, and linen.

Below right: GREEN ALL TIED UP. 1971. 91″ high, 36″ wide. Wool.

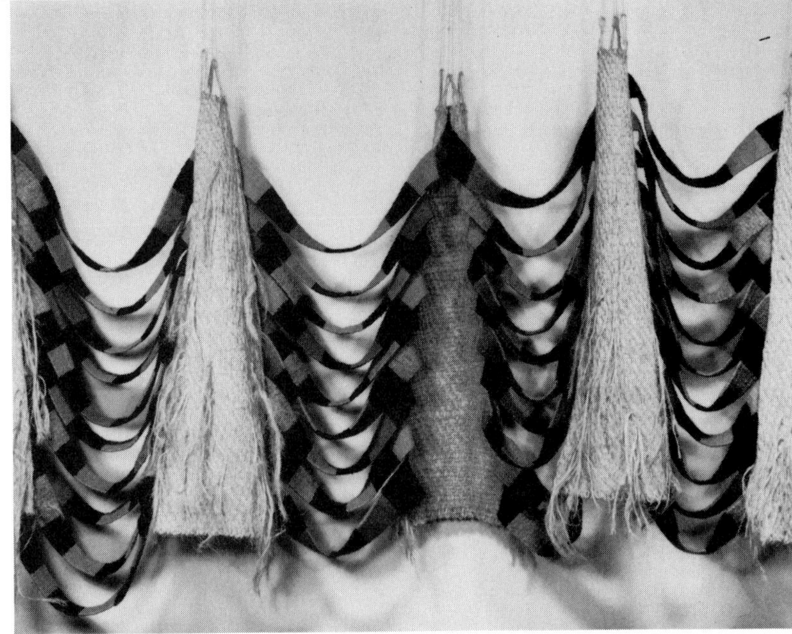

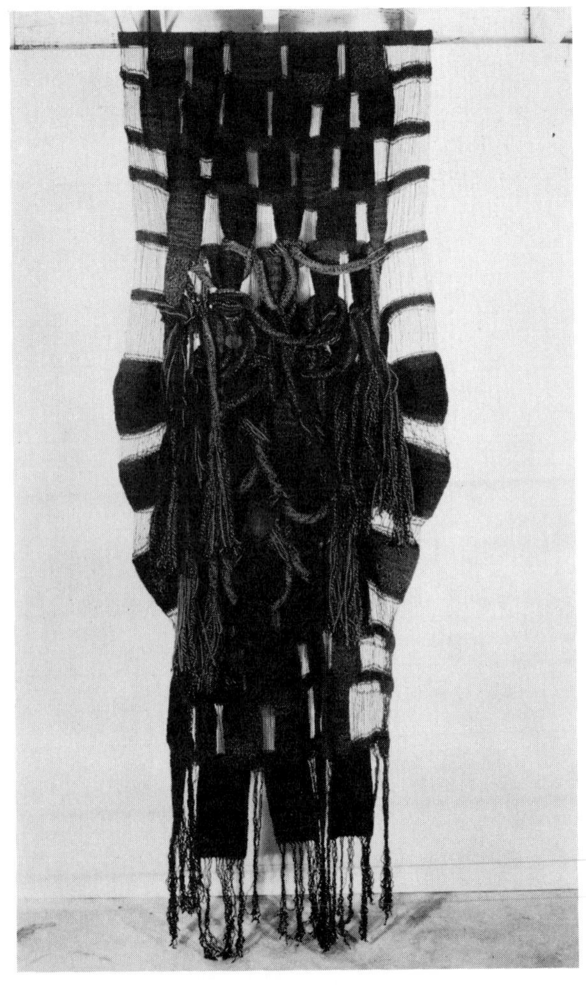

NEW RED AND BLACK. 1972. 41″ high, 41″ wide. Horsehair and wool.

BLACK AND YELLOW MOVES. 1971. 51″ high, 30″ wide. Horsehair and wool.

All photos, courtesy, artist

FLYING FORM I. Budd Stalnaker. 63″ high, 28″ wide, 17″ deep. An architectural hanging composed of wool, linen, brass, and bronze. *Collection, Mr. and Mrs. J. Grunwald, Bloomington, Indiana*

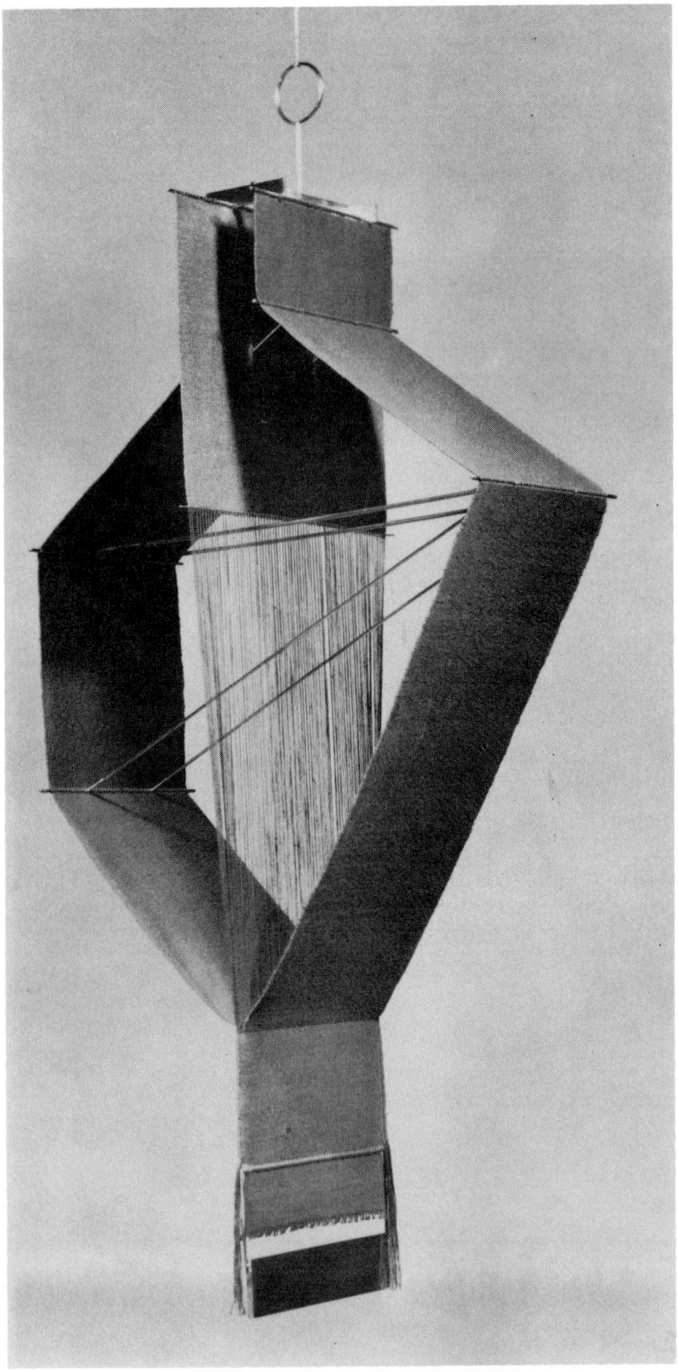

TORN PILLAR. Walter Nottingham. 1972. Approximately 7′ high, 30″ square. Sisal and mixed fibers. *Photographed at the exhibit* Fabrications '72, *Detroit*

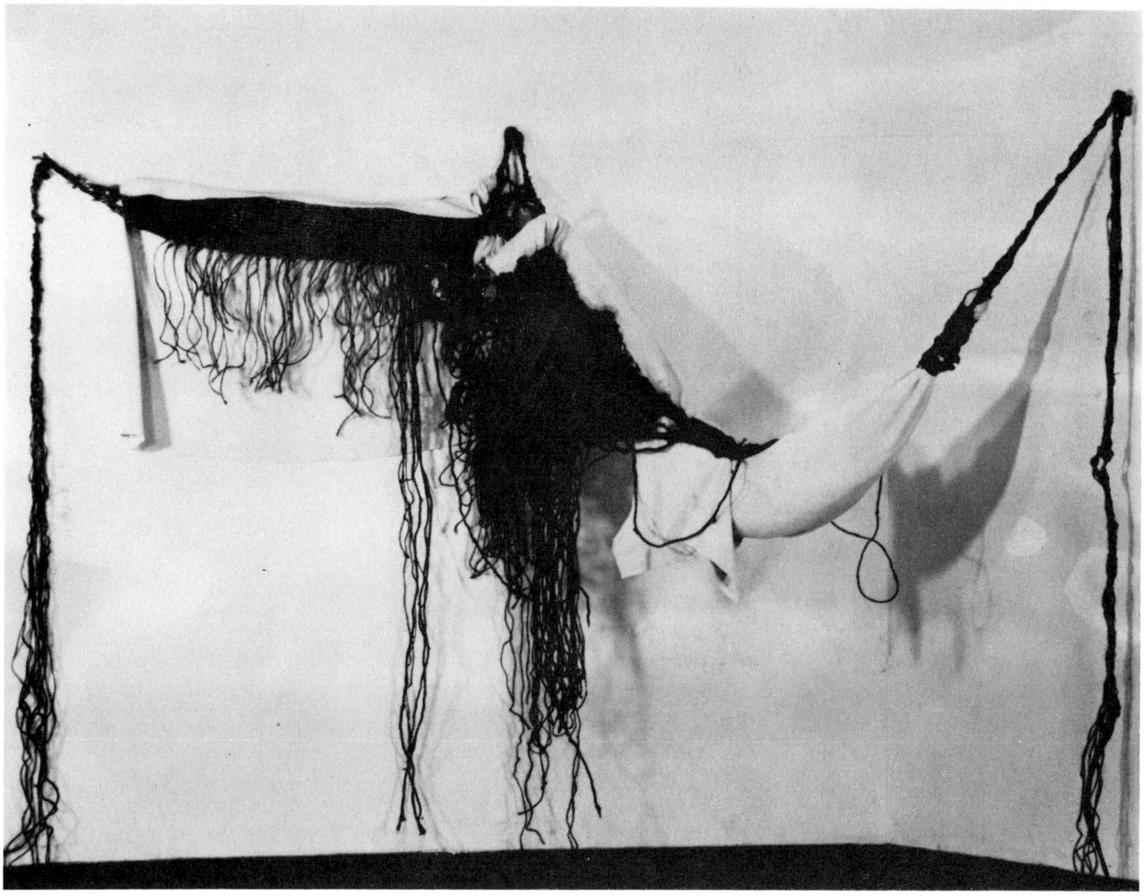

UNTITLED. Larry Peterson. 1971. 10′ wide. Sisal. Weaving and twining. *Courtesy, artist*

PROCESSION FOR A DEAD LOVER. Dorian Zachai. 1969. *Photographed at the Museum of Contemporary Art, Chicago*

UNTITLED. Art Sandoval. 1969. 6′ high, 30″ wide, 15″ deep. Belgian linen, polished linen, cow and horse hairs, raffia, and excelsior filling.

SHE FORM. Art Sandoval. 1969. Woven gold Lurex, cotton loop twist yarn, gold metallic warp, and horsetails.

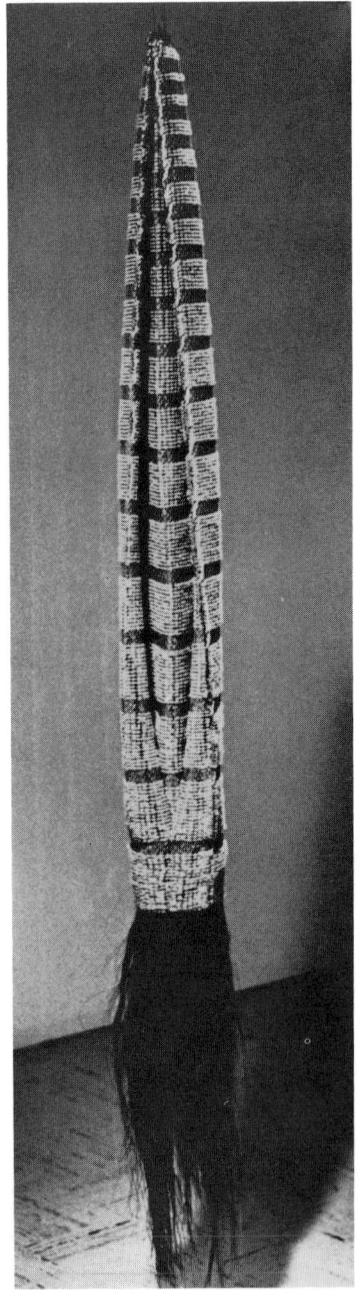

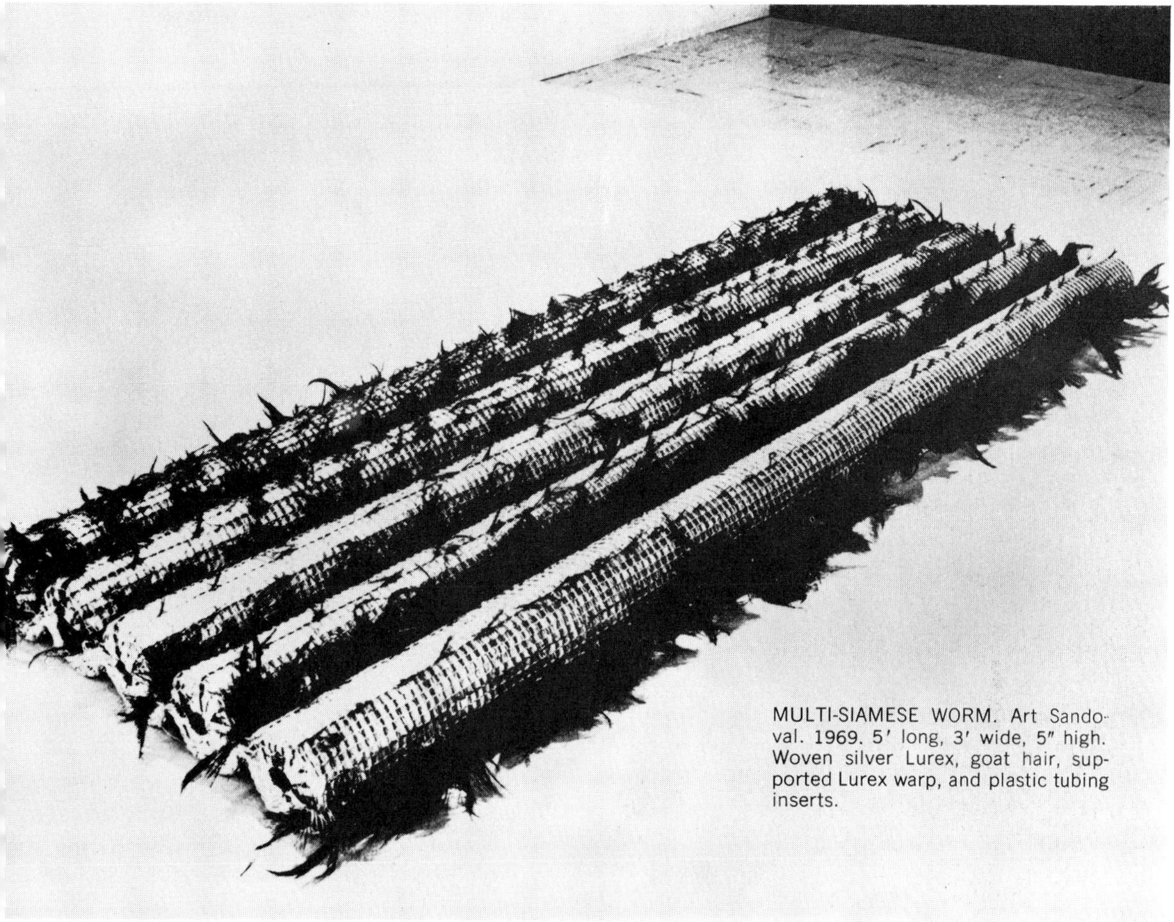

MULTI-SIAMESE WORM. Art Sandoval. 1969. 5′ long, 3′ wide, 5″ high. Woven silver Lurex, goat hair, supported Lurex warp, and plastic tubing inserts.

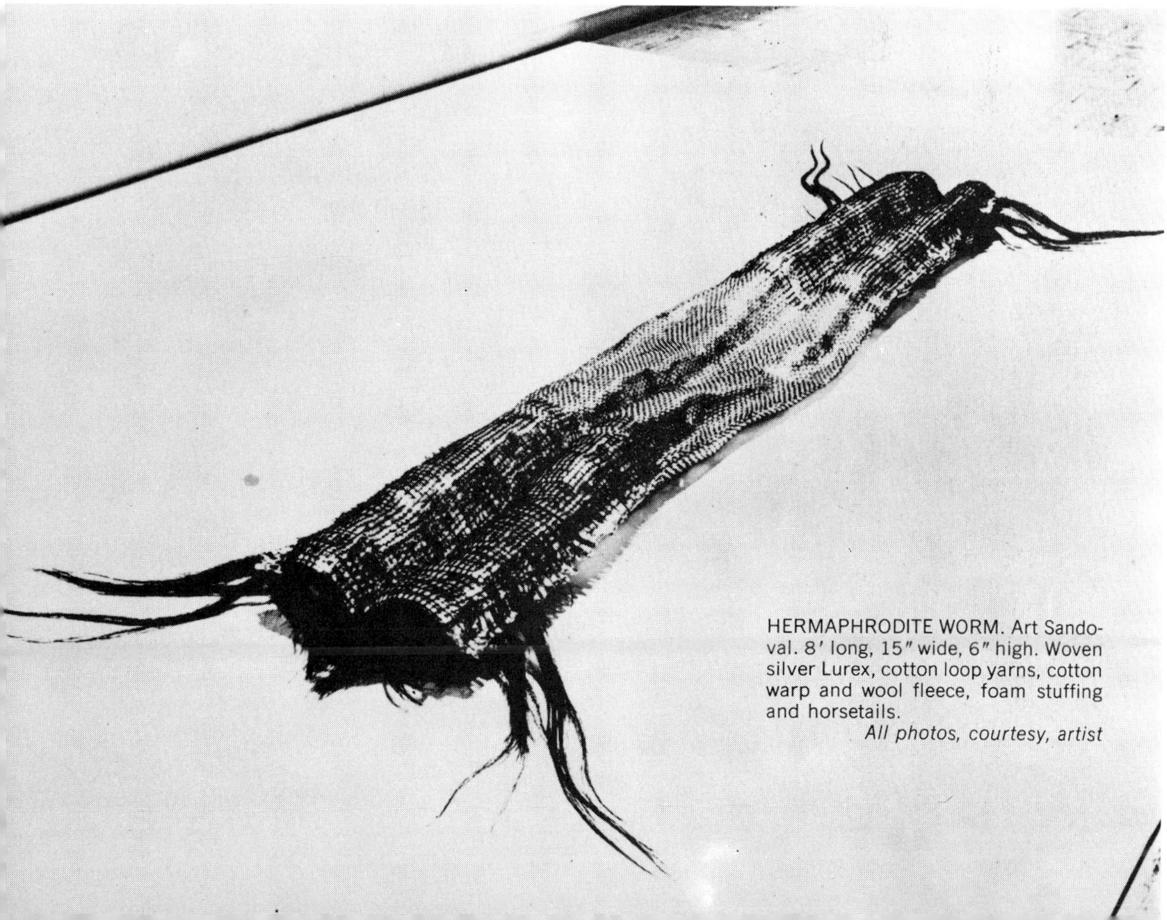

HERMAPHRODITE WORM. Art Sandoval. 8′ long, 15″ wide, 6″ high. Woven silver Lurex, cotton loop yarns, cotton warp and wool fleece, foam stuffing and horsetails.

All photos, courtesy, artist

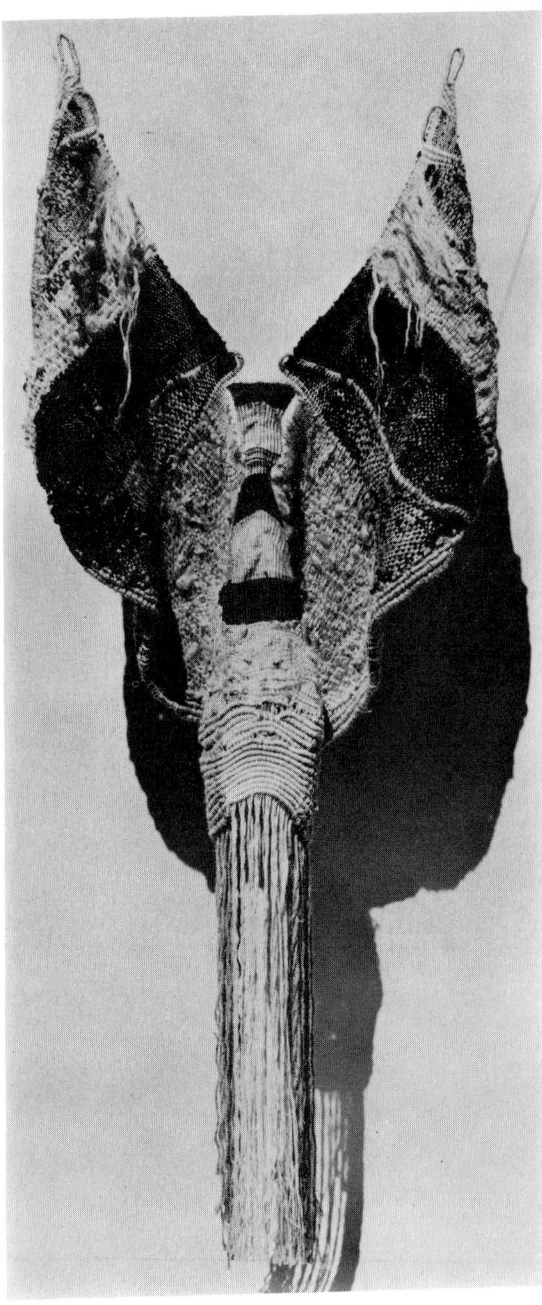

PHOENIX. Jan Wagstaff. 1971. 81″ high, 36″ wide. Flax, jute, and wool. *Right:* UNTITLED. Jan Wagstaff. 1972. 72″ high, 50″ wide. Wool, linen, and horsehair.

Photos, David Cordoni

UNTITLED. Jan Wagstaff. 1971. 72″ high, 48″ wide. Black sculpture woven of horsehair, wool, and linen with a painted, stuffed central portion. *Below left:* Detail.

Photos, David Cordoni

UNTITLED. Peg Wood Greenfield. 1972. 84″ high, 23″ wide. (One of two related forms.) Double woven with slits in each section to allow unwoven cords from one portion to be pulled through the other. French knots and wrapping.

Photo, Robert O. Hodgell

Photo of a cactus trunk illustrates nature's source of inspiration for Gary Trentham's CACTUS PHALLUS.
Photo, Mel Meilach

TRAPEZE. Ruth Geneslaw. 1972. 68″ high, 23″ wide. Tubular weave stuffed hanging in red and purple wool on a purple linen warp.
Photo, Robert Geneslaw

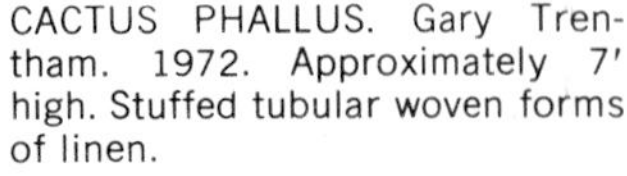

CACTUS PHALLUS. Gary Trentham. 1972. Approximately 7′ high. Stuffed tubular woven forms of linen.

WOVEN WIRE. Linda Ulvestad Fisher. 1971. 6′ high, 2′ wide. Woven, knitted, and crocheted copper, bronze, silver, and alkaline soldering wires, pounded sterling silver, reinforced cement tie rods and wool, and bouclé yarns. Interior support consists of crocheted silver radio wire on a ¼″ bronze rod.

Courtesy, artist

Left: STAR VESSEL. Cynthia Fisher. 1972. 3′ high, 2′ wide. Linen and wools.

SEATED FORMS. Barbara Kasten Rice. 1971–72. All pieces are sisal, woven on a frame loom, and manipulated afterward to hold the form. "The collaboration of the chair and the woven form is an intentional effort, integrating and extending the experience of a utilitarian object and a form which relates to it in various human attitudes."

All photos, Leland Rice
Collection, Lee D. Witkin, New York

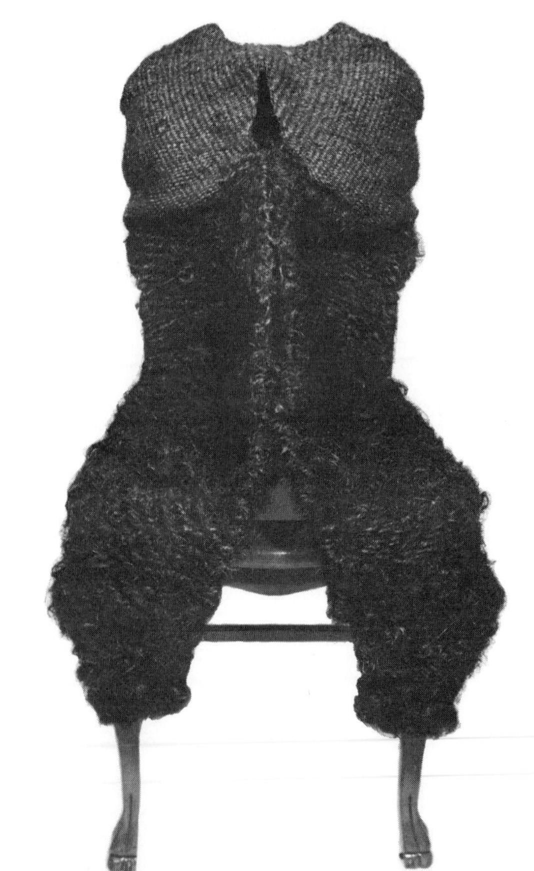

Left: Sisal and wool.
Below left: Freestanding form (without a chair).
Below: Back and front views.

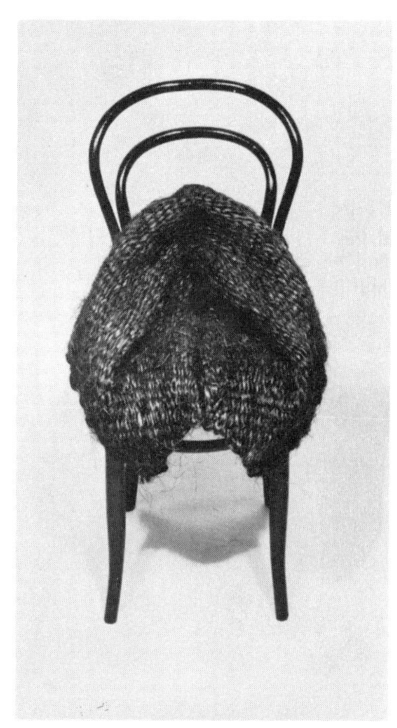

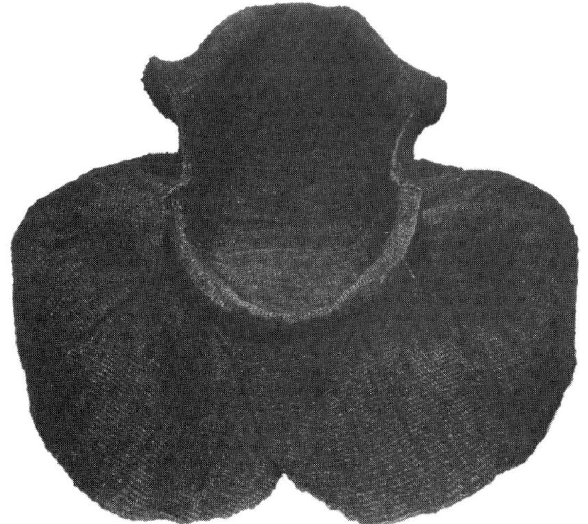

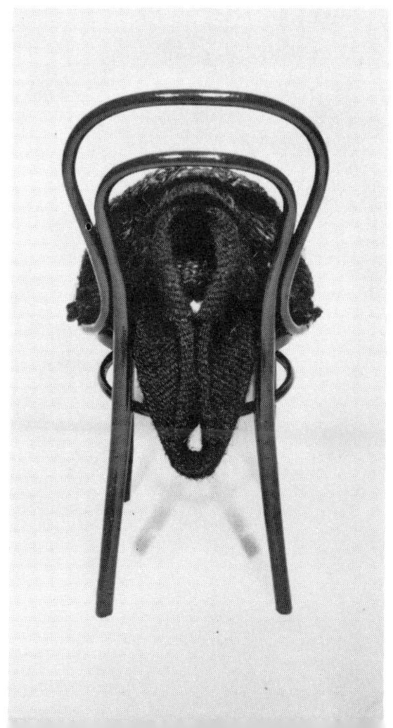

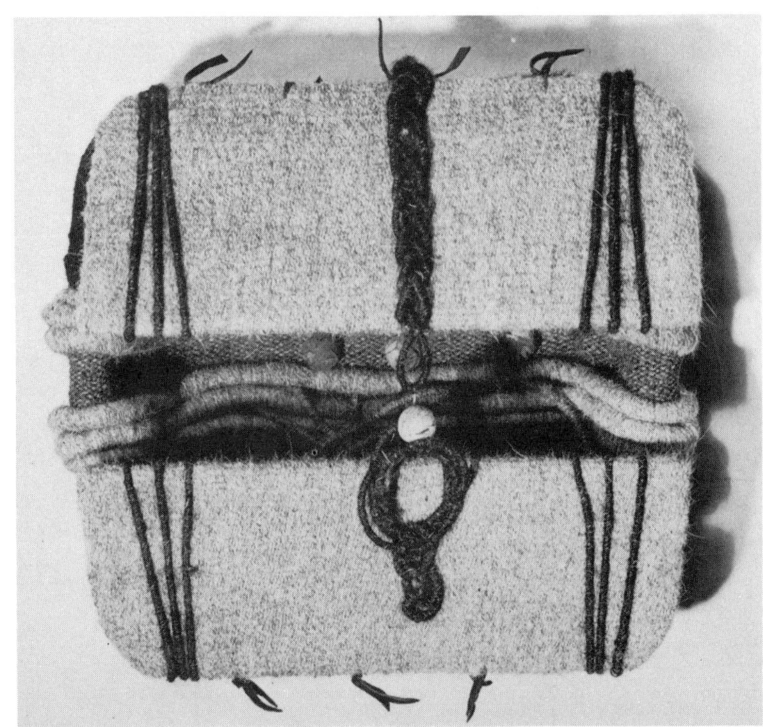

OBJECT. Ritzi and Peter Jacobi. 1970. Closed, back, and open views. Woven gray and black goat hair with polyester stuffing.

Courtesy, artists

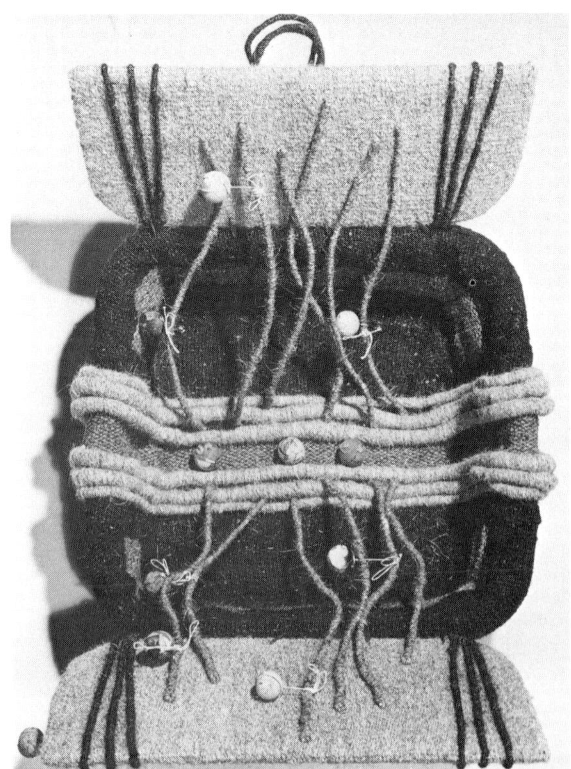

DIARY I. Elizabeth Kuhs. 1972. 15″ high, 6″ wide closed. Woven wool "book forms" with some wrapping. Mirrors and metal clamps. *Left:* Closed. *Above:* Open.

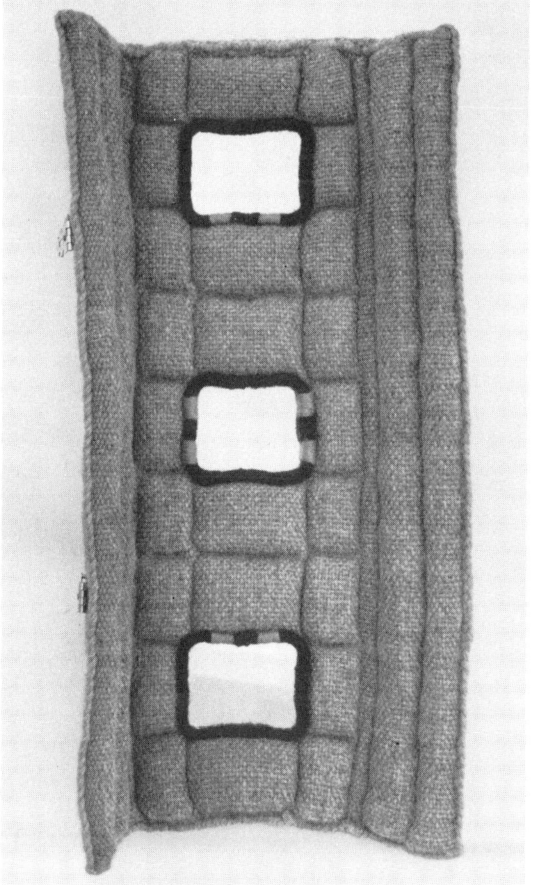

DIARY II. Elizabeth Kuhs. 1972. 5½″ square closed. 5½ x 11″ open. Woven wool with mirrors and clasps. *Left:* Open. *Above:* Closed.

Photos, courtesy, artist

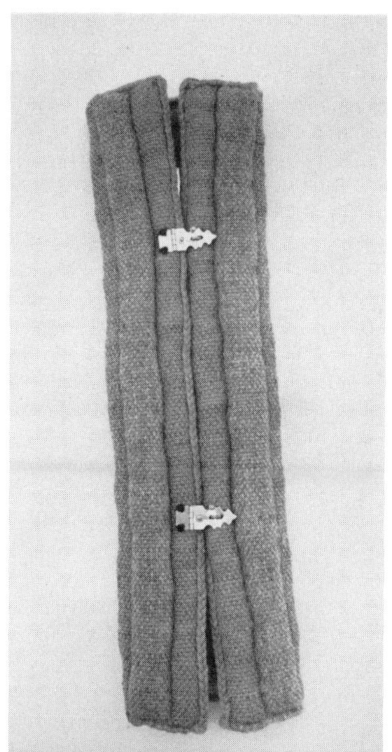

WHEAT. Ruth Geneslaw. 1972. 24″ high. Stuffed tubular weave of gray linen. Textured area at bottom is Rya knotting.
Photo, Michael Smirnoff

ENVIRONMENT. Ritzi and Peter Jacobi. 1970. 1½″ high, ½″ wide, ¼″ deep. Woven goat hair over constructed metal shapes. Soft, stuffed feather pillows.

Courtesy, artists

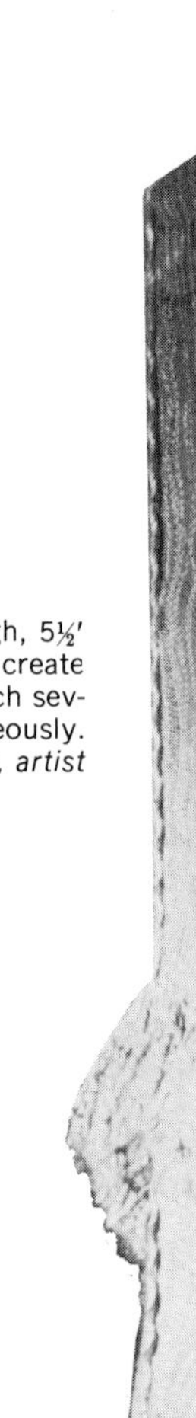

TREEHOUSE. Sue Ferguson. 9′ high, 5½′ wide. Jute, hemp, sisal, and straw create an environmental structure in which several people can interact simultaneously. *Courtesy, artist*

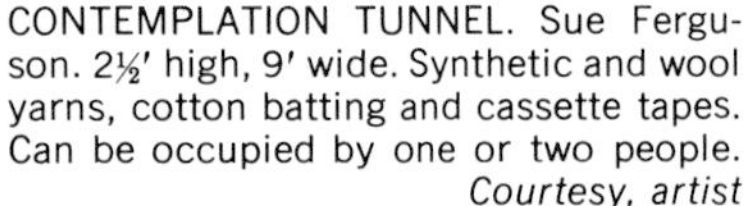

CONTEMPLATION TUNNEL. Sue Ferguson. 2½′ high, 9′ wide. Synthetic and wool yarns, cotton batting and cassette tapes. Can be occupied by one or two people. *Courtesy, artist*

BAG OF DREAMS. Yvonne Porcella. 1972. Handwoven sleeping bag of wool and suede with deerskin and rabbit-skin hood. A "sleep" environment.
Photo, Diane Fitz

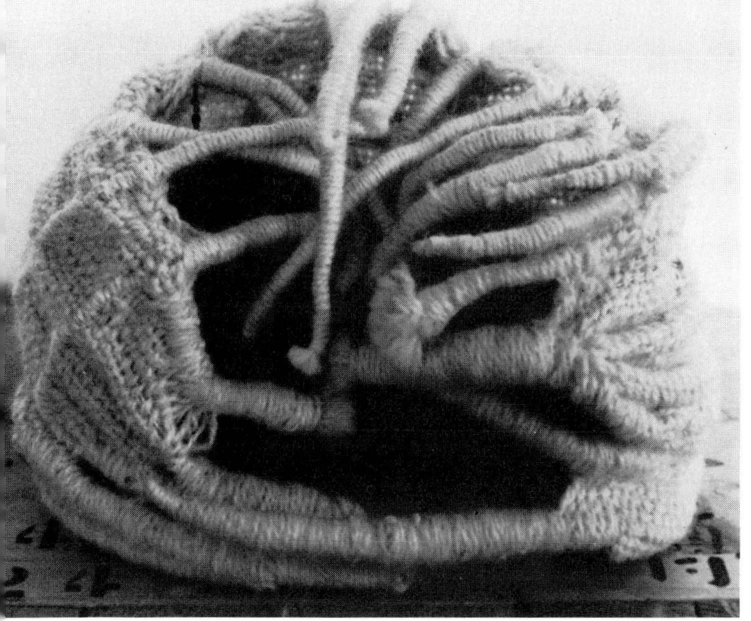

EMERALD CAVE. Jean Singerman. 1970. 7′ high, 8″ diameter. Loom-woven wool and linen small environment.
Courtesy, artist

JOURNEY SACK. Yvonne Porcella. 1972. Leather backpack with weaving and wrapping. Wool, handspun wool, and goat hair.
Photo, Diane Fitz

IN LOVING MEMORY. Sharon Giacomo. 1972. 49″ high, 7′ wide. Cowhair, jute, and human hair tapestry is stretched on bent concrete reinforcement rods. The warp and added fibers are coiled beneath. Colors are muted purples, wine, and light blue.
Courtesy, artist

TEXTILE ENVIRONMENT. Ritzi and Peter Jacobi. 1970. 6′ high, 8′ wide, 6½′ deep. Gray goat hair woven, stuffed and stretched over a frame and tubes.

Courtesy, artists

7
Knitting-Crochet-Embroidery

WE ARE SO ACCUSTOMED TO ASSOCIATING THE NEEDLECRAFTS OF knitting, crochet, and embroidery with clothing, useful household articles, and decorative purposes that it requires a mental regearing to apply them to objects as art forms. Yet, the techniques are beautifully adaptable to fiber sculptures and allow great freedom of construction.

Yarns are manipulated by the use of the necessary needles, and they are interlaced to form a fabric. With the planning and addition of stuffing, a three-dimensional form can easily be created. But as in weaving, the problem of aesthetics arises; it isn't sufficient to assume that a two-dimensional cloth, folded over, stuffed, and the ends sewn together, pillowlike, is a sculpture: It is still a pillow. But the artists, whose work is illustrated here, have thought far beyond the pillow-stuffing stage; they create works that exhibit all the attributes of sculptural form. They are expressive; they exist as mass in space; they have linear movement, texture, pattern, and have brought into a cohesive order the essential elements of design.

Many of the examples were the result of an unusual exhibit entitled *Wool Art* at the Galerie Boutique Germain, Paris, in 1972, sponsored by the Woolmark Foundation. The purpose was to provide artists with the wools and let them create *objects.* The results are humorous, serious, cynical, and so forth. Some objects were composed of strands of yarn glued over soft forms so the yarn was not worked with a needle. But the form and the material result in a convincing presentation.

MATERNITY. Abel Ogier. 1972. 27″ high. Knit wool stuffed with paper.
Courtesy, Galerie Boutique Germain, Paris

Crocheted yarns can be attached to and worked over hoops in a free-form manner. Knitting in the round may be accomplished on round needles used for making skirts. The experienced needleworker

MOTHERBALL #1. Sharon Giacomo. 1972. 3′ high, 4′ 8″ wide. White acrylic yarn crocheted and knotted and stuffed with shredded paper.

Courtesy, artist

will employ the necessary increase and decrease methods to shape the fabric to the form.

Embroidery techniques are often used to embellish a form and for fabric collages that have a relief dimension. The stitches may also be used with knitting, crochet, and with weavings. It is also possible to use needlepoint mesh backings as a base for working thick layers and projecting yarn forms in many techniques to create relief surfaces. Dimensional yarn forms can also be added together onto a backing or to one another as an assemblage. Try combining basket shapes, braiding, macramé, tubular woven pieces, and objects such as beads, feathers, hardware pieces, and so forth.

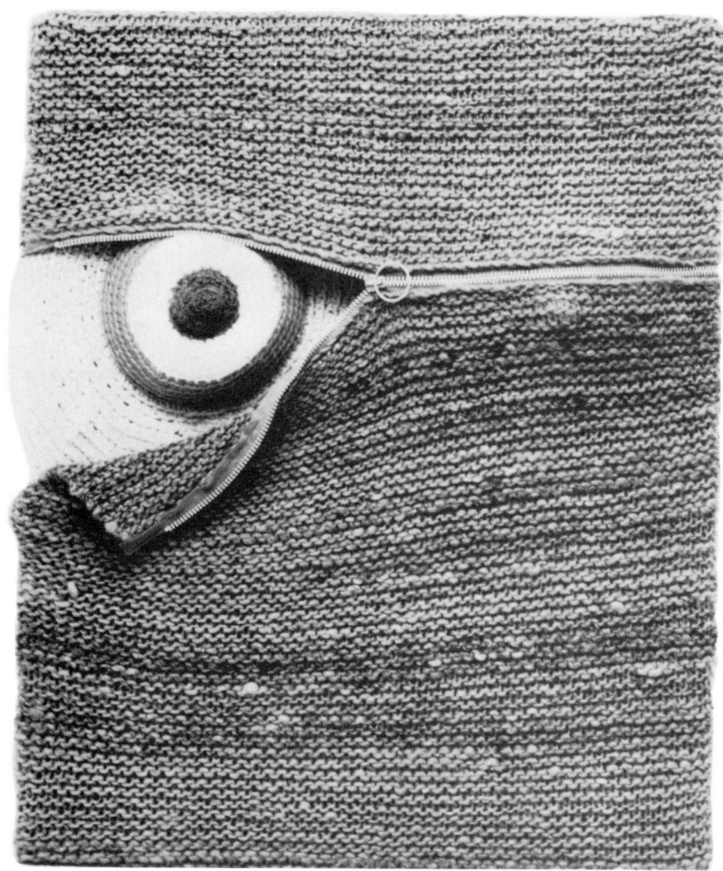

BONJOUR MONSIEUR ROYER, TRICOTAGE ET DÉSHABILLAGE SONT LES DEUX MAMELLES DE LA FRANCE. Zizine Bouscaud. 1972. 33″ high. Crocheted wool. *Courtesy, Galerie Boutique Germain, Paris*

SIT ON. Roy Adzak. 1972. 18″ high. Crocheted and stitched rug yarn.
Courtesy, Galerie Boutique Germain, Paris

ALICE'S TEA CUPS. Milivia Maglione. 1972. 4" high. Crocheted yarn.
Courtesy, Galerie Boutique Germain, Paris

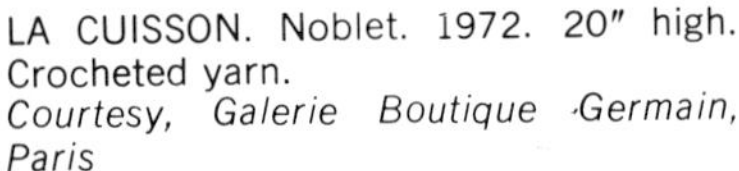

LA CUISSON. Noblet. 1972. 20" high. Crocheted yarn.
Courtesy, Galerie Boutique Germain, Paris

FIGURES. Norma Minkowitz. 12″ high, 8″ wide. Crochet and hooking.
Collection, Mrs. Kenneth Hall

PEDESTAL FORMS. Richard Daehnert. 1972. Wood and synthetic fibers woven and crocheted over ceramic bases. *Opposite page:* 18″ high, 11 ″ wide, 10″ deep. *Left top:* 18½″ high, 12″ wide, 8″ deep. *Left below:* 17″ high, 13″ wide, 6″ deep.

Photos, courtesy, artist

UNTITLED. Deborah Frederick. 1972. 6″ high, 18″ wide. Crocheted polished twine with stuffing material.
Courtesy, artist

PIG. Susan Lehman. 1972. Crocheted yarn and textiles.
Courtesy, Richmond Art Center, Richmond, California

UNTITLED. Lou Ann Musinski. 1972. 26″ high, 28″ wide. Crocheted linen and wool.

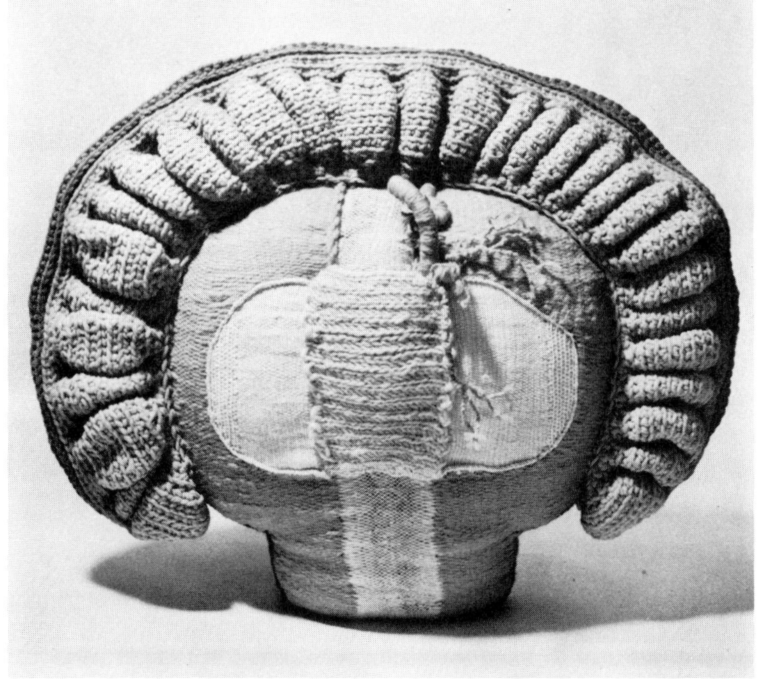

UNTITLED. Lou Ann Musinski. 1972. 25″ high, 32″ wide. Crochet added to weaving over a stuffed form.

UNTITLED. Jane Knight. 1973. Crochet.
Photo, Richard Knight

UNTITLED. Jane Knight. 1972. Crochet.
Photo, Richard Knight

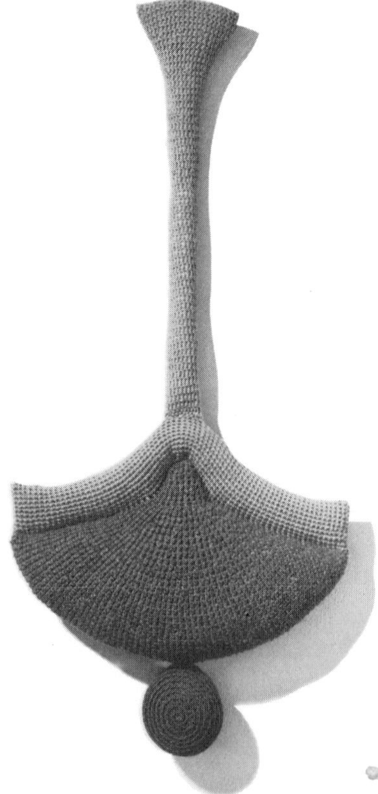

PINK PUSSY. Margaret Kaplowitz. 1973. 6″ high, 12″ diameter. Crocheted and stuffed.

KNITTED SCULPTURE IN WOOL. Ricardo Licata. 1972. 47″ high. Yarn and loose wool in brown, beige, red, and ecru.
Courtesy, Galerie Boutique Germain, Paris

L'AINARCHISTE BOURRÉ. Hugh Weiss. 1972. Silver knit yarn in ecru, black, gray, orange, and green.
Courtesy, Galerie Boutique Germain, Paris

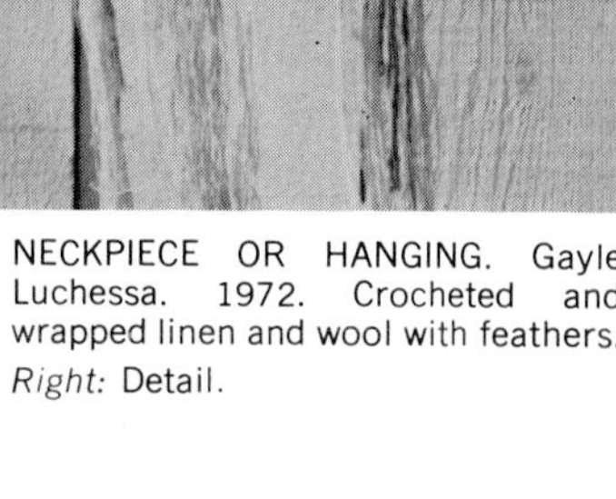

NECKPIECE OR HANGING. Gayle Luchessa. 1972. Crocheted and wrapped linen and wool with feathers. *Right:* Detail.

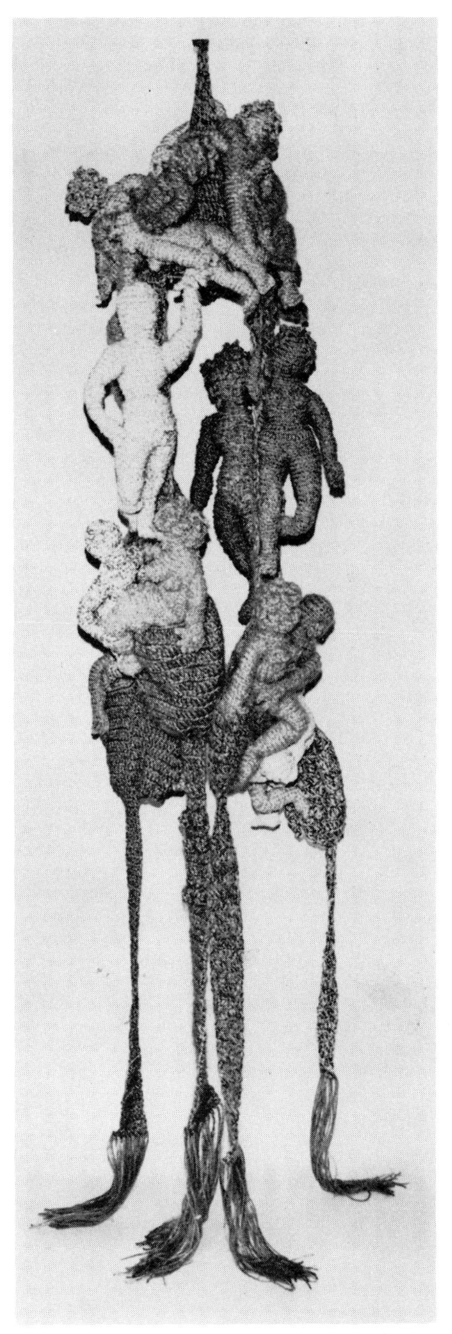

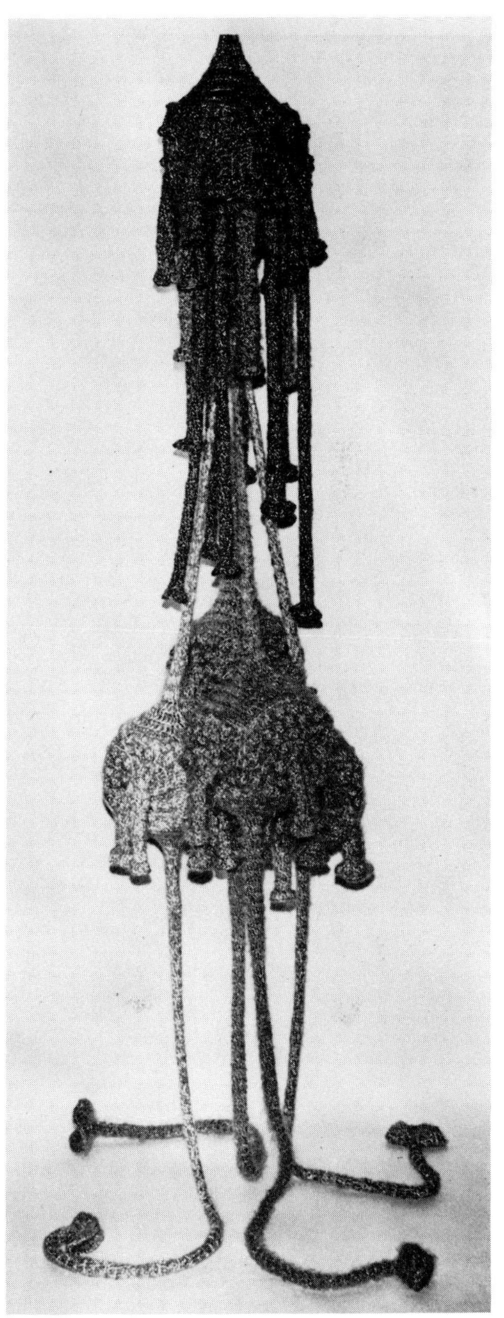

Left: MARRY-GO-ROUND. Mary Lou Higgins. 1972. 8′ high. Crocheted.

Above: ON THE GOOD SHIP LOLLIPOP. Mary Lou Higgins. 1972. 8′ high. Crocheted mohair and lamé space hanging. *Photos, Ed Higgins*

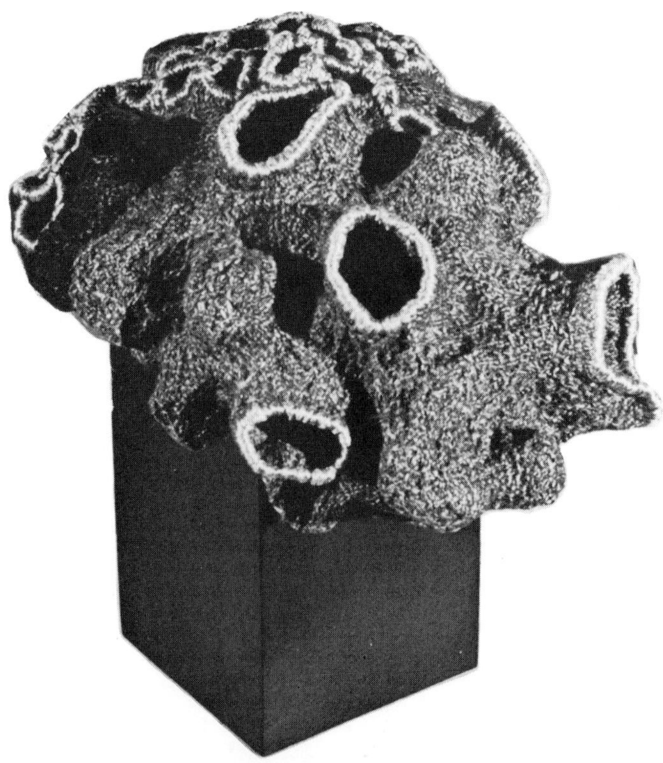

SOFT SCULPTURE I. Evelyn Svec Ward. 1970. 10″high, 12″ wide. Stitched and molded burlap, cotton, and sisal on a wood pedestal.
Collection; Irwin C. Gemlich, Twinsburg, Ohio

SMOTHER LOVE AND HER LITTLE ONES. Shirley Ribelin. 1973. 37″ high, 21″ wide, 6″ deep. Stuffed duck fabric with stitchery. *Right:* Hanging. *Below:* With the appendages wrapped around to carry out the theme.

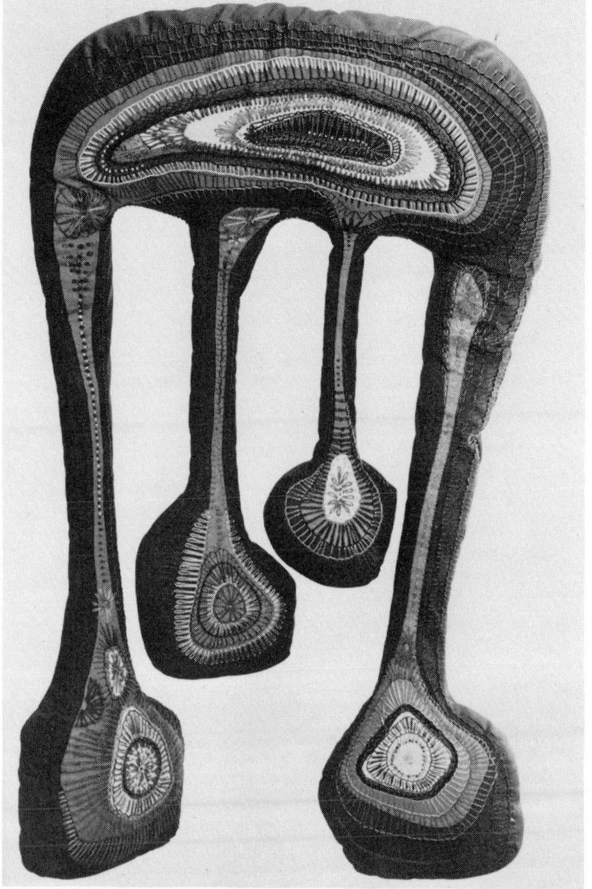

TO HAVE AND TO HOLD. Evelyn Marx. 1972. 23″ high, 20″ wide. Fabric collage made with stuffed and padded shapes that are emphasized with stitchery.
Collection; Mrs. Jack Murphy, St. Louis, Missouri

SOFT FIGURE. David Riegel. 1972. Pillowlike form is of embroidered wool on linen.
Courtesy, artist

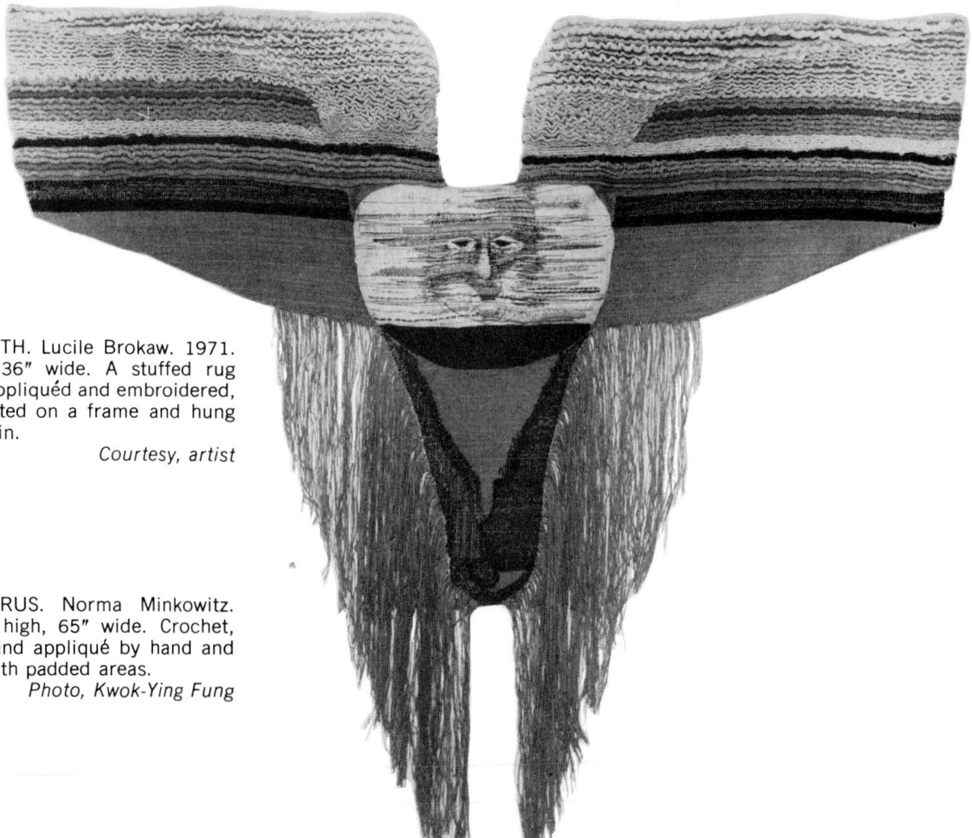

Above: MOTH. Lucile Brokaw. 1971. 31″ high, 36″ wide. A stuffed rug has been appliquéd and embroidered, then mounted on a frame and hung from a chain.

Courtesy, artist

Right: ICARUS. Norma Minkowitz. 1973. 54″ high, 65″ wide. Crochet, stitchery, and appliqué by hand and machine with padded areas.

Photo, Kwok-Ying Fung

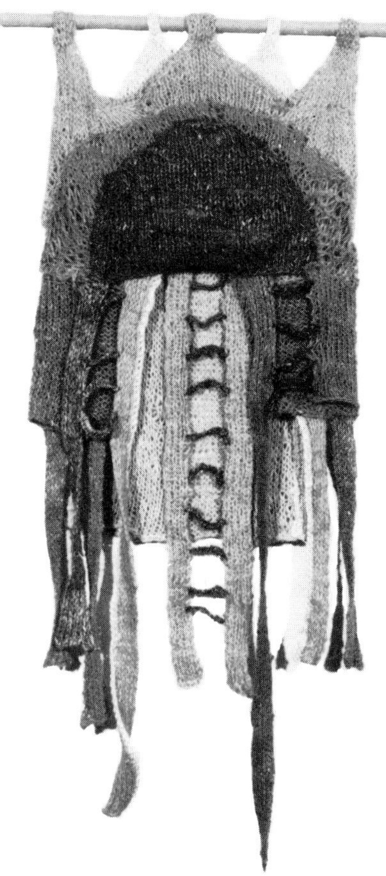

CARNIVAL. Deborah Frederick. 21″ high, 9″ wide. Knitting, crochet, and knotting using linen and stuffing materials.
Courtesy, artist

WALL OBJECT. Pat Malarcher. 1972. The cylinder is 12″ in diameter. The object is 30″ high, 7″ deep. Mylar and stitchery on linen.
Courtesy, artist

NEEDLEWORK TECHNIQUES

Generally, knitting, crochet, and embroidery fall into needlework categories because all use needles, although different types. Knitting needles and crochet hooks are available in many sizes: some are so fine they will make eye-straining loops and some are very large for use with bulky yarns and ropes. A survey of the needles and accessories at any needlework counter will help you choose the materials and needles for any particular project. Circular needles, used for knitting skirts, can be adapted to sculptural knitting.

Basic needlework procedures are presented. These are usually all that are required for creating forms. Once you learn to increase and decrease you can create any necessary shapes which can be stuffed or twisted. A free design approach is more creative than following intricate line by line and stitch by stitch instructions required for clothing. Panels and parts for knitted and crocheted work can be made separately and assembled. All the techniques illustrated throughout the book may be combined with one another.

Illustrations courtesy Spinnerin Yarn Company

KNITTING PROCEDURES

CASTING ON

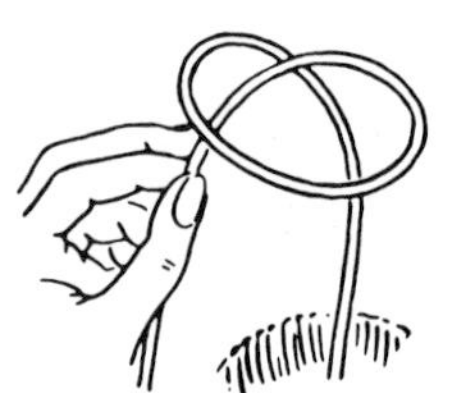

1. Make a slipknot about two yards from end of yarn—allow plenty!

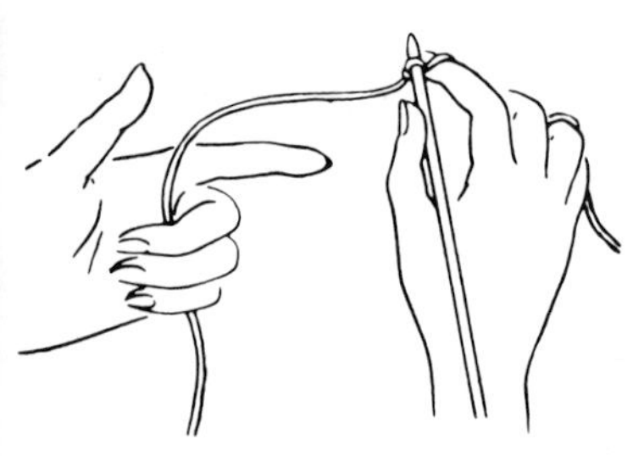

2. Place knot on needle and hold yarn end in palm of left hand.

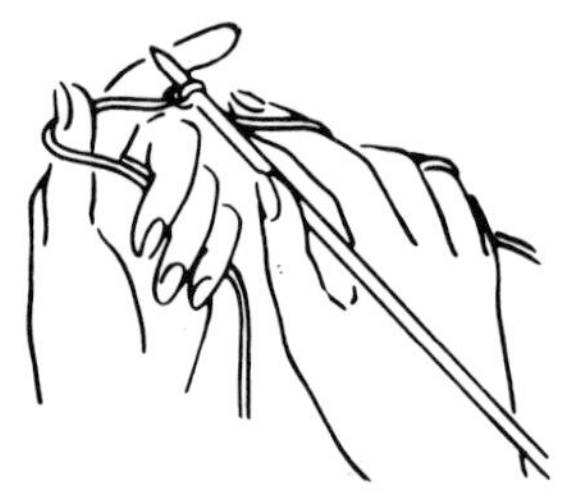

3. Loop end of yarn around your left thumb from front to back; wind yarn leading to ball loosely around fingers of right hand.

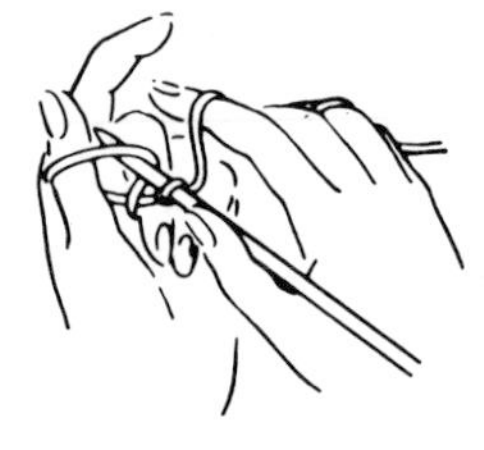

4. Hold needle in right hand as you would hold a pencil. Insert the needle into loop on thumb from front to back.

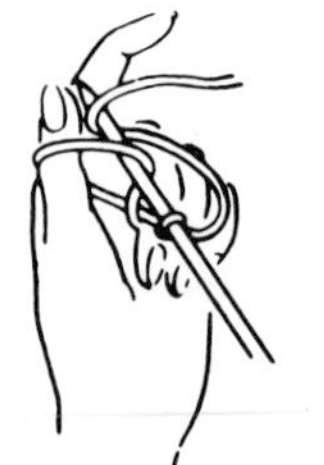

5. Pass the yarn in your right hand around the needle from back to front.

6. Draw yarn through, slip loop off thumb, pull to tighten. One stitch is cast on. Repeat for as many stitches as necessary.

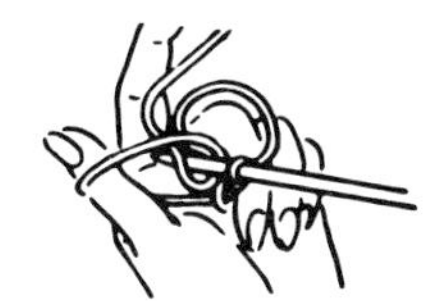

KNITTING

7. Hold needle with cast-on stitches in left hand, second needle in right, yarn in back. Insert needle into first stitch from left to right, front to back.

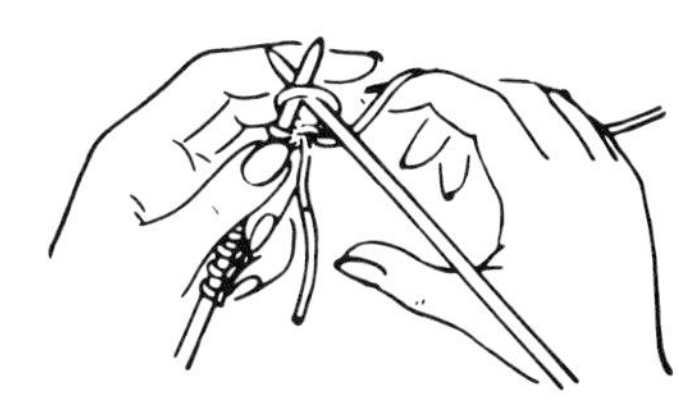

8. Pass yarn under and over the right-hand needle. (If neçessary, support both needles with your left hand in this step.)

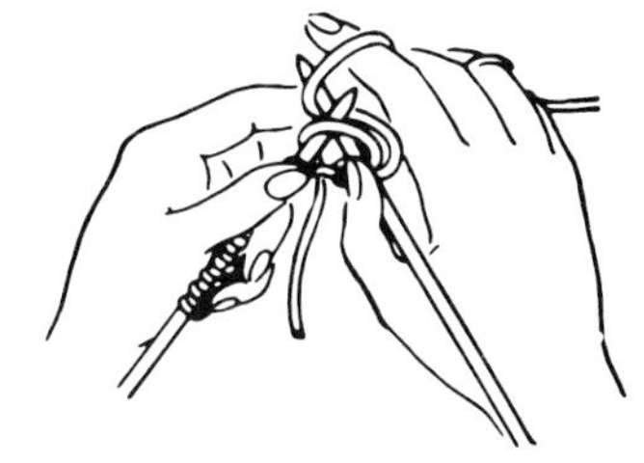

9. Draw loop on right-hand needle through the stitch on left-hand needle.

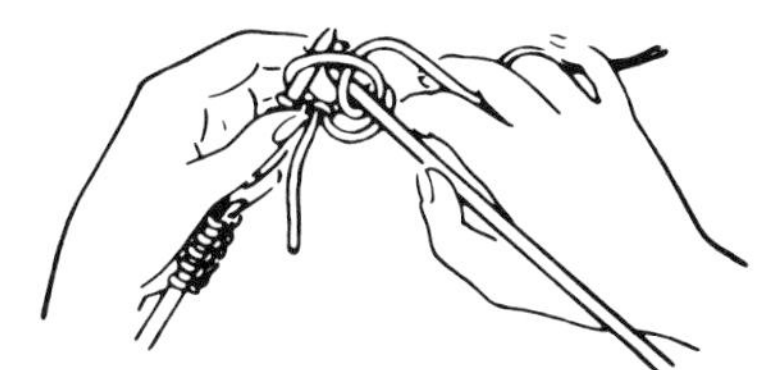

10. Slip the stitch just worked in off left-hand needle. One knit stitch made. Repeat in every stitch.

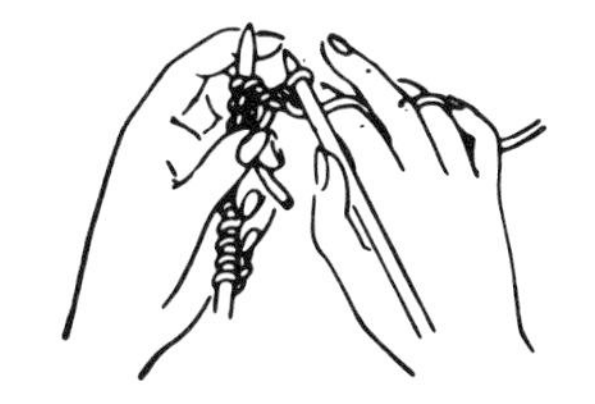

PURLING

11. Hold needle with stitches in left hand and second needle in right, yarn at front. Insert the right-hand needle into first stitch from right to left, back to front. Pass yarn over and under right-hand needle, draw loop through, slip the stitch just worked in off left-hand needle.

12. Stockinette stitch is produced by alternating knit and purl rows. It has two different surfaces; the back, as shown in Figure 11, and the front, as shown in Figure 12. "Reverse stockinette" means that the back of stockinette knitting is used as the front, or the "right," side.

INCREASING

13. To increase in *knitting,* knit the stitch as usual, but do not slip the stitch just worked in off left-hand needle. Knit again in the same stitch, inserting the needle into back of stitch. Now slip the stitch worked in off left-hand needle.

14. To increase in *purling.* purl the stitch as usual, but do not slip the stitch just worked in off left-hand needle. Purl again in the same stitch, inserting the needle into back of stitch. Now slip the stitch worked in off left-hand needle.

DECREASING

15. To decrease in *knitting,* knit two stitches together from left to right.

16. To decrease in *purling,* purl two stitches together from right to left.

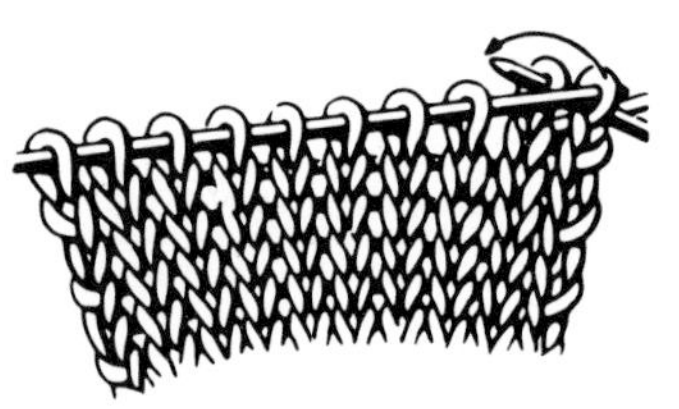

BINDING OFF

17. Work the first two stitches as you would in a regular pattern row. Insert tip of left-hand needle from left to right into the first stitch worked, which is now on the right-hand needle.

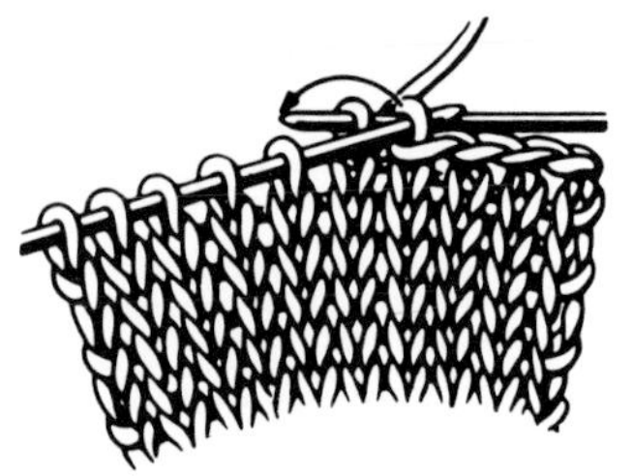

18. Pass the first stitch over the second stitch and off tip of right-hand needle—one stitch bound off. Repeat until as many stitches are bound off as desired.

CROCHET

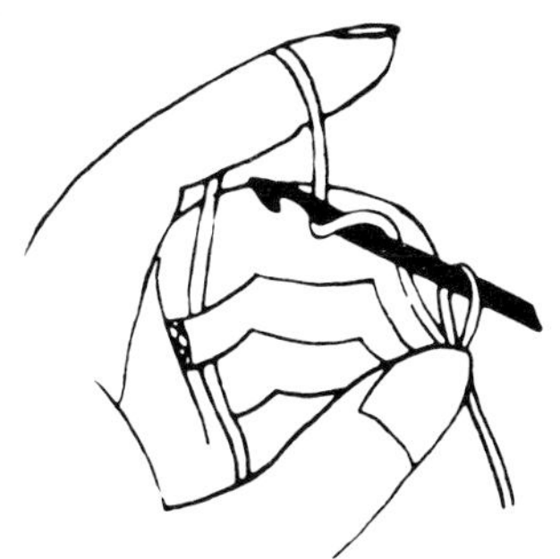

All crochet begins with a simple chain accomplished with a plastic, wood, or metal crochet hook. Large crochet loops can be made using your fingers as the hook, and this is often referred to as "finger crochet."

CROCHET CHAIN

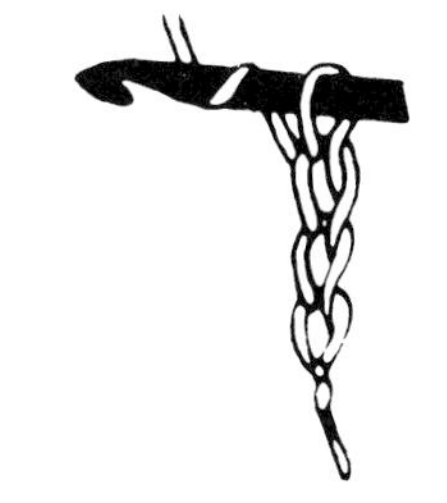

1. Place a slipknot on hook held with the point toward you, as you would hold a pencil. Hold yarn in the other hand over your ring finger, under middle and over index finger, loosely enough so the yarn feeds smoothly as the hook pulls it.
2. Pass hook under and over yarn and draw it through the loop on the hook for as many stitches as you want the chain to be.

SINGLE CROCHET

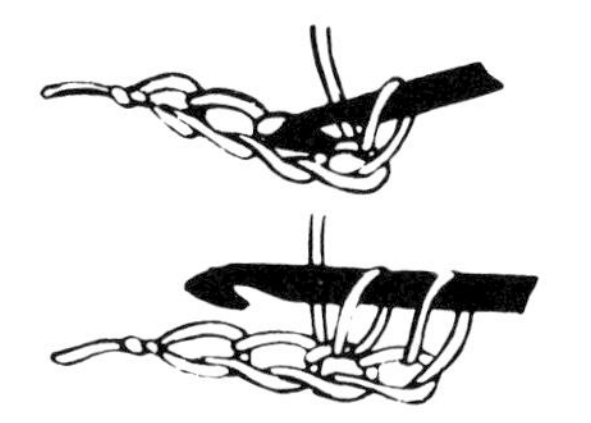

1. Insert hook under two top strands of second stitch from hook. *For all crochet, hook is always inserted under both top loops* unless a different motif is desired.
2. Pass hook under and over yarn and draw it through the stitch to give you two loops on the hook.

3. Pass hook under and over yarn again and draw it through the two loops.

HALF DOUBLE CROCHET

1. Pass hook under and over yarn, insert hook into third stitch from hook.

2. Pass hook under and over yarn and draw it through stitch. Pass hook under and over yarn again and draw it through the three loops on the hook.

DOUBLE CROCHET

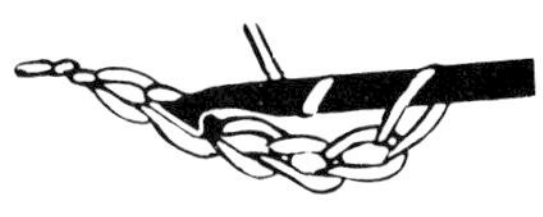

1. Pass hook under and over yarn, insert hook into the fourth stitch from hook.

2. Pass hook under and over yarn and draw it through the stitch. Pass hook under and over yarn again. Draw yarn through the first two loops only on the hook. Pass hook under and over yarn again and draw it through the remaining two loops on hook.

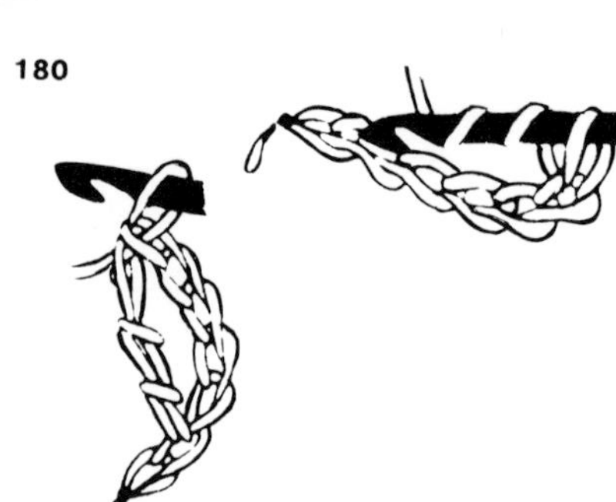

TRIPLE CROCHET

1. Pass hook under and over yarn twice. Insert hook into the fifth stitch from hook.

2. Pass hook under and over yarn and draw it through the stitch. * Pass hook under and over yarn and draw through two loops, repeat from * twice.

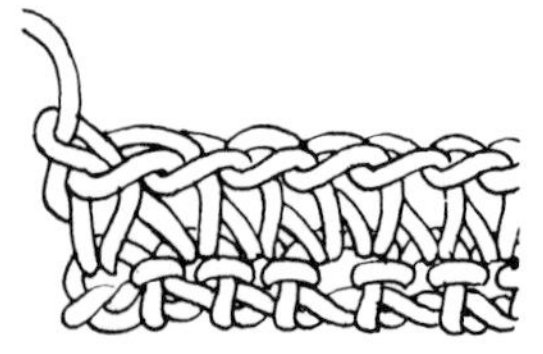

INCREASING

Increasing is simple. You work two of whatever stitch you are doing anywhere in the row or at the end. Increasing is usually done with a single or double crochet.

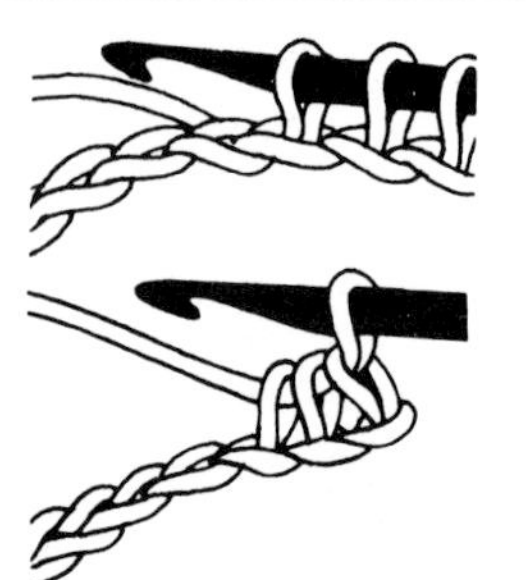

DECREASING

Decrease can be made at any point and is usually done in a single or double crochet; each one is slightly different.

To Decrease in Single Crochet

1. Insert hook in stitch next to loop and draw yarn through (two loops on hook), insert hook in next stitch and draw yarn through (three loops on hook).

2. Pass hook under and over yarn and draw through all three loops. You actually work two stitches together to give a decrease of one.

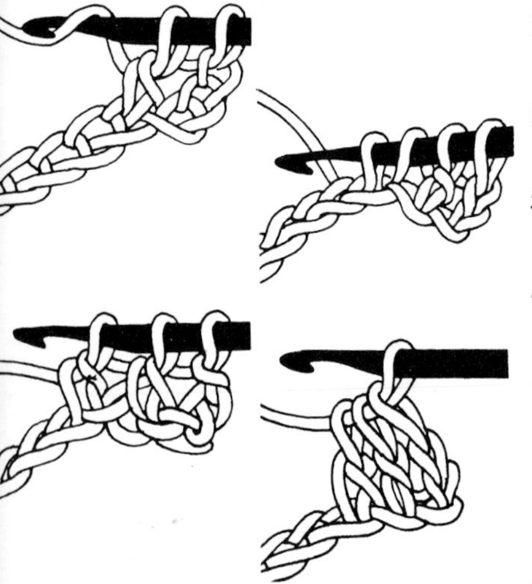

To Decrease in Double Crochet

1. Pass hook under and over yarn, insert hook in next stitch and drawn yarn through. There are three loops on hook.

2. Pass hook under and over and draw through two loops with two remaining on hook. Hook under and over yarn again.

3. Insert hook in next stitch and draw yarn through; four loops on hook.

4. Catch yarn again and draw through two loops; three loops remain on hook.

5. Catch yarn and draw through the three loops. A decrease of one double crochet is completed.

To Form a Circle

1. Make a chain of any number of stitches. Insert hook in first chain made. Catch yarn with hook. Be sure chain is not twisted.

2. Draw yarn through *both* the chain and the loop on hook. This is a "slip stitch," which can be used for any kind of joining. You now have a circle that can be expanded to any size you like using the same number of stitches to form a straight tubular crochet; or it can be shaped by increasing and decreasing.

EMBROIDERY STITCHES

Embroidery, also called stitchery, is done with a large eye needle into a fabric surface. The same stitches can be applied to mesh backings using crewel and needlepoint yarns.

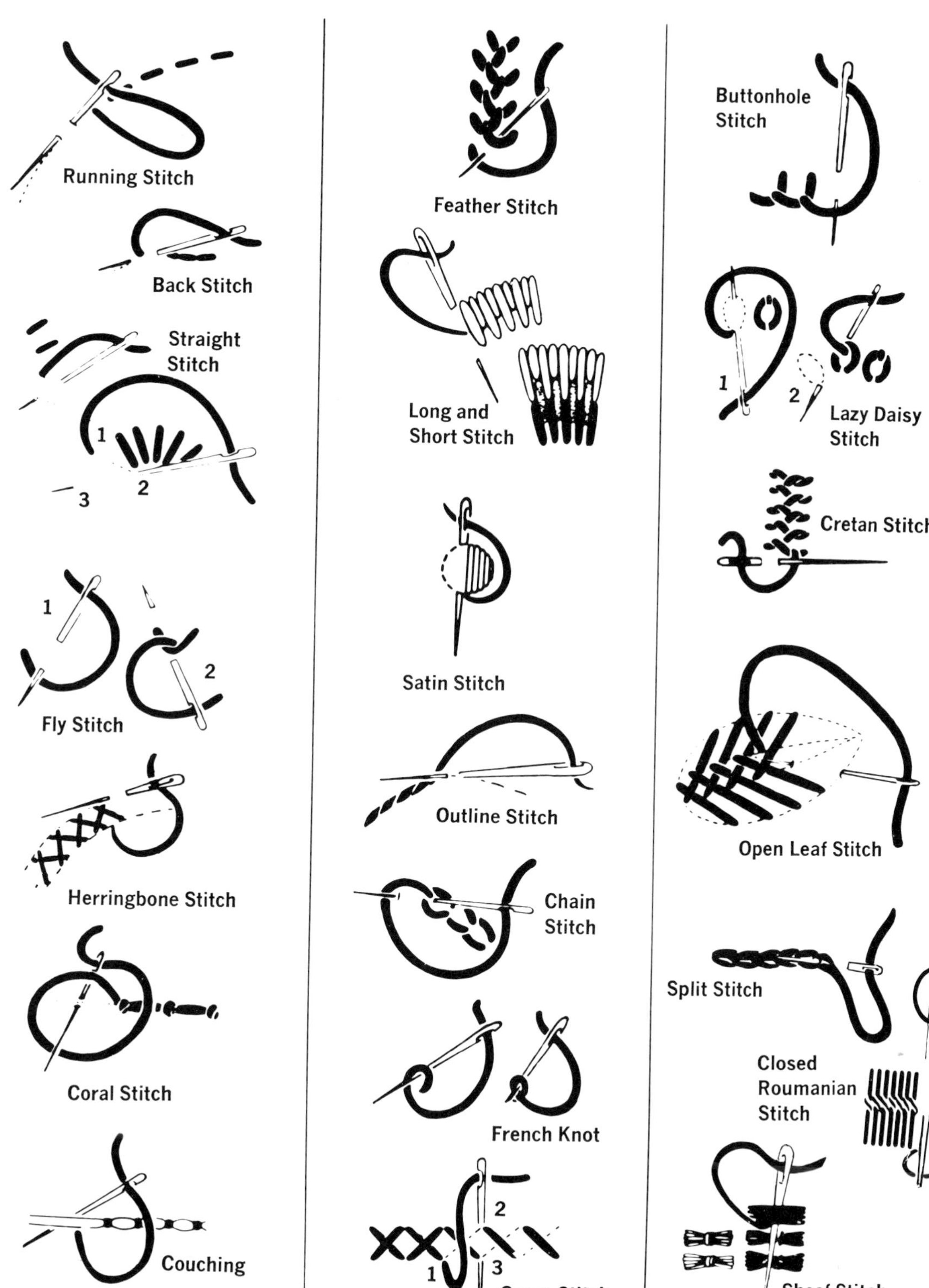

8
Body Adornments

ANIMA HEADDRESS. Rita Shumaker. 1972. Four-layer loom-woven double tubular weave construction with wool carpet yarn warp and hand-dyed yarns. Hot pink, magenta, rust, and gold.
Photo, John Daughtry

FOR CENTURIES CRAFTSMEN HAVE CREATED JEWELRY AND BODY adornments by casting and forming metals for rings, bracelets, and necklaces; ceramics for beads; leather for clothing and accessories and so forth. It was inevitable that the concept of soft sculpture be explored. Stuffed fabric, weaving, sewing, knotting, wrapping, crochet, knitting, and all the other methods mentioned in previous chapters are also being used to create items that can be worn in any variety of ways. These items often have a sculptural basis in the arts as opposed to a decorative, flat look normally associated with mass-produced fashions.

The examples were selected to show the direction that artists are taking in evolving forms and designs of their craft that can be worn. In some cases they are practical, almost conservative; others are way out, avant-garde, and probably would be worn by the brave rather than the meek.

Inspiration for body adornments are extremely varied. Nature and its organic forms (see Chapter 2) continue to inspire shape and design concepts in this medium as they have in every other for centuries past. African, Oceanic, and other primitive cultures dominate for their suggested use of unusual natural materials and for their methods. A necklace may have feathers, shells, bones, yarns, and strings in a combination of sewing, knotting, and finger weaving. A headdress may be constructed of tubular loom-woven fibers, supported by a metal armature, and be finished off with knotting or hand weaving.

Stuffed fabrics may combine hand-batiked and silk-screened materials; polyester double knits, suedes, cottons, rayons, and the entire range of cloth and designs.

Following pages:
BREASTPLATE. Rita Shumaker. Hand-dyed silk and cotton with linen and stoneware beads.

Backview with inset of Plexiglas.
Photos, John Daughtry

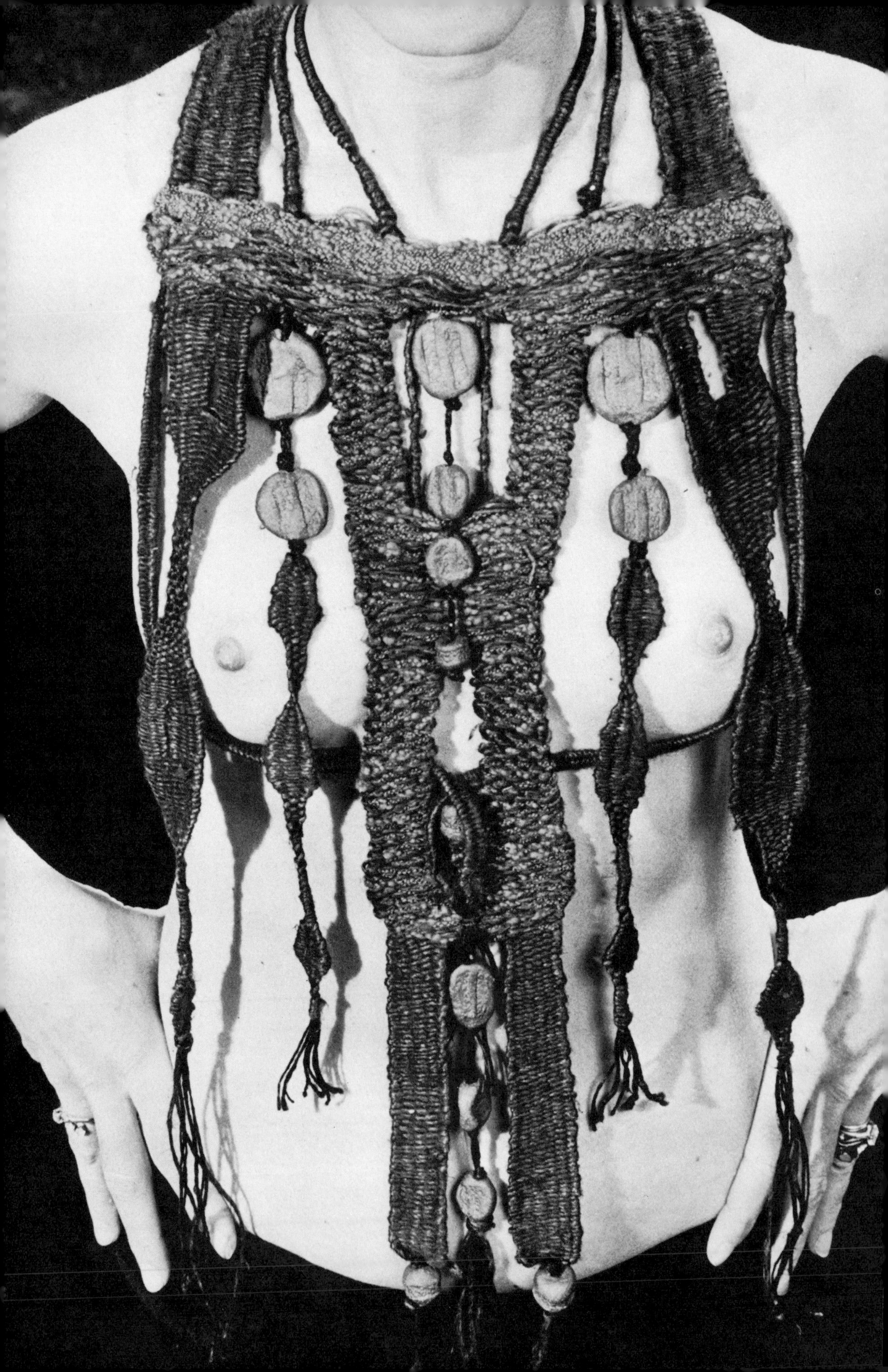

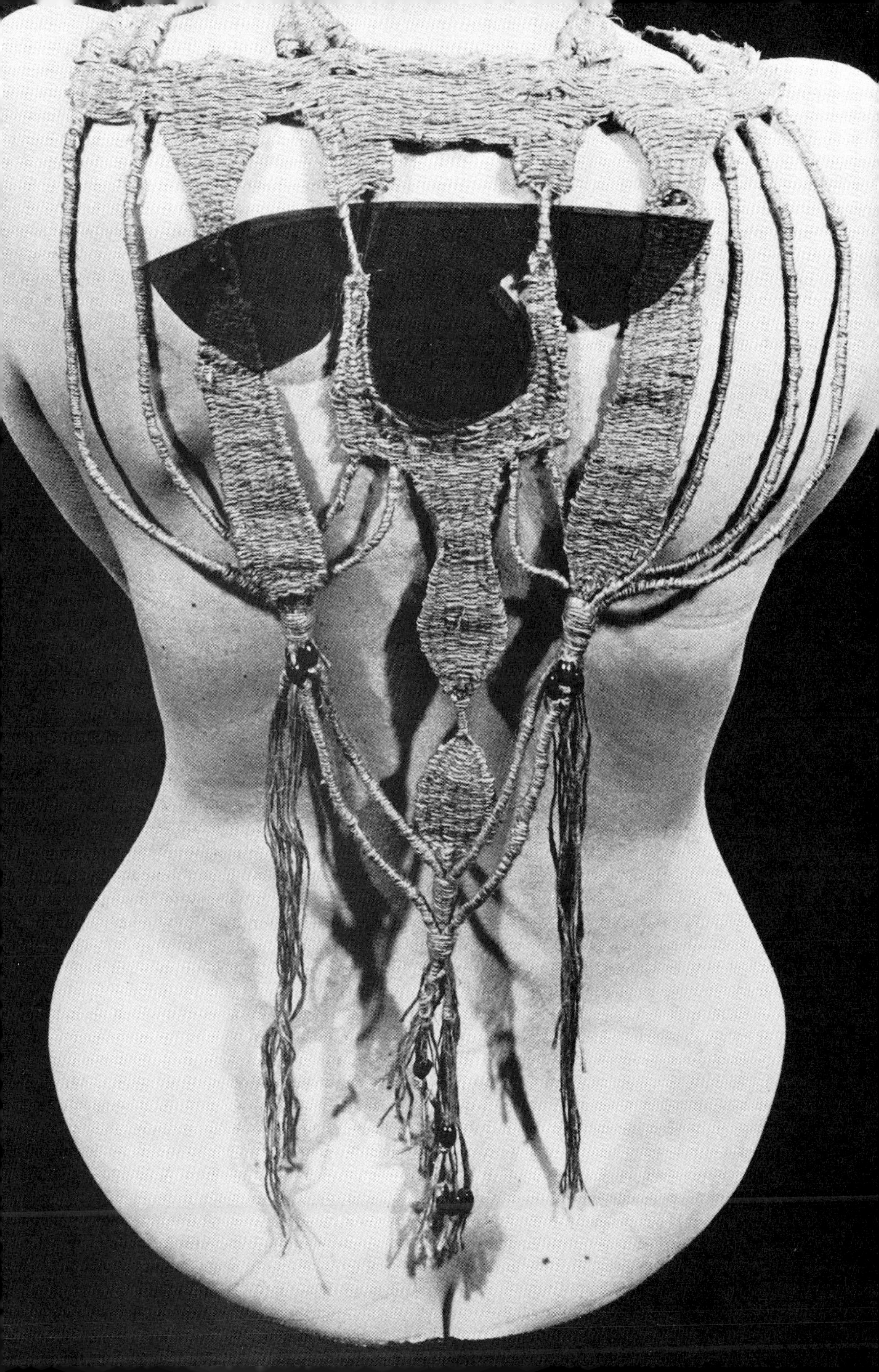

For surface decoration, look to examples from India, Spain, Afghanistan, Mexico, and Poland. You will find beads, mirrors, buttons, found objects, and bells are all part of the costuming. Locating the materials you want to use can present a problem; in addition to the Sources of Supply listed, one must continually haunt resale shops, costume supply companies that cater to theatrical productions, garage sales, and grandparents' attics. Then you must learn to recognize the potential of these objects and materials in a new context.

Opposite page: Another view of EARTH, AIR, FIRE AND WATER.
Photos, Hosea Fumero

QUEEN OF HEARTS. Rita Shumaker. 1972. 72″ high, 18″ circumference. Four-layer double tubular weave construction with wrapping and macramé.

EARTH, AIR, FIRE AND WATER. Rita Shumaker. 1972. 65″ high, 18″ wide. Headdress of double tubular weave with feathers, raku, and tiger eyes.

QUILTED VELVET YOKE. Lou Ann Musinski. Velveteen-padded neck adornment with stoneware, Egyptian paste glass beads, and silver studs along edge. Front and back views.

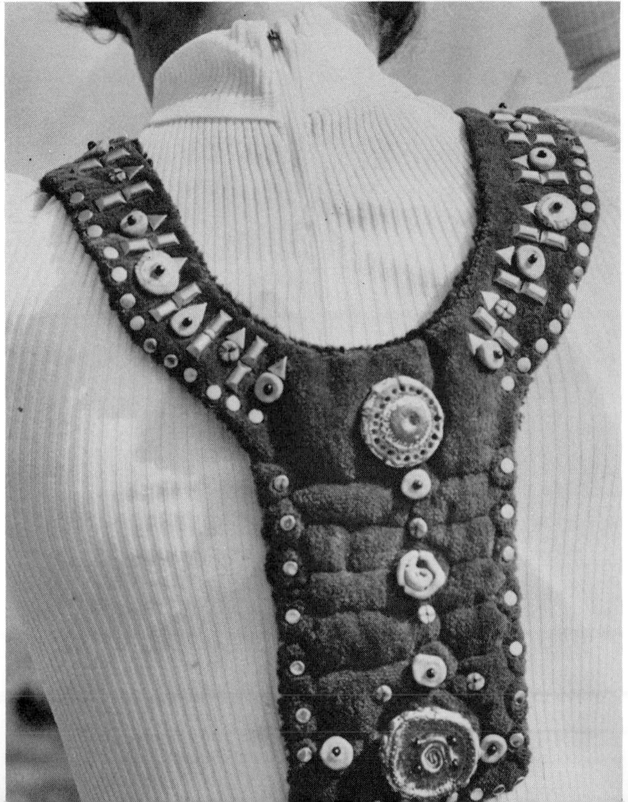

SOFT CHOKER. Lou Ann Musinski. Three different colored stuffed jersey tubes hook in the back. Handmade American Indian buttons, stoneware, and Egyptian paste beads are stitched to the center tube. Each tube is an individual unit also.

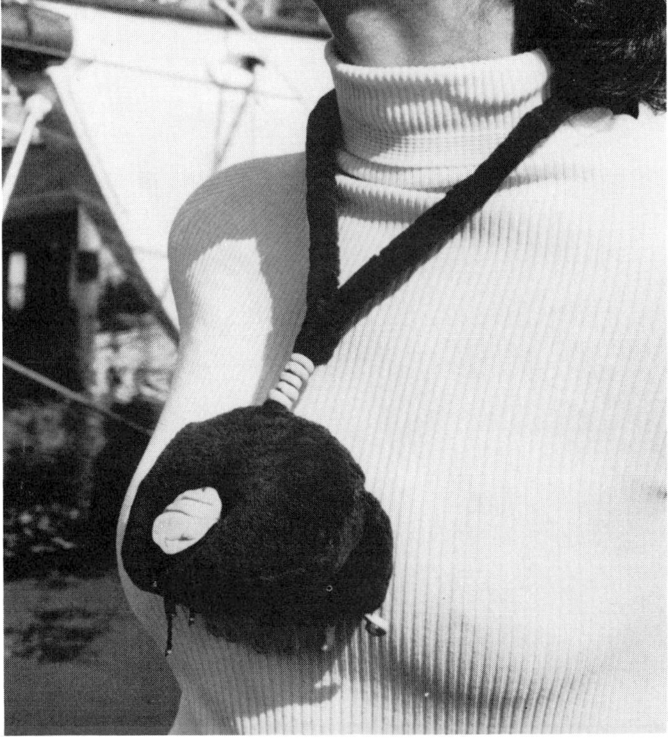

SOFT NECKLACE. Lou Ann Musinski. Velveteen adornment inspired by a Venus's-flytrap has a porcelain medallion that is stitched off-center. Glass beads hanging from the bottom simulate the leaf's tentaclelike action.

SOFT MEDALLION. Lou Ann Musinski. Padded cotton batik neckpiece with glass beads. *Below:* Construction of shape.

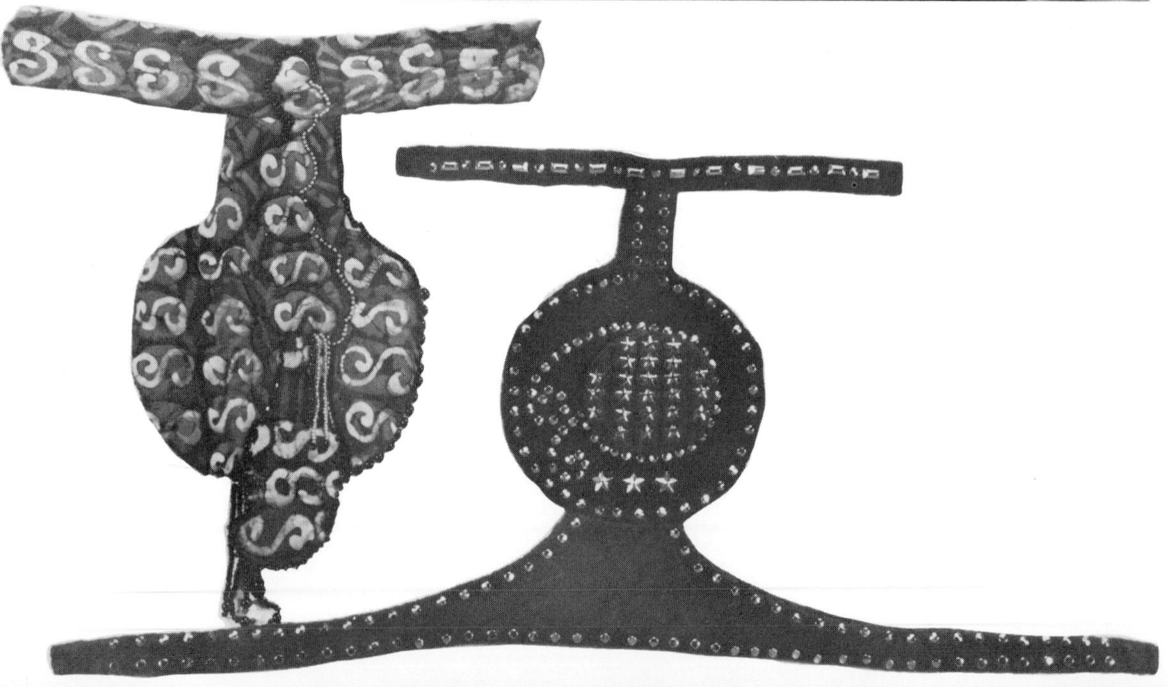

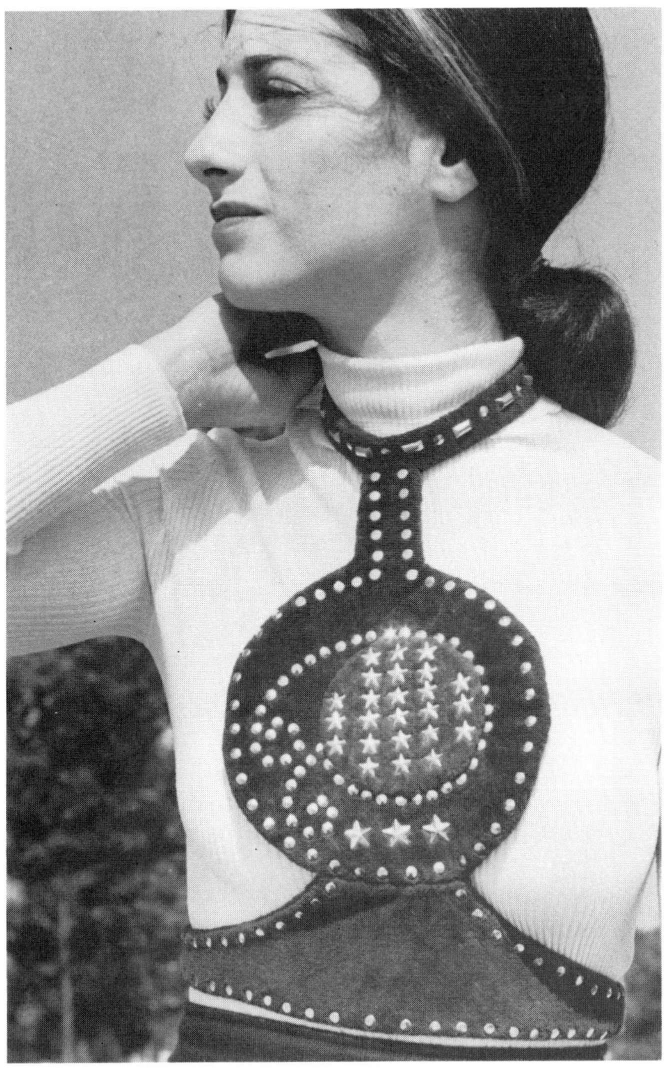

QUILTED VELVET BREASTPLATE. Lou Ann Musinski. Silver round and star-shape studs clip through the fabric. See construction on opposite page.

SOFT SHELL BREAST COVER. Lou Ann Musinski. Tie-bleached cotton breast adornment inspired by seashell shapes. Glass and stoneware beads. Piece pins to dress front.

FEATHER COLLAR. Rita Shumaker. 1972. Woven yarns and feathers.

Photo, John Daughtry

NECKPIECE. Kathy Pittman. 1972. Gray wool wrapping over a jute core. Feathers and beads.

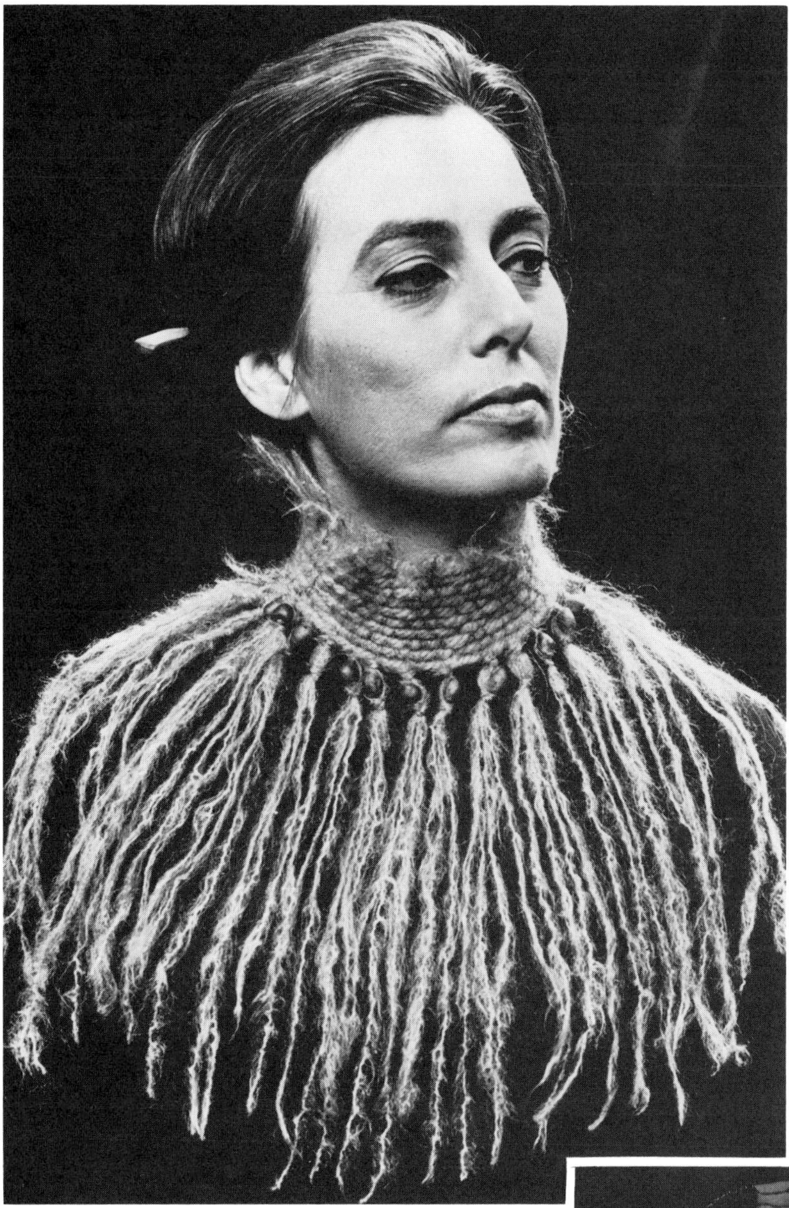

COLLAR. Rita Shumaker. 1972. Finger-woven wool and mohair with stoneware beads.
Photo, John Daughtry

ALBATROSS NECKPIECE. Maggie Nicholson. White leather, tan suede, gray velvet, and embroidery details. Velcro closing.
Courtesy, artist

Feather Jewelry

Feather jewelry is an attractive and natural development of "soft" art. It is relatively simple to create; the feathers themselves have magnificent colors and textures. Design depends upon the shaping, combination of feathers with one another and with other materials and techniques.

Generally, feathers, purchased by the ounce or pound, are mounted on a backing of scrim, needlepoint canvas, or leather, with glue or by sewing. When scrim or canvas is used, it should be lined with a layer of felt or thin leather. Circles can be drawn with a dish, water glass, or compass; other shapes can be cut from a paper pattern and then transferred to the backing. Seashells, ceramic pieces, beads, buttons, and other ornaments are compatible with feathers. Hanging parts for necklaces can be lengths of leather or suede, or sennits of knotted or braided cords and yarns.

Simply arrange the feathers on the backing and attach by stitching or gluing. Overlap layers to fill out the basic shape. Glue a decorative item over the central stems where desired. Hanging cords should be glued or sewn to the backing also. Line with a circle of felt, suede, or leather, glued and whipstitched around the edges for a neat finish.

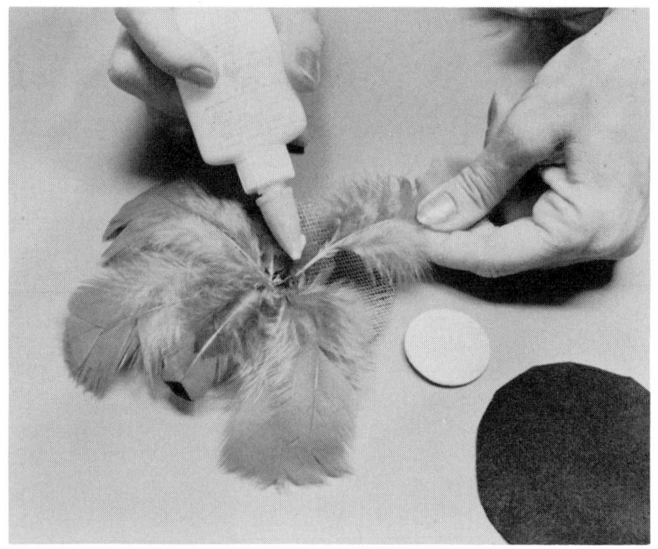

Two necklaces by Eileen Bernard combine; *Left;* Duck feathers in brown and oranges with a ceramic piece in the center and amber rings tied into the linen macramé cord. *Above:* Speckled goose feathers are arranged radially. The center is a sea urchin shell with a bead glued on the top. Jute macramé hanging parts are strung with cowrie shells. Necklaces of seashells can be purchased and unstrung so that holes are already in the shells. Otherwise holes may be drilled with a fine drill bit. If shells are soft, holes can be made with a large needle.

Feather neckware and cuffs by Karen Naïma Weiss illustrate different shapes, combinations of feathers, and objects that can be created.
Courtesy, Anneberg Gallery, San Francisco

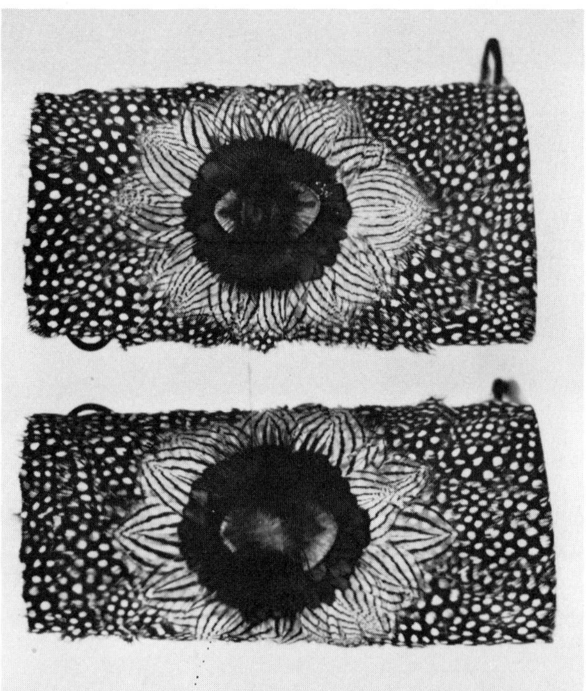

HEADPIECE. Karen Naïma Weiss. Feathers are used in the same manner as jewels for a tiara that is different and sculptural.
Courtesy, Anneberg Gallery, San Francisco

FETISH NECKPIECE. Dona Z. Meilach. White duck and gray speckled goose feathers with touches of orange are mounted on a curve-shaped piece of canvas that conforms to the neckline of a dress. Cowrie shells are glued to the edge and a white jute macramé sennit buttons onto the dress at the back.

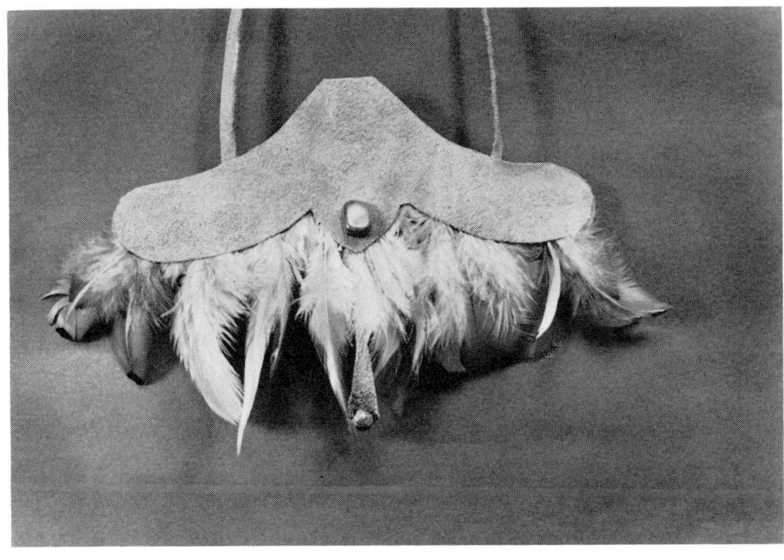

SOFT NECKLACE. Dona Z. Meilach. Feathers are sandwiched between two pieces of garment leather. An extra piece of leather is attached at the center front. A bead is glued to the top and the dangle to unify the parts.

BREAST ORNAMENT. Marquesas Islands, Polynesia. One of many examples in museums that can serve as inspiration for contemporary jewelry.
Courtesy, Field Museum of Natural History, Chicago

Opposite page:
JEWELRY. Doreen Uhl Worob. Pheasant feathers are combined with leather and silver tubing in a necklace and pin. A cast silver pin *(left bottom)* is constructed with various colored pheasant feathers.

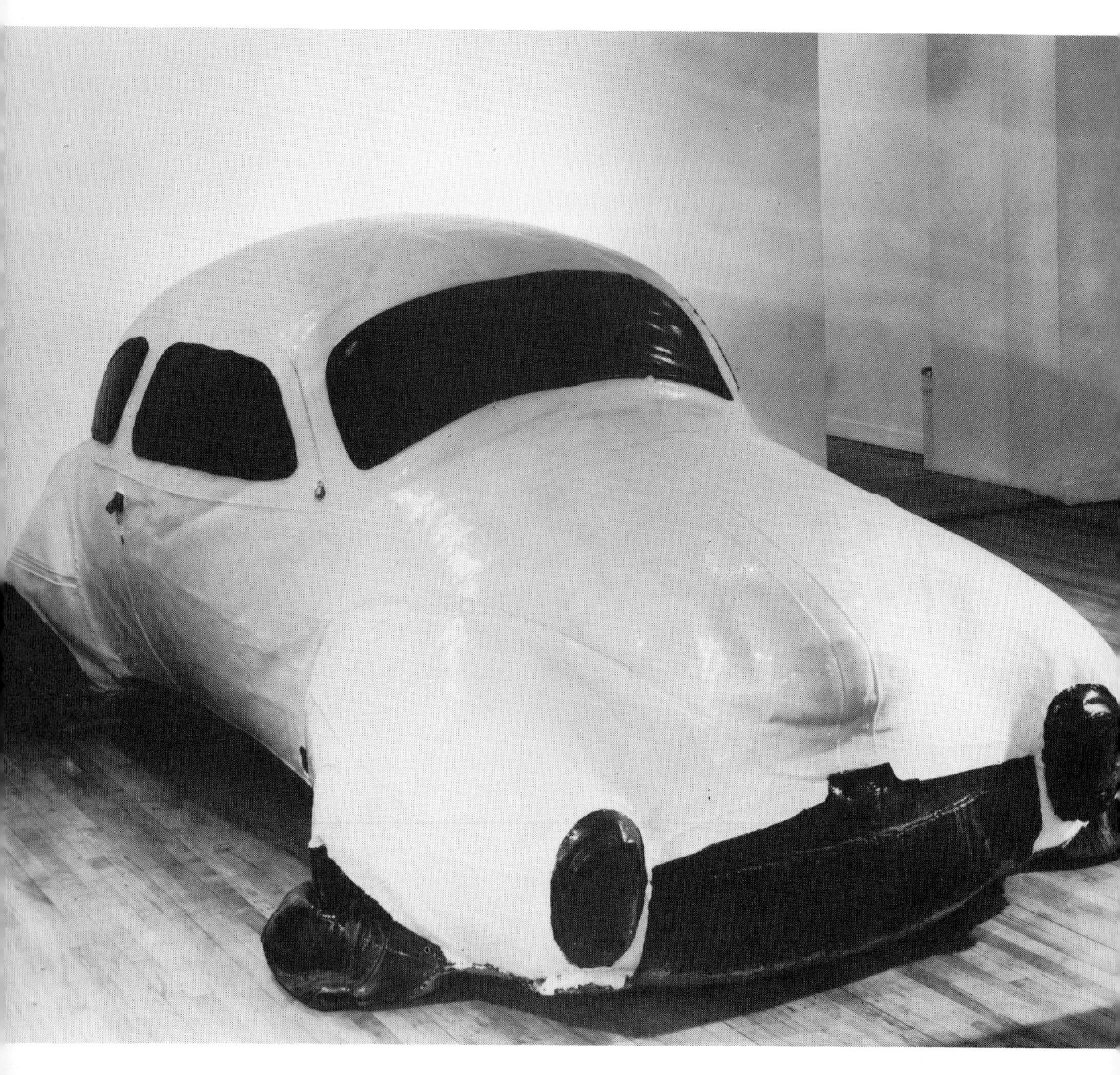

9

Rubber and Plastics

AS THE SCOPE OF SOFT SCULPTURE IS CONTINUALLY EXPANDED, materials other than fibers and fabric are being explored. Several artists are developing unique expressive statements in rubber and various plastics, by themselves, and in combinations with other materials.

Liquid latex, or rubber, usually is associated with mold making in the arts. Its viscosity and ability to reproduce minute hairline textures also makes it adaptable to soft concepts. The material is being used by sculptors to create inflated and stuffed forms. A demonstration of the technique begins on page 208. You will also discover applications for polystyrene (Styrofoam, Ethafoam) and polyurethane (foam rubber).

Clear polyethylene sheeting is a versatile material that may be shaped, sewn, and stuffed with other plastics, rubber, and so on. Howard Woody, professor of art, University of South Carolina, has adapted clear plastic sheets in a conceptual relationship to space and movement. His "atmospheric sculptures" (pages 218, 219) exploit the properties of open-air space. Instead of space considered as a partially encompassed negative area displaced by an important mass, the atmospheric systems feature positive space as the essential element. The theory is that space is not a frozen neutral block, rather these are diverse and changing forces that activate the ethereal block of flexible sheets in a flowing, fluid manner.

Mr. Woody's sculptures, containing blocks of free-hanging polyethylene sheeting, employ the elements of motion, time, light, and sound as major qualities. Ideally, they are presented outdoors with winds less than 15 mph that gently undulate the forms. The result is a flamboyant aerial ballet based on the oscillating currents of wind flow that activate the pieces as they are attached to their guy lines.

YELLOW '42 FORD. Sig Rennels. 1972. Inflated rubber latex colored with acrylic.
Courtesy, O. K. Harris Gallery, New York

AIR FLO. Gerhardt Knodel. 1972. 7″ high, 30″ wide. Plastic foam (Ethafoam by Dow Chemical Co.) in soft rod shapes are partially covered with tie-dyed fabrics and wound with monofilament.

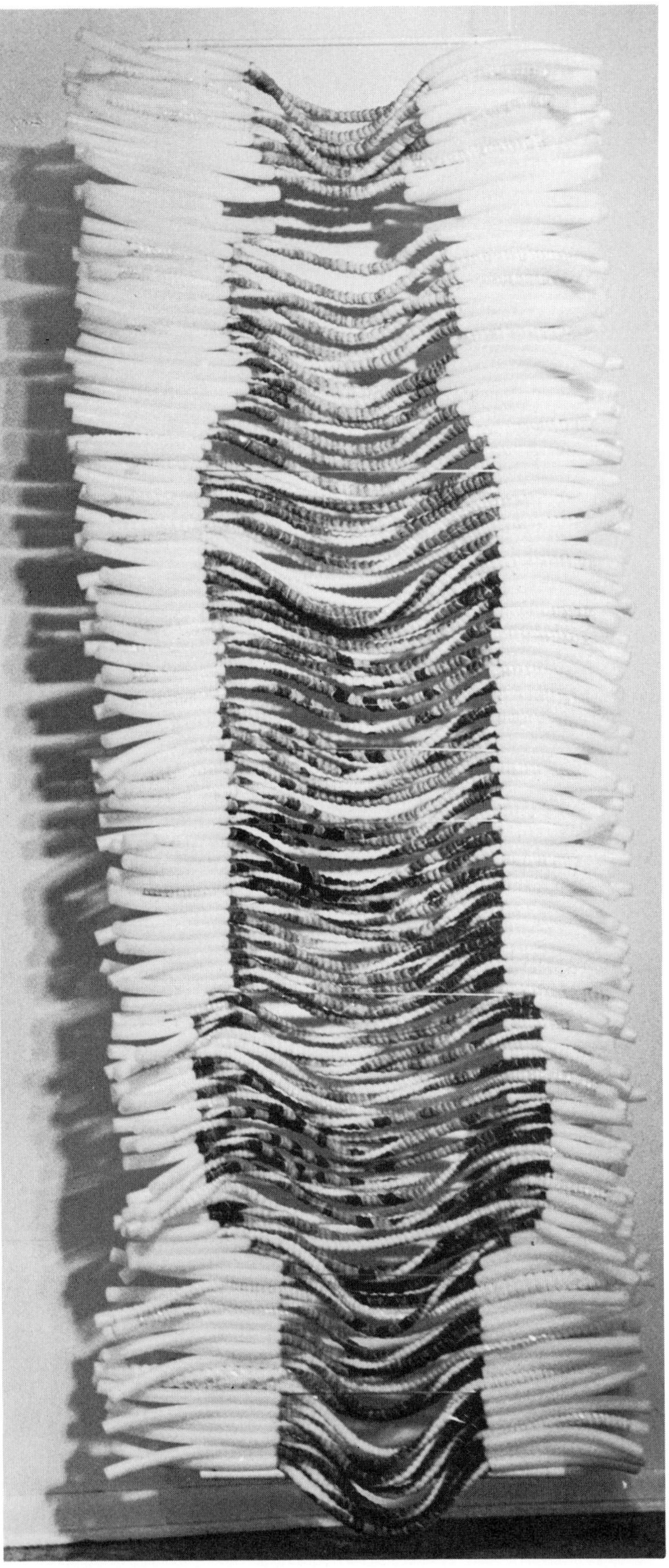

Opposite page: Several pieces on display. At left of photo, SANTA FE. 7′ high, 7′ wide. From the show *Eleven Aerial Acts* by Gerhardt Knodel. *Photographed at the James Yaw Gallery, Birmingham, Michigan*

Opposite page below: Detail shows the construction of wrapped and unwrapped portions of the foam.

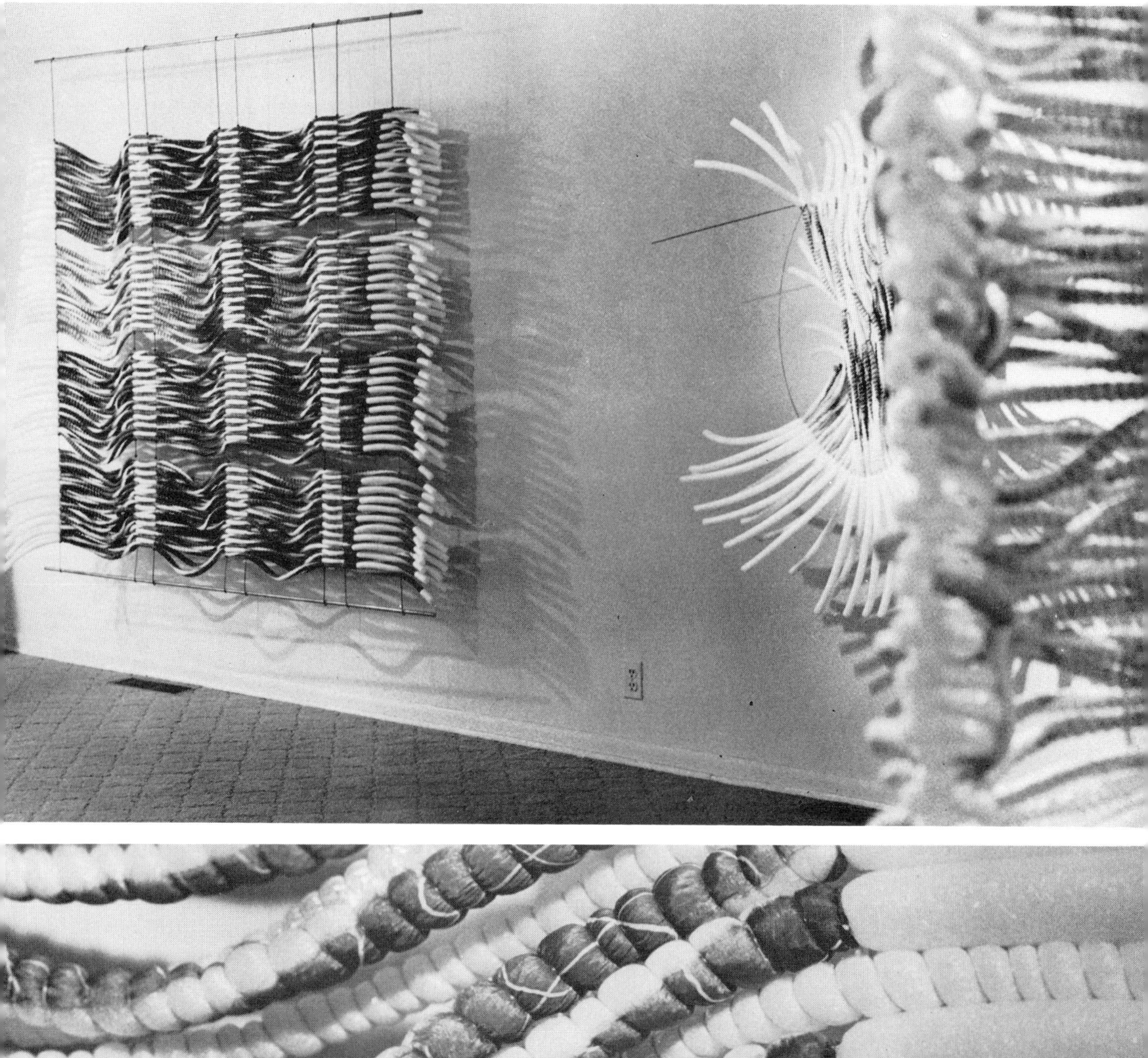

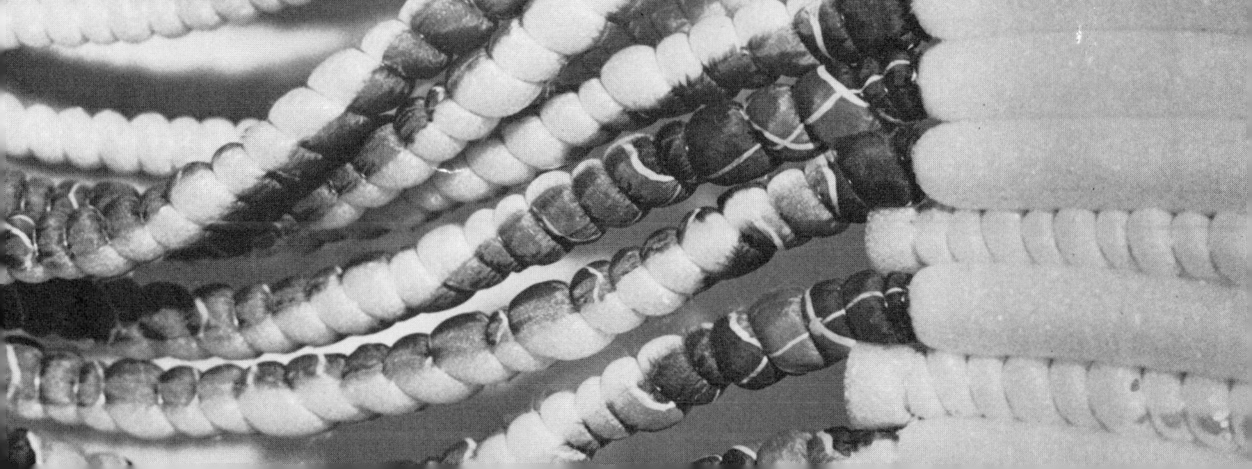

A SLICE OF LIFE. Arlene Seitzinger. 1973. 15″ high, 24″ long, 18″ wide. Different densities of polyurethane foam cut, colored, shaped, and assembled.

Polyurethane (often called foam rubber) is cut with a band saw to the overall large shapes required. Smaller details are cut with a curved blade manicure scissors. Some foams cut more easily when they are wet; it avoids distortion. Cutting with surgeon's shears and scalpels yields a variety of interesting textures.

Foam is colored by dipping it in household dye, and details are drawn with India inks. Details can also be burned in with cigarettes or woodburning tools. Use silicone seal and bathtub caulking for adhesion but hold the parts together with pins and needles while adhesive is drying. Foams already cut for packaging can be readily adapted to this art form.

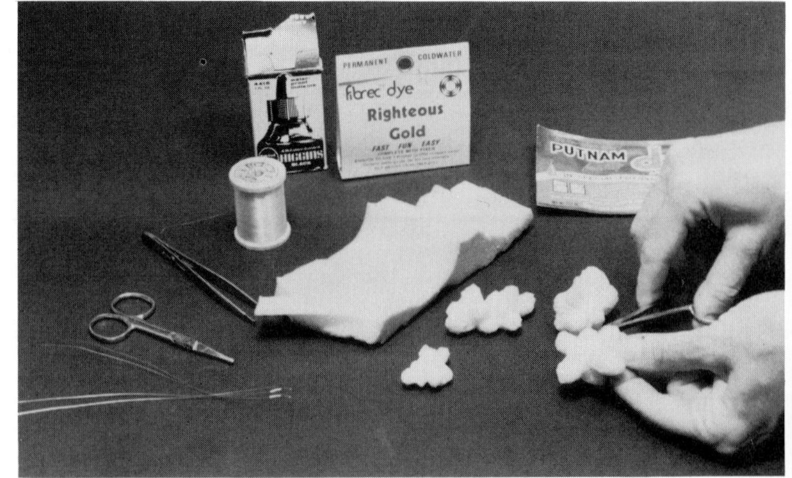

MAN'S STRUGGLE. Arlene Seitzinger. 14″ high, 10″ wide, 10″ deep. Head and hands cut from white Styrofoam are inset into a gray piece of polyurethane with holes that remained from packaging.

THE PROTECTRESS. Arlene Seitzinger. 1973. 40″ high, 18″ wide. Polyurethane foam cut, shaped, and colored.

Detail of THE PROTECTRESS.

POMMES TOMBÉES AVEC ÉCHELLE. Piero Gilardi. 1966. 133″ deep, 78″ wide. Polyurethane cut and colored. *Courtesy, Galerie Ileana Sonnabend, Paris*

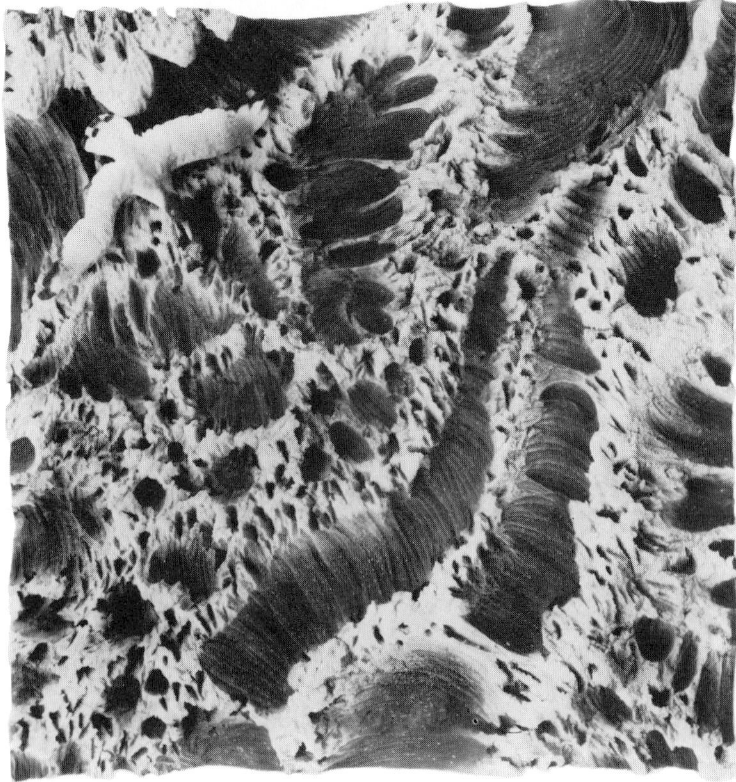

MER AGITÉE. Piero Gilardi. 1966. 67″ square. Polyurethane cut and colored. *Courtesy, Galerie Ileana Sonnabend, Paris*

SOUTH SHORE DRIVE. Tom Ladousa. 1972. Rubber latex waves, beach, and toys.
Courtesy, artist

RUBBER LATEX PRONG PIE. Tom Ladousa. 1972. 45″ high, 33″ wide.
Courtesy, artist

RUBBER LATEX SOFT SCULPTURES

Latex, which is actually liquid rubber, is normally used for a mold material in casting. It has been adapted to finished soft sculptures by Tom Ladousa, Clayton Bailey, and Sig Rennels. The following demonstration and information were provided by Mr. Ladousa.

The liquid latex Mr. Ladousa uses is marketed by General Latex Corp. (of Ohio) in 5 and 55 gallon containers, and from art supply dealers. Similar products are available from other manufacturers (see Sources of Supply, page 242, and/or consult your yellow pages).

Latex has a heavy viscosity which runs very little when applied to a form by brushing or dabbing. It has superior tear resistance. It comes ready to use and cures at room temperature. With these rubbers it is possible to produce thin lightweight sculptures so flexible that they can be turned inside out without cracking or tearing. They pick up the finest detail from almost any type of form no matter how severe the undercutting may be. They have the property of great release ability so the mold material is easy to eject and no mold releases are necessary. Various fillers, colors, and retarders or accelerators may be

A rubber latex wall (see finished sculpture, page 211) will be formed over bricks held together by clay coils built up approximately ¼" above the top level of the bricks. This positive will become the negative when the latex skin is pulled away. The clay coil will simulate the appearance of mortar in the finished piece.

Rubber latex is dabbed, not brushed, onto the surface to give a heavy even coat and to minimize the number of coats needed. *Allow latex to dry between each coat*—3 to 4 coats are usually required. The final coat should be about ⅛" thick. Apply latex with a nylon bristle brush. If bubbles or pinholes form, blow against the rubber gently to break the trapped air.

Extra care is taken to coat the holes in the bricks completely. A fourth coat is being applied. Note the other latex forms in the background.

On the fourth coat the entire surface is dabbed for the final buildup. It is allowed to dry at least 48 hours in a warm dry room with a fan circulating the air. When dry, dust it with baby powder to remove stickiness.

The latex skin is carefully pulled from the bricks. A finished sculpture can be cleaned by gently washing with soapy water. The form should not be allowed to soak, and any residual water should be dried off. Excess water tends to weaken the latex and cause it to rot. If the latex looks milky when it is wet, do not be alarmed; it will return to normal color after drying.

Demonstration and photos, courtesy Tom Ladousa

Detail shows the prongs from the bricks and the mortar joints from the clay coils.

added for altering the textures, color, and workability of the prepared latex. Finished latex pieces should be kept indoors.

Latex can be used over almost any material and will yield a detailed surface from clay, wood, metal, bricks, ceramics, plastic, and so forth. The latex becomes the negative mold of the positive item. The finished latex sculpture can be loosely hung or supported; it can be stuffed; if the piece is properly sealed, it can be inflated.

The general procedures involve:

1. Preparing the original by forming or cleaning the object that is to be reproduced in rubber.
2. Applying the prepared latex by dabbing or brushing. (For large surfaces the latex can be sprayed or poured on but there is more waste.) Three or four layers usually are required to build up a ⅛" thickness. Each layer must dry thoroughly before applying the next layer.
3. The dried latex skin is removed either by peeling it back from the mold, or by removing the form, depending upon the material used.
4. Always keep the latex can tightly closed when not in use.

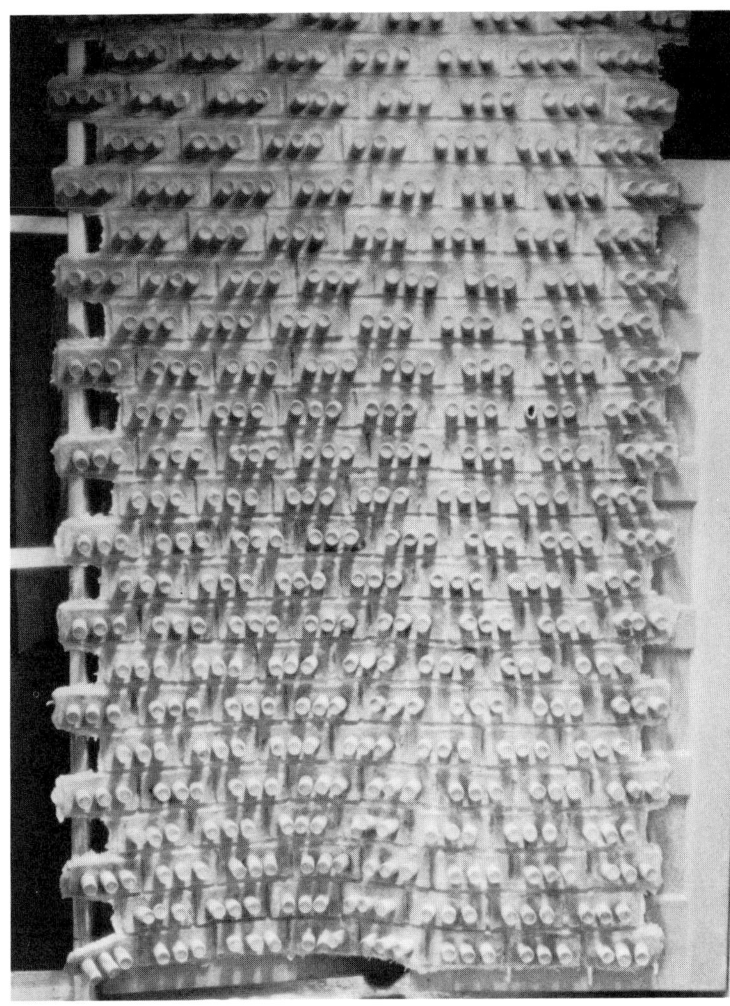

RUBBER LATEX PRONG WALL. Tom Ladousa. 1973. 8′ high, 5′ wide.
Courtesy, artist

Latex Over Clay Forms

Clay is a practical, versatile material for creating three-dimensional soft latex forms. The clay object is made and must be allowed to dry leather hard. If the clay is too soft and moist, the latex coatings will take too long to cure and they will remain moist and weak and tear easily. Where crevices in the clay cause the latex to puddle, the puddles must be brushed out or a dry film will form on top of the puddle and prevent the latex underneath from drying. A fan will hasten the drying. When the first coat of latex changes color from a milky white to a light tan color, a second coat may be applied.

Apply liquid latex with nylon bristle brushes. They are easily cleaned and cared for with soapy water. When not in use keep the brushes in water. Dab or brush on the latex all over the clay. If you can't make it adhere all around, and on the bottom, build up all possible surfaces with the necessary coats. Then turn the mold over and repeat. When dry, trim away any excess rubber rims with a sharp knife.

Always dust the dried latex with baby powder to remove stickiness. Make a slit in a convenient place, usually at the bottom, and

DOUBLE HUMP BIRDIE FOWL. Tom Ladousa. 1972. 18″ high, 36″ wide, 15″ deep.
Courtesy, artist

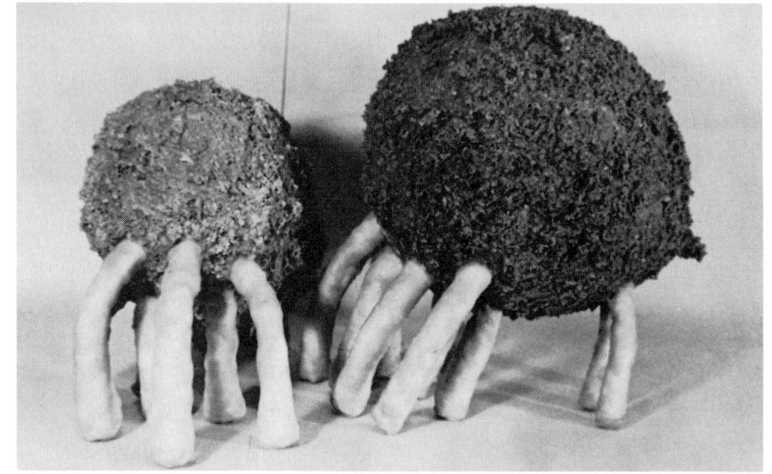

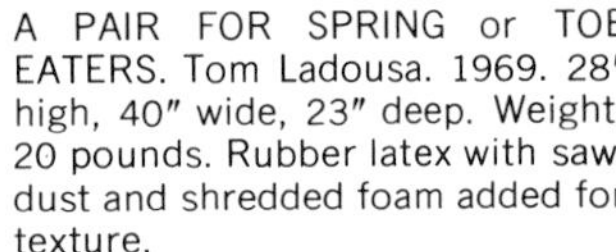

A PAIR FOR SPRING or TOE EATERS. Tom Ladousa. 1969. 28″ high, 40″ wide, 23″ deep. Weight, 20 pounds. Rubber latex with sawdust and shredded foam added for texture.
Courtesy, artist

break up and remove the clay. The latex form can be turned inside out by pulling it through the slit, and this first coat will have picked up the texture of the object.

You now have a collapsed rubber form that can be reshaped by stuffing with a hard or soft material. When the form is filled out, the slit can be sewn up and a line of rubber beaded over the sewn area. Be sure to clean all talc off the surfaces to be reattached so the new rubber can weld properly. A zipper can also be sewn into the rubber.

Airtight Rubber Sculpture

To make inflatable forms, such as Sig Rennels's cars, the process is the same as the clay procedure except the slit is sewn up and sealed without stuffing. A prepared air valve is added to the piece through which air can be blown into the form by mouth with a tire air-pump or a vacuum cleaner. However, latex rubber alone is slightly porous and

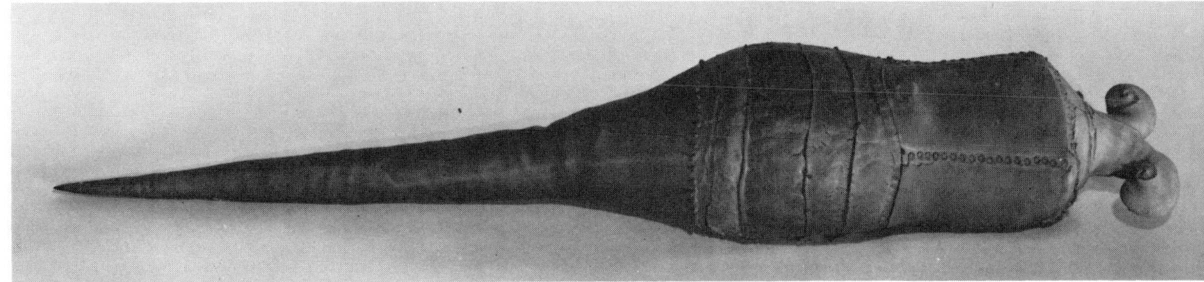

STUFFED RUBBER GRUB. Clayton Bailey. 1966. Rubber latex stuffed with shredded polyurethane.
Courtesy, The Art Institute of Chicago

Clayton Bailey removes the leather-hard clay from inside the rubber skin. He breaks up the clay first so it will come out in small pieces and only a small slit is necessary in the skin.
Courtesty, artist

the pieces require repumping frequently to retain their inflation. To avoid deflation Mr. Rennels uses the latex for a base coat to pick up details and then alternates that with a coat of Butyl Rubber (B. F. Goodrich), which is long lasting and provides an airtight seal.

Patching and Joining

If the rubber forms spring holes or tears, they can be patched. In the same way separate pieces can be assembled to create larger forms. The areas to be joined must be cleaned by moistening the areas with a thin coat of latex and then rubbing until the latex dries and rolls off. Then the edges of both pieces are coated and allowed to dry to its tacky stage and recontacted. Pieces may also be sewn together at the edges and then the sewn area coated with latex.

Coloring

A complete range of colors can be obtained by using acrylic colors mixed with the liquid latex. (Do not use oil colors as they are destructive to natural rubber.) A small amount of acrylic color is thinned with latex, but thinning does not change the color. To color, squeeze a few drops of acrylic color into a small paper cup, add a few drops of water, and stir. Then add latex to make ¾ cup and mix again until the color is thoroughly blended. This amount will coat a form about 15″ square.

Color can also be painted onto the finished form. Another effect can be achieved by using different colors in each coat of latex applied.

Adding Textures

The thickness and texture of the rubber can be changed by adding fillers such as sawdust, wood shavings, clay dust, sand, cork, and ground cork rubber filler. The procedure is to mix the material into the liquid rubber as thick or thin as you like and then apply. Color can be added to the mix by stirring in. When coating with a filler latex, allow a longer drying time between coats; about 24 hours is recommended.

GRUB. Clayton Bailey. Rubber latex form made over clay.
Courtesy, artist

Vulcanizing

The liquid latexes are self-curing at room temperatures. However, additional vulcanizing, or curing, may be accomplished by placing small forms into an oven for 40 minutes at 240° F. Another way is to boil the collapsed latex forms in boiling water for 40 minutes. This treatment tends to prevent the piece from stretching out of shape and gives it a longer life. Collapsed skins can also be heated in an oven as above, but the odor is irritating and lasting so proper ventilation must be provided.

The normal aging of the latexes can be improved with an additive called Antioxidant #9–I–P–708 (General Latex Corp. of Ohio). The recommended use is 1 pound of additive to 100 pounds of latex.

Deterioration

Rubber will deteriorate if it is exposed to outdoor conditions for a long time; it cannot withstand ultraviolet light exposures. It will also deteriorate rapidly in the presence of materials such as copper or manganese. Avoid contact with oil, grease, and other petroleum products because they are destructive to rubber. Extended dampness and temperatures above 180° F. will also cause deterioration. The life expectancy of such sculptures is about six years.

Safety Precautions

Wear old clothes. Have good ventilation and use exhaust fans when containers are open. Avoid getting latex on skin since it will pull out the hairs on which the latex has dried. Wash off skin promptly with warm soapy water. Latexes are flammable, so do not smoke or strike matches around open containers. Use with adequate ventilation and do not breathe in too much of the vapors. Keep the container tightly closed when not in use; if a skin forms on the liquid, remove it before using the latex.

UNTITLED. Robert Morris. 1968. Approximately 10′ high. Rubber. *Courtesy, Detroit Institute of Arts*

DOWNBEAT. Helen Beling. 1972. Rubber tormented and glued. *Courtesy, artist*

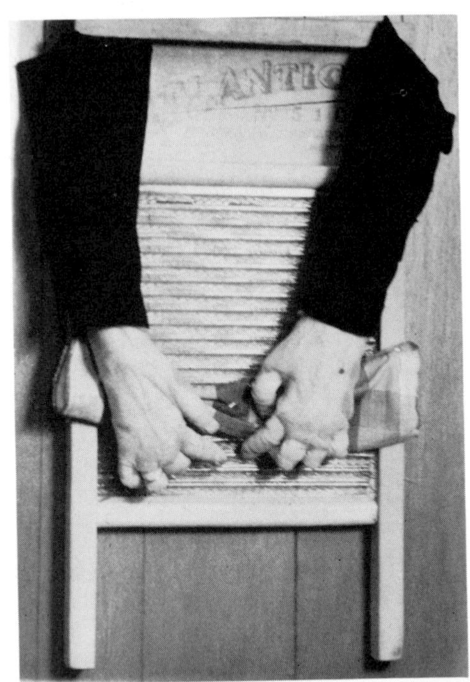

GRANDMA. Susan Sabin. 1972. Vinyl gloved hands stuffed and assembled with fabrics and objects.
Photo, Lee Milner

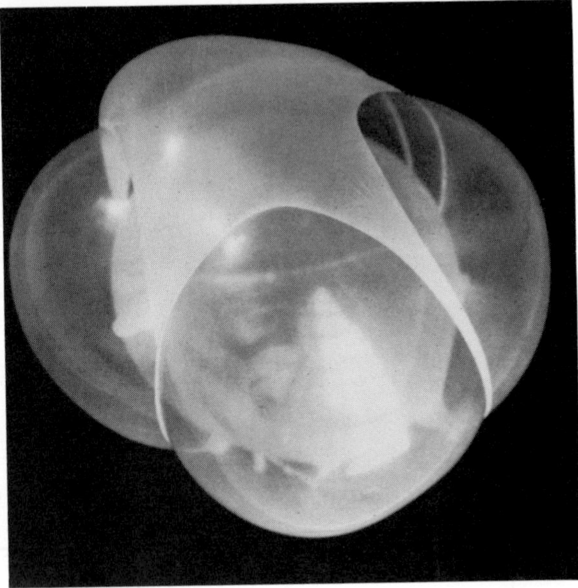

SURGICAL GLOVES. Jack Bakke. 1972. Approximately 30″ high, 24″ diameter. Inflated surgical gloves create unusual forms. One of the pieces was sprayed inside with acrylic paint before inflating.
Courtesy, artist

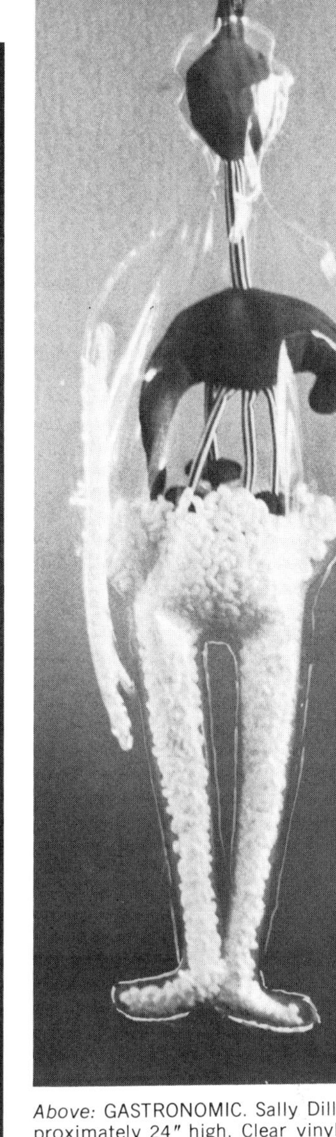

Above: GASTRONOMIC. Sally Dillon. 1972. Approximately 24″ high. Clear vinyl, stuffed with fabric and foam pellets.

Courtesy, artist

Left above: SUN SETTING, OCEAN AND OYSTERS AND SEA-URCHIN. Sally Dillon. 1972. Approximately 30″ high, 12″ wide. Clear vinyl with soft objects of stuffed fabrics, fur, and leather.

Courtesy, artist

Left below: THE THINKER ENCLOSED. Sally Dillon. Stuffed fabrics inside of clear vinyl.

Courtesy, artist

LIGHT BULB. Student. 18" high, 12" wide. Clear plastic with a colored element inside and a tie-dye socket.
Collection, Robert Falwell, DeKalb, Illinois

WALL HANGING. Edie Danieli. 1972. 52" square. Transparent vinyl stapled and stuffed with kapok.

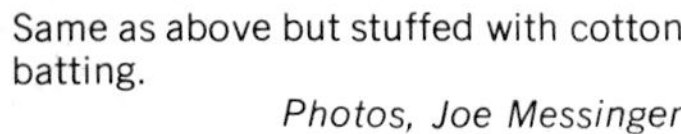

Same as above but stuffed with cotton batting.
Photos, Joe Messinger

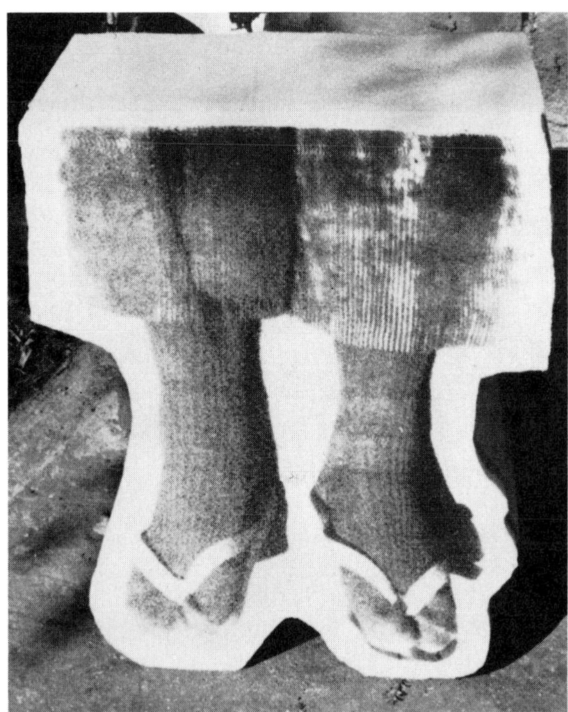

DON'T STEP ON MY FEET. Pat Tavenner. 1972. 19″ high, 11″ wide, 7″ deep. The feet have been silk screened onto a 1″ slab of polyurethane, which was laminated onto another 6″ block for rigidity.

4 ALARM FIRE. Carol Tranter. 1972. 6′ 4″ high, 4′ wide. Plastic, newspapers, rock salt, drawer pulls, photo emulsion, watercolors, and ribbon.
Courtesy, artist

TRANSPARENT CUBES. Edie Danieli. 1971. 11″ cubes. Transparent vinyl stapled and stuffed with various materials including hay, cellophane, wood shavings, sawdust, plastic foam, kapok, foam rubber, cotton batting, and polyester fibers.
Photo, Joe Messinger

REDUCTION. Howard Woody. 1971. 4½′ cube hung 1½′ above floor. Ten 4½′ square 1 mil vinyl sheets are hung from steel hangers above four 14″ × 54″ mirrors. Atmospheric sculptures displayed in a gallery depend on air currents for their kinetic properties.

Opposite page above:
SPACE BARRICADE. Howard Woody. 1971. 30′ high, 60′ wide, 20′ deep space block. Clear ½ mil polyethylene sheets weighted, weather balloons, and helium. A sky sculpture that emphasizes the relationship between human scale and vastness of space.

Opposite page below:
AMBIGUOUS SPACE. Howard Woody. 1971. 20′ high, 70′ wide, 20′ deep space block. Clear polyethylene sheets appear to float from invisible lines as it subdivides the space block in equal sections.

All photos, courtesy, artist

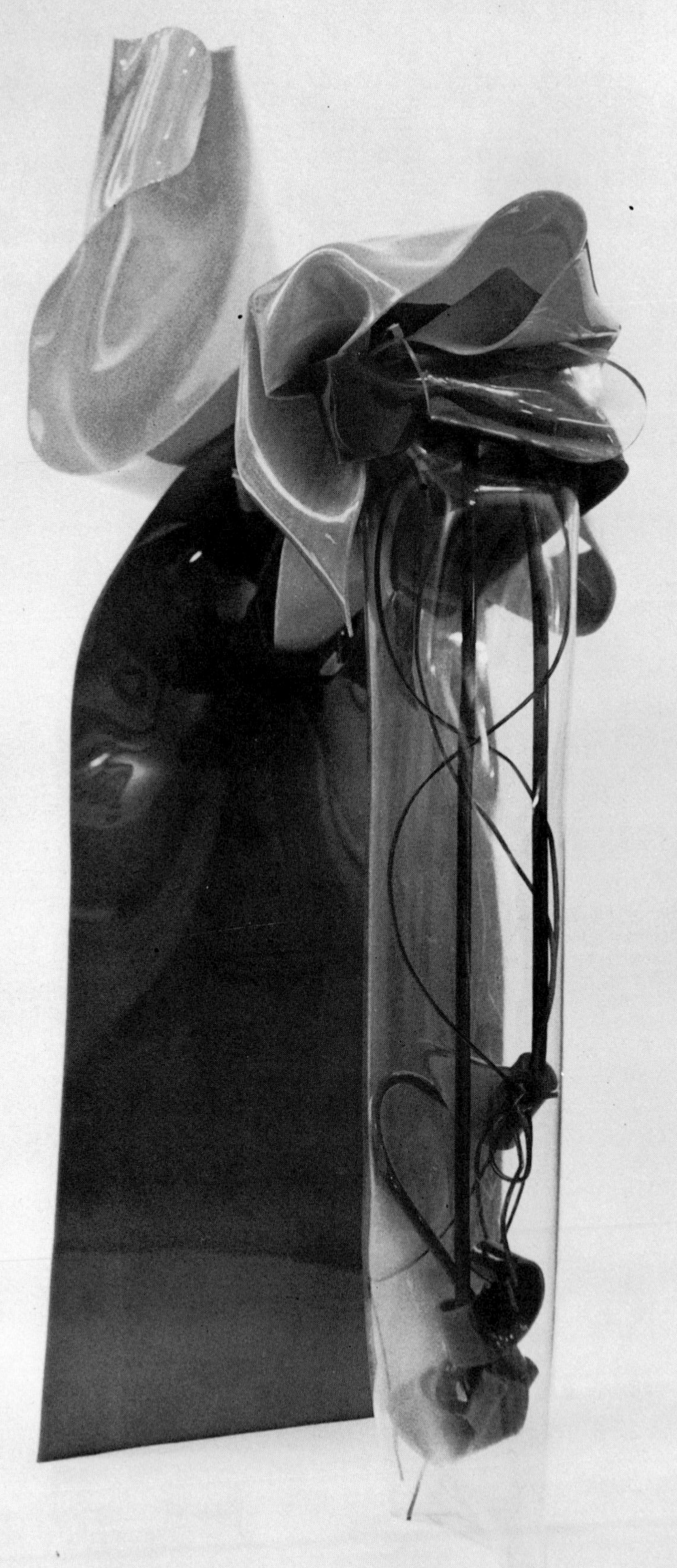

10
Soft-Hard

ARTISTS CONSISTENTLY DEAL WITH ILLUSION. THE ILLUSION OF three-dimensionality often is created by the painter who works on a two-dimensional surface. Trompe l'oeil, which means "fool the eye," refers to an illusion that is usually spatial such as in the painting *Sunday Dinner* by Harnett. The depiction of landscapes in depth on a painted canvas is also an optical illusion. Picasso and Braque accomplished an illusion of real objects on a painted canvas. Often the artist will present visual cues that create illusions for a particular purpose, such as distorting and circumventing reality as the viewer recognizes it. Psychological literature is filled with references to illusions, which has been defined as "any visual perception which does not harmonize with physical measurements."

Soft sculpture provides another set of illusions which, for any other classification, can be termed *soft—hard.* In this category are those materials that are worked soft, become hard, but still retain a soft appearance such as Plexiglas or other acrylic plastic as handled by Kenneth Weedman. The materials are formed in a soft, or melted, state. The mixture of transparent plastic with colored plastic within also suggests the concept of softness even after the material has hardened.

Screen wire mesh, woven from a hard wire, still retains a softness and is worked into an illusion of undulating moiré patterns by Jonathan Bauch, accompanied by and accomplished with colored blinking lights.

The shaped canvases by Zareh Maranian over pegged wood frames are both soft and hard; they are treated as two-dimensional surfaces, but the result is a relief dimension with qualities unique to the method.

INSIDE OUTSIDE MOVEMENT VI. Kenneth Weedman. 1971. 42″ high, 35″ wide, 23″ deep. Plastic, colored and clear.
Courtesy, artist.

Maxine McClendon uses the concept of stretched canvas, but stuffs the form and then stitches it with threads and paints it with acrylics.

Soft materials can be added to a canvas in the same manner as collage, and then painted upon for another expression in soft art. Any and all materials and techniques can be combined with restraint, good taste, and the ultimate statement that is expressive of the artist's feeling, his visual perceptions, and the goal he wishes to achieve.

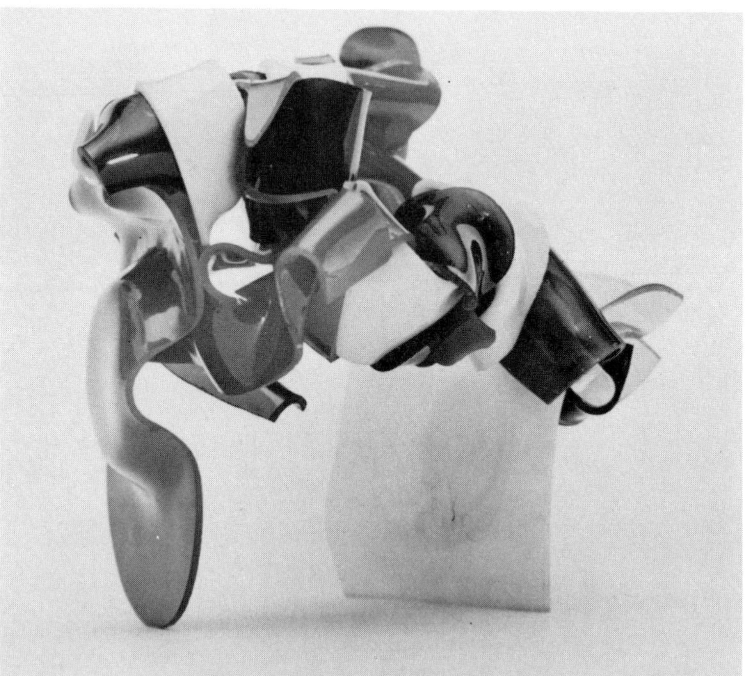

EXTERIOR MOVEMENT. Kenneth Weedman. 1969. 10″ high, 12″ wide, 8½″ deep. Plastic.

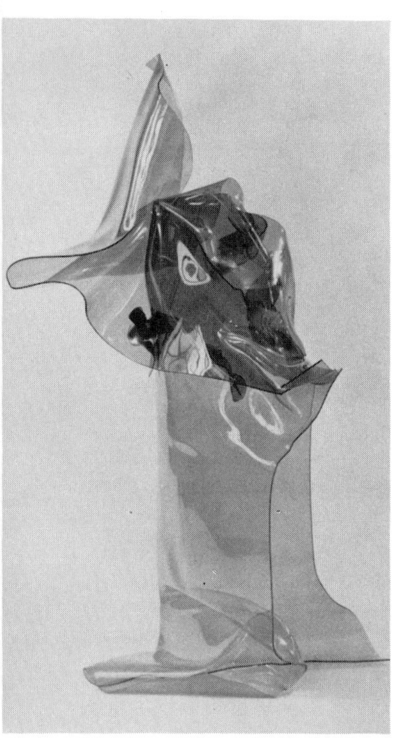

TRANSPARENT MOVEMENT IN GREEN AND ORANGE. Kenneth Weedman. 1971. 48″ high, 27″ wide, 24″ deep.
Photos, courtesy, artist

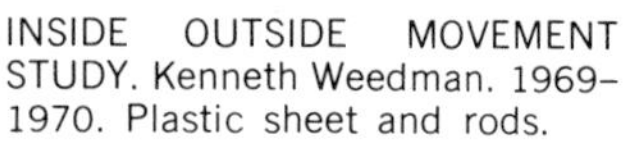

INSIDE OUTSIDE MOVEMENT STUDY. Kenneth Weedman. 1969–1970. Plastic sheet and rods.

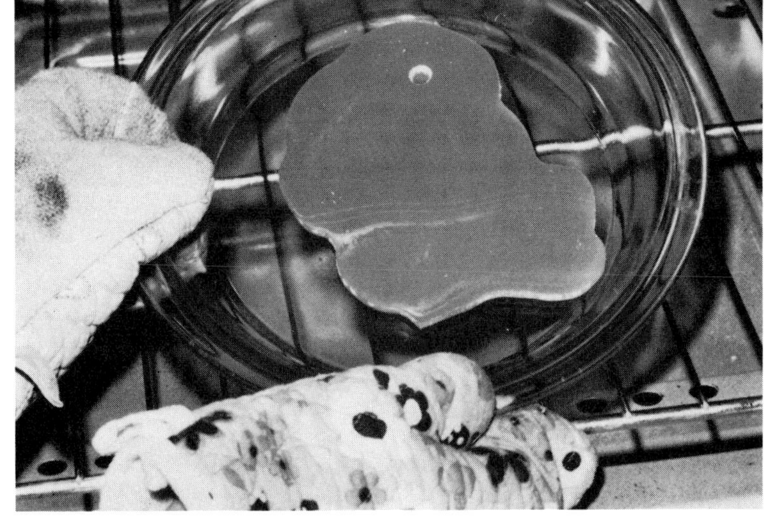

General procedures for working with acrylic plastic involves heating it to its "pliable" temperature, which requires some experimentation. The easiest place to heat plastic is in a kitchen oven and to work with the door open and heavy gloves on your arms. Depending upon room temperature, the oven will be between 250° and 400° F. Heated rods and tapes may also be used for bends. These are available from plastic suppliers.

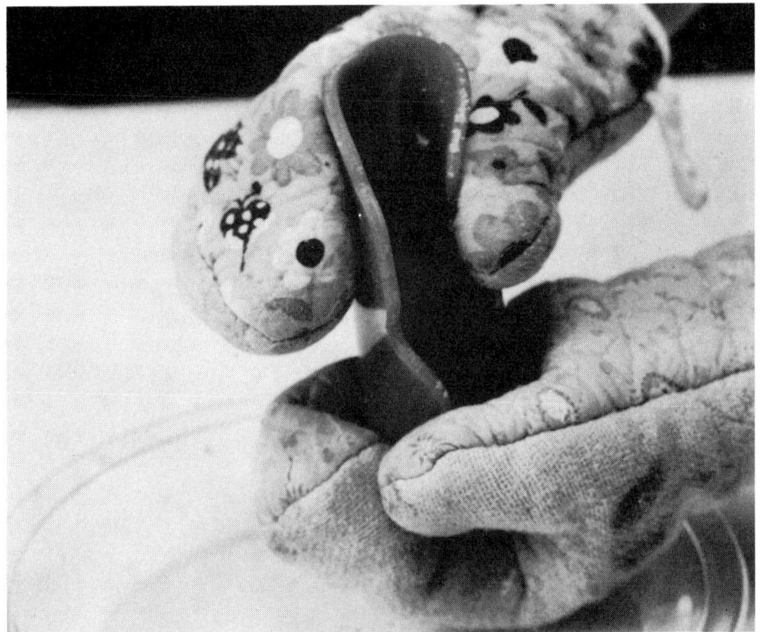

Small pieces can be shaped with a gloved hand. Large pieces can be quickly removed and shaped over a blanket draped over a chair or other form to give the shape you want. With large pieces it may be necessary to work one section at a time, then the next section; the problem is to keep the section you don't want reshaped cool while you are shaping another section. An assistant working with a cool wet sponge can help, but this may create a texture on the plastic.

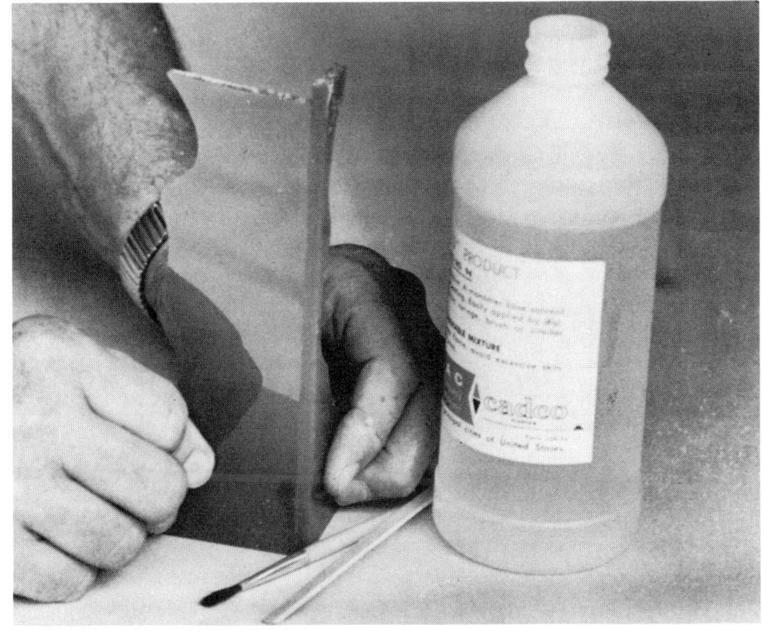

Finished plastic portions are adhered by a special plastic solvent, not a regular glue. Plastic adhesion depends upon the intermingling of the molecules of the joined surfaces. To effect this intermingling, and cohesion, the surfaces to be joined are softened with the solvent. After the pieces adhere, the solvent evaporates and the material hardens to result in a clear joint.

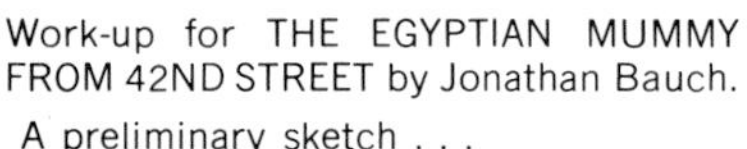
Work-up for THE EGYPTIAN MUMMY FROM 42ND STREET by Jonathan Bauch.

A preliminary sketch . . .

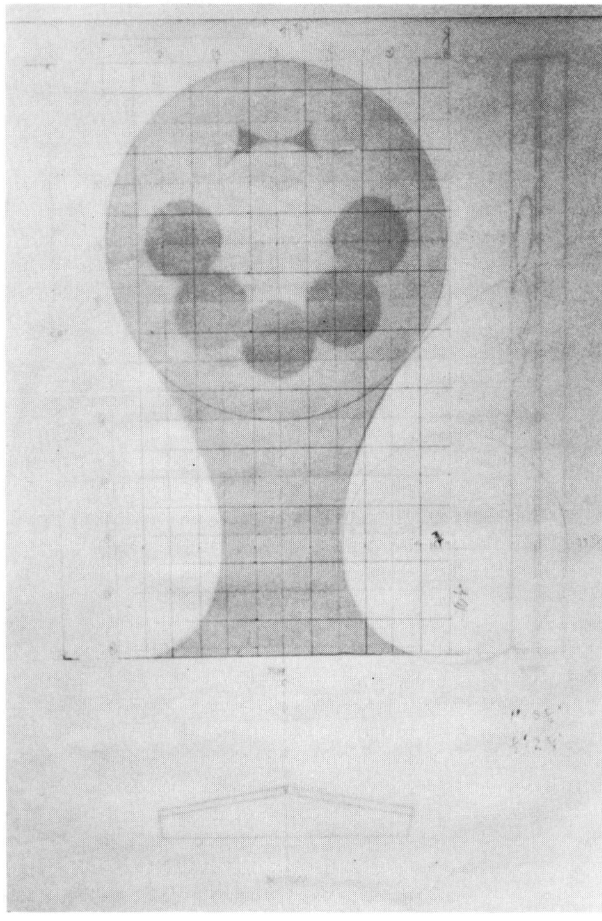
. . . is overlaid with a size scale.

The wood construction frame is built, which will hold the lights and several layers of aluminum hardware screen. Some layers have color added; kinetic and blinking lights add to the moiré effect.

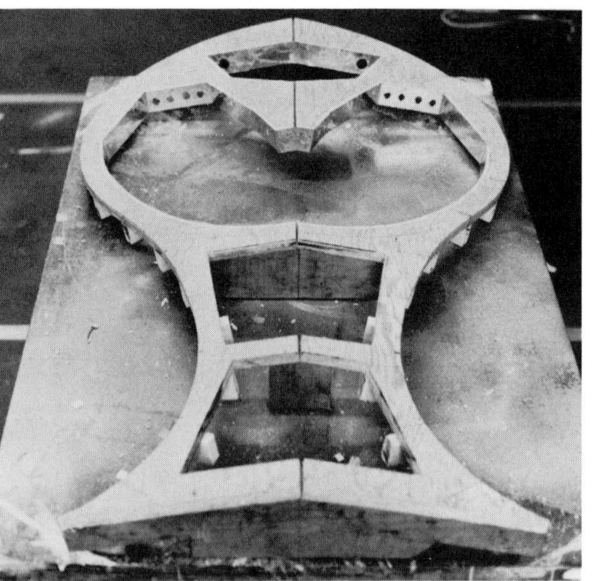

Side view shows the screening attached to the form.

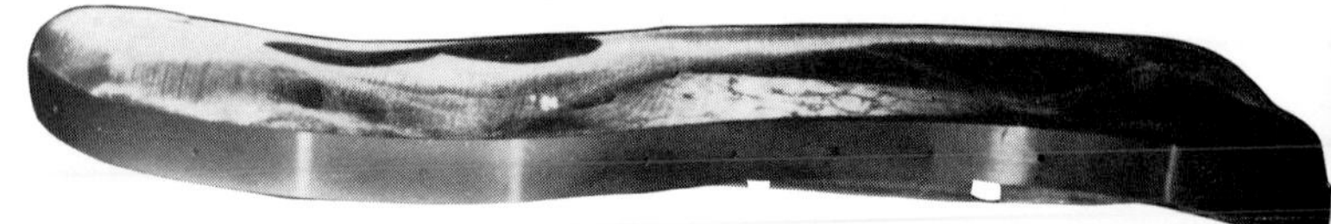

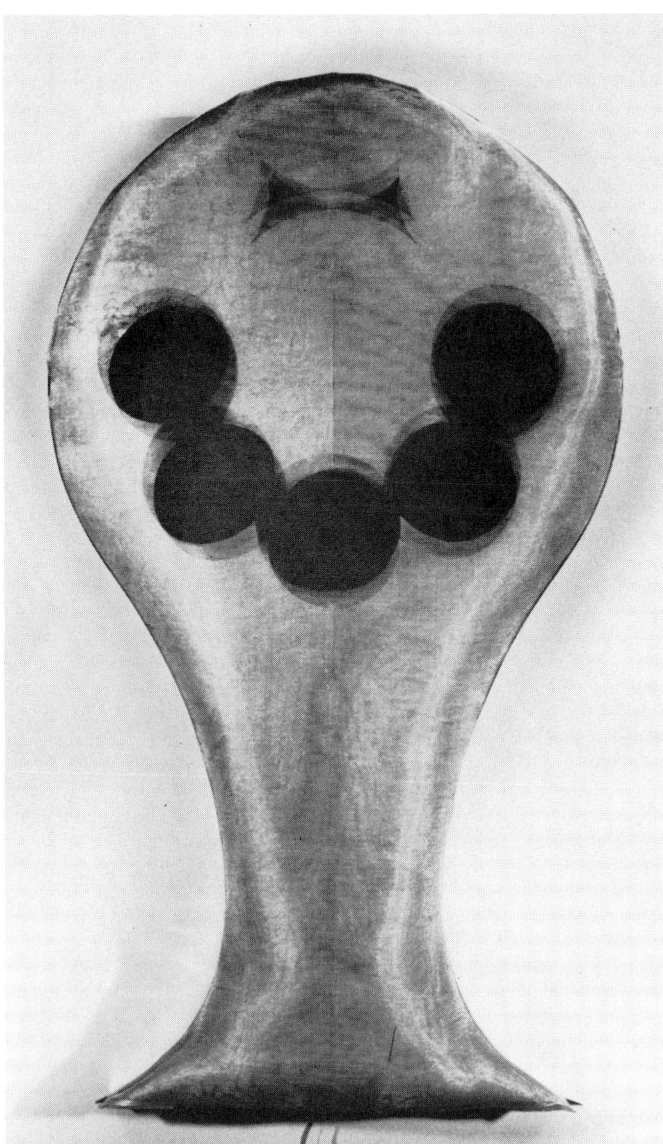

THE EGYPTIAN MUMMY FROM 42ND STREET. Jonathan Bauch. 1972. 120″ high, 32″ wide, 10″ deep. The work is in the form of relief sculpture where common materials, such as highly polished aluminum and layers of screening, interrelate with painted backgrounds and colored lights to form moiré patterns and shadows. The works have blinking colored lights to emphasize the three-dimensional effect. Says Mr. Bauch, "In essence, an ambiguity occurs when the inanimate hard materials appear to be soft in form and texture."

BANGLADESH. Jonathan Bauch. 1972. 60″ high, 44″ wide, 10″ deep. The moiré effect gives a soft look to the screening, which is lit from behind kinetically.

Photos, courtesy, artist

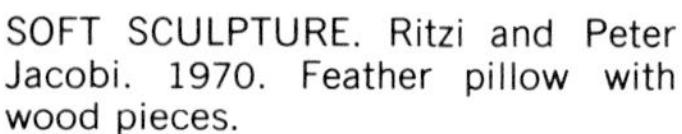

SOFT SCULPTURE. Ritzi and Peter Jacobi. 1970. Feather pillow with wood pieces.
Courtesy, artists

Right:
ALICE'S MIRROR. Cynthia Schira. 1972. 50" high, 38" wide. Woven aluminum with linen pile and mirrors.
Courtesy, artist

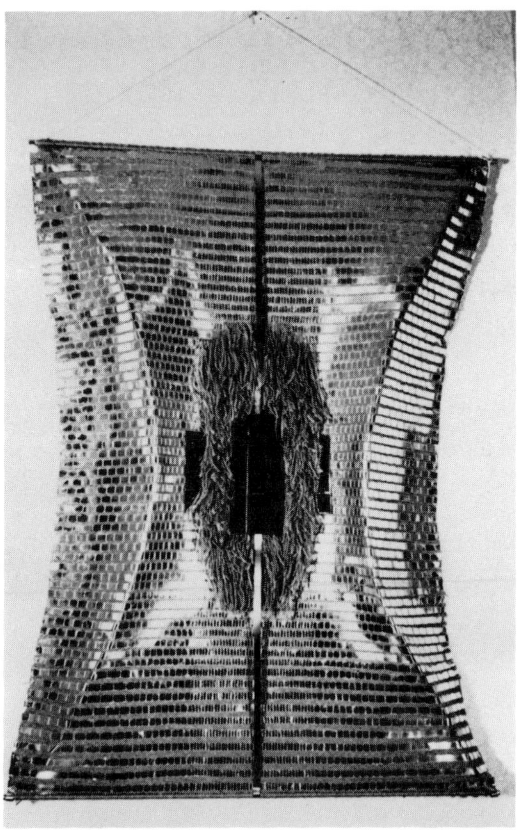

BLOOPER BLACK'S BRAZEN BLOBS. Richard Herr. 1973. 40" high, 28" wide. Aluminum and stuffed purple, blue, and orange vinyl.
Courtesy, artist

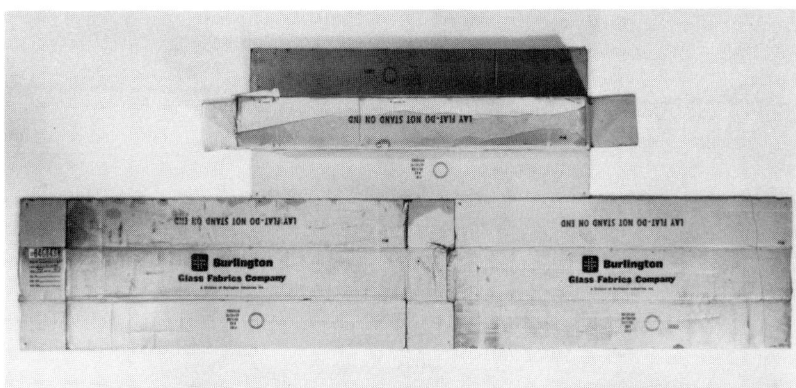

VOLON. Robert Rauschenberg. 1971. 55½″ high, 147″ wide, 10″ deep. Cardboard and plywood.

Courtesy, Leo Castelli Gallery, New York

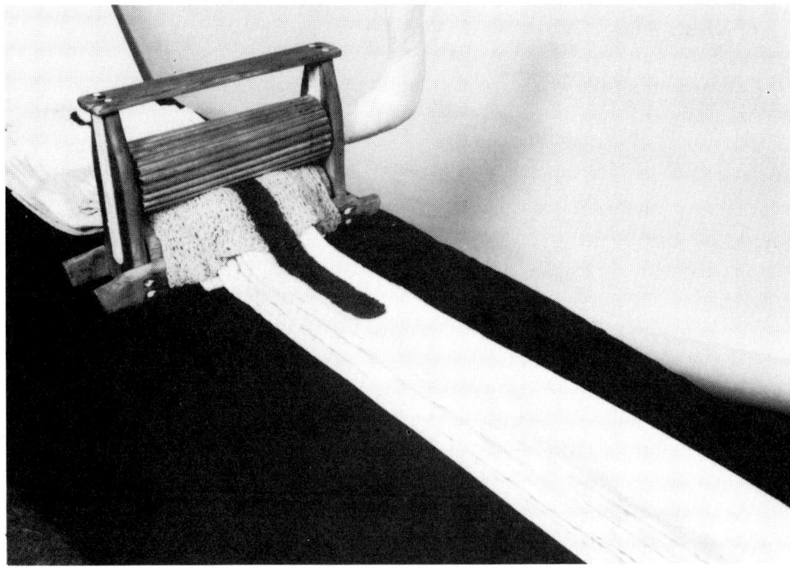

ROLL-OUT. Linda Ulvestad Fisher. 1973. 1′ high, 2¼′ wide, 8′ long. Oak rollers, layer of muslin, and crocheted bouclé yarns and crocheted string shapes.

Courtesy, artist

JESUS SAVES (two views). G. Klauba. 1972. 34″ high, 15″ wide, 11″ deep. Jackets are decorated like tattooed bodies that are meant to reflect a person's inner feelings through visual symbols.

Photographed at the American Craftsman Gallery, Chicago

EUROPA. James T. Soult. 24″ high, 21″ wide, 4″ deep. Gessoed muslin stuffed with polyurethane foam, then drawn and painted upon with silver point and acrylic paint. It was mounted on a rigid board.
Courtesy, Richmond Art Center, Richmond, California Photo, artist

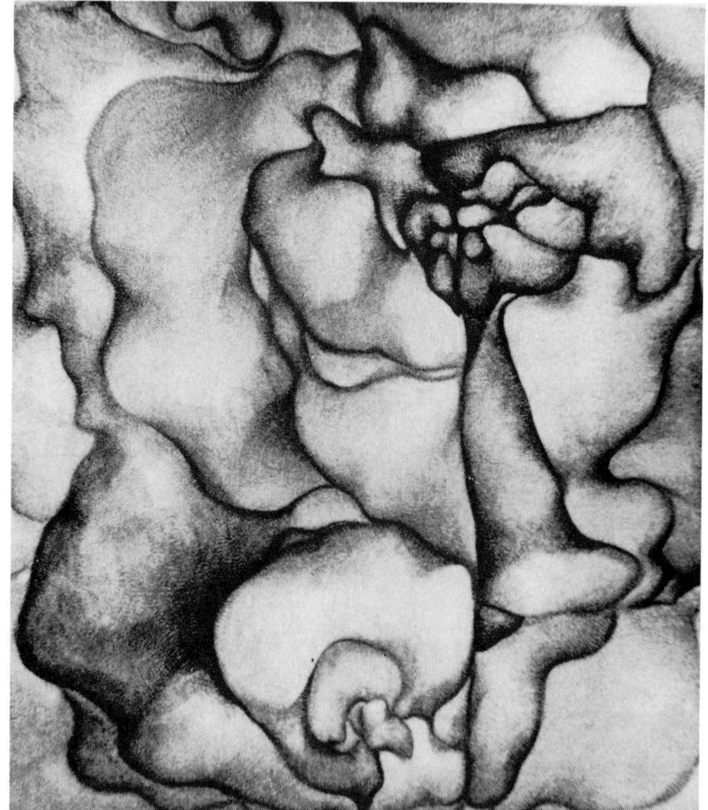

TOUCH PAINTING #8. Charles Meyers. 1972. 84″ wide, 96″ high. A synthetic acrylic fleece material used commercially for lining boots is cut and pieced as shapes, and glued onto a stretched canvas. Portions of the fleece are etched out by cutting, and then the surface is painted with thinned oil paints. The work is meant to be touched as well as viewed.
Courtesy, artist

Shaped, stretched canvases are motorized and have a kinetic construction. Zareh Maranian.

Left: A room full of shaped constructed kinetic pieces.

This piece has a rubberized surface so that the kinetic movement is more pronounced for a soft feeling.

Photos, courtesy, artist

The artist puts the finishing touch on a canvas.

NIGHT VISION. Maxine McClendon. 1972. Stretched canvas stuffed from back and/or front with cotton batting and then stretched over a wood frame. Painted with acrylics.

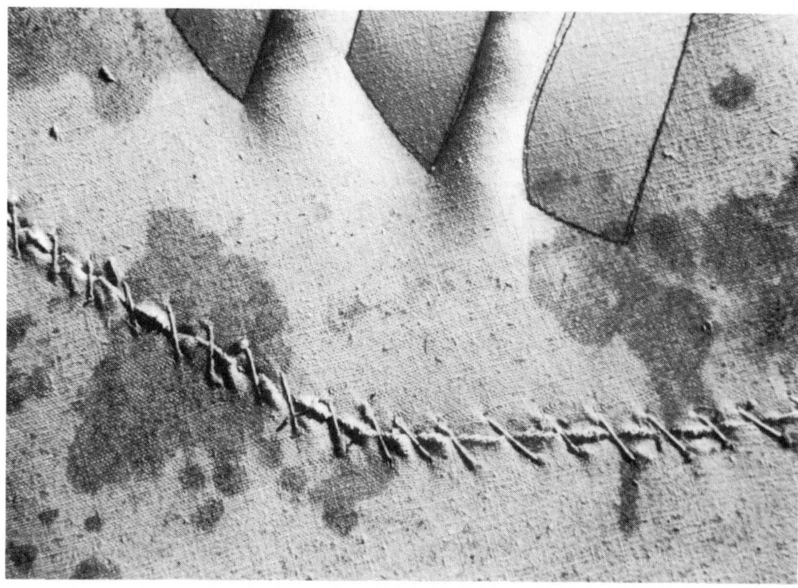

Detail of NIGHT VISION.

DIRECTORY. Maxine McClendon. 1972. Same technique as on opposite page.

SABBATH. Maxine McClendon. 1972. Same technique as on opposite page.

All photos, Edward E. Nichols

Appendix

HEATING AND SHAPING ACRYLIC SHEET

Plexiglas, Lucite, and other brands of acrylic sheet can be developed into soft art media and used in conjunction with various materials and techniques. The sheet can be scored and snapped apart, sawed, drilled, and sanded. Softening and bending, and shaping large pieces pose certain problems (for small pieces heating can be accomplished in an ordinary oven). Rohm and Haas Co., distributor of Plexiglas, suggests the use of a strip heater, which you can make yourself for about $10. A special heating element manufactured by the Brisco Mfg. Co. (Briskeat RH–36) can be mounted to form a narrow heating surface that allows you to melt only portions of the acrylic plastic for spot shaping. It is available from Plexiglas dealers and from local hardware stores that handle Plexiglas or from Cadillac Plastic Co. (See Sources for Supplies.)

The strip heater can be mounted for convenient use with the directions shown here. Using this same procedure, other heating techniques could be improvised using available heating elements, heating irons, and so forth.

HOW TO MAKE THE STRIP HEATER

1. Cut a piece of ½″ plywood 6″ x 42″.
2. Cut two ¼″ plywood strips 2⅝″ x 36″. Center the two strips (2) on top of the base (1), leaving a ¾″ channel down the center and nail this to the base.
3. Cut two pieces of heavy duty aluminum foil 6″ x 36″ and fold to fit the ¾″ channel.
4. Attach a ground wire to the aluminum foil with a nail, as shown.

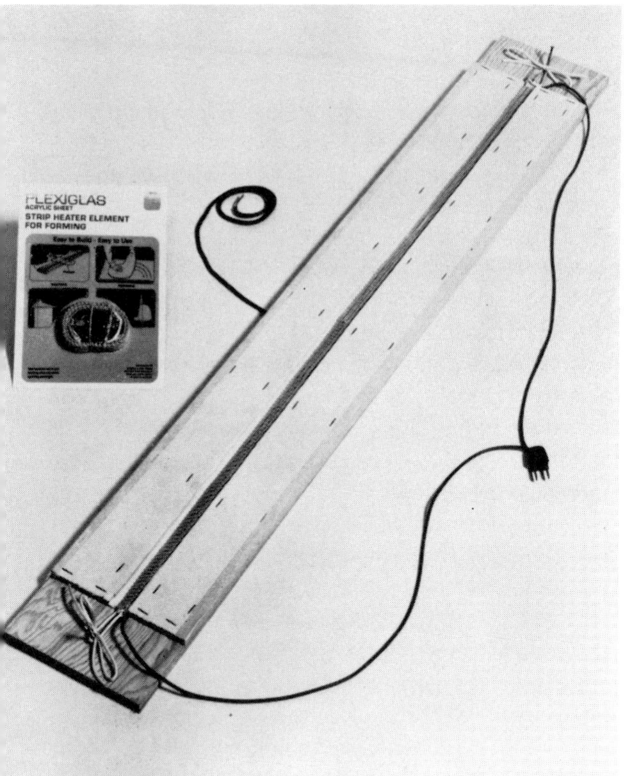

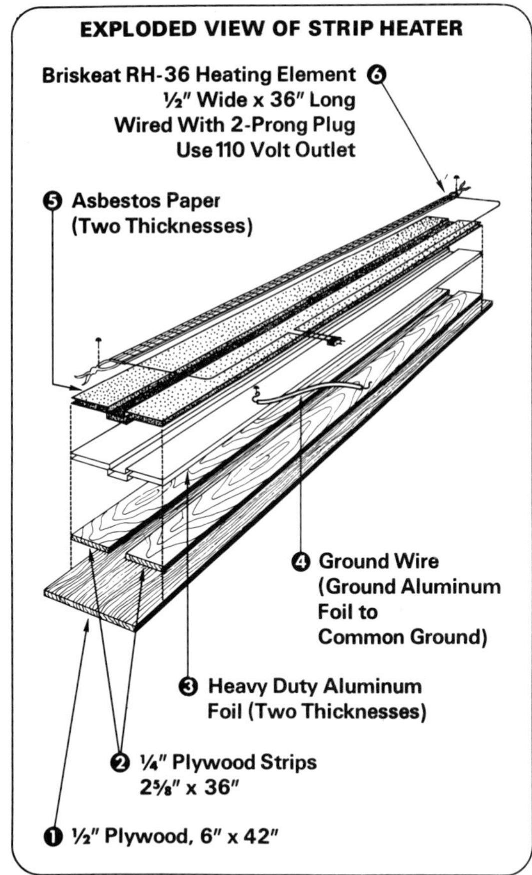

Left: Strip heater.
Above: Exploded view of a strip heater.
Photos, courtesy, Rohm and Haas Company

Note: The ground wire should be long enough to attach to a common ground such as the cover plate screw on an electrical outlet.

5. Cut two pieces of asbestos paper 6¼″ x 36″ and fold to fit the ¾″ channel on top of the aluminum foil. Staple asbestos paper and aluminum foil to ¼″ plywood strips (2) along the outside edges.
6. Lay the Briskeat RH–36 heating element in the channel. Drive a nail 1½″ from each end of the base (1) along a center line and the end strings of the heating element to the nails. Slide two pieces of plug together. Attach ground wire to common ground and you're ready to plug the strip heater into a 110-volt outlet.

FLAMEPROOFING

Artists and craftsmen who create work on speculation or commission for use in public areas such as window displays, stage settings, hotels, banks, museums, convention booths, and similar settings may find it necessary to flameproof their work. Many states have fire ordinances for fiber and fabrics and require strict adherence to their codes.

Generally, flameproofing requires immersing or spraying materials, or the finished piece, with a flameproof chemical. It is necessary to know the content of the material because the type of chemical required for natural fibers, cotton, rayon, linen, silk, wool, jute, burlap, and so on, is different from that used on synthetics. There are special chemicals for different plastics.

Chemicals used for flameproofing are usually a concentrate liquid or powder to which water is added. You can purchase the chemicals and do the flameproofing yourself. However, any washing or dry cleaning will remove the chemical and the piece must be re-treated.

Commercial flameproofing may be accomplished with certain chemicals that permit the piece to be dry cleaned with a special solvent several times before re-treatment is necessary.

If you are planning to create a sculpture that will require flameproofing, be sure to know the content of the materials you are using. You can send samples to a company that distributes such chemicals and ask them to recommend the type of chemical for the specific material. When you purchase the chemical, pretest samples of the material by immersing or spraying and then setting a match to it. This is a much safer procedure than treating a finished piece and then trusting to luck. Also test the possibility of treating yardage or cords before working them, providing the treatment does not stiffen them.

When spraying with flame retardant solutions, always spray heavier at the top, edges, and seams of the piece. You can use any paint spray equipment or fruit tree sprayer for applying the chemicals to hangings or sculptures.

Hand-dyed fabrics can pose a problem because some dyes will run when they are treated with the chemical. Batiks, tie-dyes, silk-screen prints, and so forth should all be pretested for color fastness and/or for amount of chemical that the piece can accept before the colors run.

When spraying, care must be taken *not* to overload the fabric and get it dripping wet. Overloading may cause the cloth to be stiff when it is dry. To do a thorough job, every thread of the fabric must be wet. One gallon of flameproofing solution will treat twelve to twenty yards of fabric, depending on its weight.

Consult your classified pages under "Flameproofing" for sources in your area and for information specifically geared to your needs. A free booklet about flameproofing and the chemicals for different materials is available from:

California Flameproofing and Processing Co.
170 N. Halstead Street
Pasadena, California 91107

Additional chemicals and information are available from:
Keystone Aniline Co., 321 N. Loomis, Chicago, Illinois 60600
Ballantyne Flameproofing Co., 2722 N. Lincoln Avenue, Chicago, Illinois 60657
Bay Ridge Flameproofing Co., 274–87th Street, Brooklyn, N.Y. 11209
Local distributors of DuPont X–12

Sources for Supplies

The following supply sources are listed for your convenience. Materials offered and charges for samples and catalogs are subject to change without notice. No endorsement or responsibility is implied by the author. Price lists are free unless specified. A large self-addressed stamped envelope is suggested.

Note: Stuffing materials such as polyester fill, cotton batting, Dacron padding, etc., are usually available from dime stores, fabric departments, and fabric shops. All kinds of foams and padding materials can be ordered from any of the catalog supply stores such as J. C. Penney, Sears, Montgomery Ward, and so forth.

YARNS, THREADS, DYES, BEADS, AND MISCELLANEOUS ITEMS

AAA Cordage Co., Inc. 3238 N. Clark St. Chicago, Ill. 60657	Twine, rope.	Samples: \$.50—twines. \$.50—ropes. \$1.00—twine and rope.
Colonial Woolen Mills, Inc. 6501 Barberton Ave. Cleveland, Ohio 44102	Handweaving yarns, macramé and craft yarns. Weaving accessories.	Samples: \$.50. Minimum order: \$5.00.
Contessa Yarns P.O. Box 37 Lebanon, Conn. 06249	Yarns of all kinds.	Samples: \$.25.
Craft Kaleidoscope 6551 Fergeson St. Broad Ripple Village Indianapolis, Md. 46220	Wide variety cords, yarns, and beads. Books. Weaving supplies. Dyes.	Send stamped self-addressed envelope for supply and price lists.

Craft Yarns of Rhode Island, Inc. 603 Mineral Spring Ave. Pawtucket, R.I. 02862	Weaving, rug making, macramé, and accessories. Hand looms.	Samples: $.50.
Creative Handweavers P.O. Box 26480 Los Angeles, Calif. 90026	Tremendous variety of unusual yarns, cords, etc. Fleece, hair. Basketry supplies. Weaving supplies.	Wool and hair sample set: $1.00. Cotton and jute sample set: $1.00. Minimum differs with yarns ordered. Wholesale prices on large amounts.
Dharma Trading Co. P.O. Box 1288 Berkeley, Calif. 94701	Yarns, cordage, dyes.	Samples: $.50. Minimum order: $5.00.
Earthworks 624 W. Willow St. Chicago, Ill. 60614	Stoneware beads—10 colors. Small and large holes and sizes.	Large bead samples: $1.00.
Earthy Endeavors P.O. Box 817 Whittier, Calif. 90608	Ceramic, stoneware, and porcelain glazed and unglazed beads.	Minimum order: $1.50–$3.00. Wholesale information available.
El Mercado Importing Co. 9002 8th NE Seattle, Wash. 98115	Natural Argentine and Mexican homespun sheep's wool; natural, gray, and dark brown.	Samples and price list: $.50.
Fibrec, Inc. 2815 18th St. San Francisco, Calif. 94110	Fiber reactive dyes for batik and for yarns, cords, fabrics.	Free sample card of 23 dyed fabric swatches. Minimum order: $10.00. Wholesale information.
Frederick J. Fawcett 129 South St. Boston, Mass. 02111	Linen yarns for stitchery, macramé weaving. Large variety of textures and colors.	Samples: $1.00.
Freed Co. Box 394 Albuquerque, N.M.	Coral, glass beads, wampum Indian-made strands, turquoise, wool fleece, mohair and wool yarns, sheepskins, goatskins, leathers, wool carders, seashells.	Free price lists and fliers.

Gooleni 11 Riverside Dr. Suite 5 VE New York, N.Y. 10023	Seashells of many varieties.	
Greentree Ranch Wools Countryside Handweavers 163 N. Carter Lake Rd. Loveland, Colo. 80537	Wide variety of fat yarns as well as traditional yarns.	Free price list.
Grey Owl Indian Craft Mfg. Co., Inc. 150–02 Beaver Rd. Jamaica, Queens, N.Y. 11433	American Indian craft supplies.	Catalog: $.25.
P. C. Herwig Co., Inc. Rt. 2, Box 140 Milaca, Minn. 56353	All types of yarn for weaving, macramé. Beads, batting, books.	Catalog and samples: $.50.
Hollywood Fancy Feather 512 S. Broadway Los Angeles, Calif. 90013	Assorted natural and dyed feathers for weaving, macramé, etc.	Minimum order: $5.00.
International Handcraft and Supply 32 Hermosa Ave. Hermosa Beach, Calif. 90254	Yarns and cords for weaving, macramé, etc. Basketry supplies, goat hair, raw silk, leathers, assorted beads.	
Keystone Aniline & Chemical Co., Inc. 321 N. Loomis St. Chicago, Ill. 60607	Fabric dyes. Flameproofing materials.	
Lamb's End 165 W. 9 Mile Ferndale, Mich. 48220	Weaving yarns, spinning fibers, Dacron and polyester stuffing, feathers, beads, seashells.	Yarn samples: $1.00. Minimum order: 1 lb. of fibers.
Las Manos, Inc. 12215 Coit Rd. (in Olla Podrida) Dallas, Tex. 75230	Imported and domestic yarns, weaving supplies, macramé cords, beads, and miscellany.	Samples and price list: $.75. Minimum order: $10.00.
Lemco Box 40505 San Francisco, Ca. 94140	Cords, beads, books, bells.	Catalog free.

Lily Mills Co. Shelby, N.C. 28150	Weaving, stitchery, and macramé yarns and threads. Weaving supplies.	Charge for samples.
Macramé and Weaving Supply Co. 63 E. Adams #403 Chicago, Ill. 60614	Macramé, weaving, knitting, and stitchery yarns and supplies; beads, belts, seashells, feathers, bones.	Catalog free. Samples: $1.00.
The Mannings-Creative Crafts Handweaving Studio and Supply Center East Berlin, Pa. 17136	Wool, cotton, linen, and synthetic yarns; beads, buckles, cords, and all miscellaneous macramé supplies. Weaving and spinning supplies. Books.	Catalog and samples: $.50. Minimum order: $5.00.
Naturalcraft 2199 Bancroft Way Berkeley, Calif. 94704	Beads, seashells, feathers, yarns, and cordage. Basketry, spinning fibers, and miscellaneous weaving supplies.	Catalog and samples: $.50. Minimum order: $5.00.
Northwest Handcraft House 110 West Esplanade North Vancouver, B.C., Canada	Weaving supplies. Imported yarns, fleece, raw sisal and manila, dyes, books.	Catalog: $.50.
Oregon Handspun Wool P.O. Box 132 Monroe, Ore. 97456	Handspun yarns.	Samples: $.50.
The Pendleton Shop Handweaving-Knitting Studio 407 Jordan Road P.O. Box 233 Sedona, Ariz. 86336	Weaving, knitting, crochet, and macramé yarns. Weaving supplies. Metal rings, buttons, beads.	Send stamped self-addressed envelope for catalog and samples.
Progress Feather Co. 657 W. Lake St. Chicago, Ill. 60606	Assorted feathers. Pelts.	Free price list. Minimum order: $15.00. Wholesale only for quantity purchases.
Rip Neal THREADS 9621 Seeley Lake Drive SW Tacoma, Wash. 98499	Macramé and weaving threads. Beads, bells, books.	Free price list.

Schacht Spindle Co. 1708 Walnut St. Boulder, Colo. 80302	Looms and wood weaving accessories.	Catalog free.
School Products Co., Inc. 312 East 23rd St. New York, N.Y. 10010	Wool and linen handweaving yarns. All types of looms and accessories.	Catalog and price list free. Minimum order: $10.00.
The Silver Shuttle 1301 35th St., N.W. Washington, D.C. 20007	Weaving and spinning yarns and supplies. Looms, spinning wheels, etc.	Catalog and samples: $1.00. Minimum order: $5.00.
Siphon Art Products Durable Arts Division 74–D Hamilton Dr. Ignacio, Calif. 94947	Versatex textile paints for silkscreening, stenciling, and hand painting. Also leather paints.	Sample card of colors. Free catalog and price list.
Tahki Imports, Ltd. 336 West End Ave. New York, N.Y. 10023	Greek, Irish, and Columbian handspun yarns. Various stuffings.	Free catalog with information for ordering samples.
3 Gables Homecrafts 1825 Charleston Beach Bremerton, Wash. 98310	Handcrafted glazed ceramic beads with large openings for weaving and macramé.	Free brochure with sample bead. Also wholesale to shops and schools.
Tuxedo Yarn and Needlepoint 36–35 Main Street Flushing, N.Y. 11354	Beads, polyester fill, cotton batting. All yarns and supplies for knotting, knitting, and stitchery.	Free catalog.
The Unique 21½ East Bijou Colorado Springs, Colo. 80902	Imported yarns and threads for weaving, macramé, knitting, crochet, etc. Looms.	Sample card: $1.00. Catalog of looms: $1.00. Complete portfolio of yarns and looms and catalogs: $8.00. Free price list.
Warp Woof & Potpourri 514 N. Lake Ave. Pasadena, California 91101	Weaving, macramé, spinning, basketry and stitchery supplies.	Catalog–samples $.50.
The Yarn Depot, Inc. 545 Sutter St. San Francisco, Calif. 94102	Assorted yarns, beads, supplies, books for all crafts.	Samples: $.50–$1.50. Bimonthly samples club.

The Yarn Loft Upstairs—1442 Camino Del Mar Del Mar, Calif. 92014	Fibers for all crafts. Metallic yarns, canvases, basketry supplies, burlap, suede lacing.	Catalog: $1.00.
Yarn Primitives P.O. Box 1013 Weston, Conn. 06880	Handspun yarns from Greece, Ecuador, Peru, Bolivia, India, and Haiti Wools, goat hair, cotton blends.	Samples: $2.00.

PLASTICS AND LATEX

Adhesive Products Corp. 1660 Boone Ave. Bronx, N.Y. 10460	Latex, plastic, foams, polyester.	Minimum order: $10.00.
Berstead's Hobby Craft, Inc. Box 40 Monmouth, Ill. 61462	Latex and general craft supplies.	Catalog.
Cadillac Plastic & Chemical Co. P.O. Box 03000 Detroit, Mich. 48203	Acrylic sheet, rods, tubes and heating tapes, adhesives, etc.	Buyer's guide: $1.25.
General Latex and Chemical Corp. (of Ohio) P.O. Box 498 Ashland, Ohio 44805	Latex.	Minimum order: $30.00.
Mail Order Plastics 56 Lispenard St. New York, N.Y. 10013	Acrylic sheet, cubes, balls, tubes, discs, domes. Styrofoam flexible vinyl tubing, polypropylene and polyethylene.	Free catalog. Minimum order: $10.00.
Rohm and Haas Company P.O. Box 9730 Philadelphia, Pa. 19140	Plexiglas ® brand acrylic sheet and accessory products.	Catalog: $.25.

GENERAL ARTS AND CRAFTS SUPPLIES CATALOGS AVAILABLE

Dick Blick
P.O. Box 1267
Galesburg, Ill. 61401

Sax Arts and Crafts
207 N. Milwaukee
Milwaukee, Wisc. 53202

Lee Wards
840 N. State
Elgin, Ill. 60120

Triarco Arts and Crafts
P.O. Box 106
Northfield, Ill. 60093

BOOK DEALERS SPECIALIZING IN ARTS AND CRAFTS

The Book Barn
P.O. Box 256
Avon, Conn. 06001
Catalog $.50

K. R. Drummond, Bookseller
Hart Groves
Ealing Common
London, W. 5, England

Museum Books, Inc.
48 E. 43rd St.
New York, N.Y. 10017

The Unicorn
Craft and Hobby Book Service
Box 645
Rockville, Md. 20851

PERIODICALS OF SPECIAL INTEREST

Artisan Crafts
Star Rt. 4 Box 179–F
Reeds Spring, Mo. 65737
Quarterly

Artweek
P.O. Box 2496
Castro Valley, Calif. 94546
Weekly

Craft Horizons
American Craftsmen's Council
44 W. 53rd St.
New York, N.Y. 10019
Bimonthly

Craft Midwest
Box 42 B
Northbrook, Ill. 60062
Quarterly

Handweaver & Craftsman
220 Fifth Avenue
New York, N.Y. 10001
Quarterly

Quarterly Journal of the Guilds of Weavers, Spinners & Dyers
1 Harrington Road
Brighton 6, England

Shuttle, Spindle & Dye-pot
(with membership to Handweavers Guild of America)
339 North Steele Road
West Hartford, Conn. 06117
Quarterly

The Tie-up
Southern California Handweavers Guild, Inc.
Magazine with membership
P.O. Box 60211
Terminal Annex
Los Angeles, Calif. 90060
10 times a year

Warp & Weft
533 N. Adams St.
McMinnville, Oregon 97128
10 times a year

Bibliography

Atwater, Mary Meigs. *Byways in Hand Weaving.* New York: The Macmillan Company, 1954.

Blumenau, Lili. *Creative Design in Wall Hangings.* New York: Crown Publishers, Inc., 1967.

Emery, Irene. *The Primary Structure of Fabrics.* Washington, D.C.: The Textile Museum, 1966.

Harvey, Virginia, and Tidball, Harriet. *Weft Twining.* Lansing, Michigan: Shuttle Craft Guild (Monograph Twenty-Eight), 1969.

Haskell, Barbara. *Object into Monument.* Pasadena, California: Pasadena Art Museum, 1971.

Hastie, Reid, and Schmidt, Christian. *Encounter with Art.* New York: McGraw-Hill Book Co., 1969.

Kroncke, Grete. *Simple Weaving.* New York: Van Nostrand Reinhold Co., 1969.

Lewis, Fred Allan. *The Mountain Artisans Quilting Book.* New York: The Macmillan Company, 1973.

Meilach, Dona Z. *Contemporary Batik and Tie-Dye.* New York: Crown Publishers, Inc., 1973.

———*Creating Art From Fibers and Fabrics.* Chicago: Henry Regnery Co., 1972.

———*Macramê Accessories.* New York: Crown Publishers, Inc., 1972.

———*Macramê: Creative Design in Knotting.* New York: Crown Publishers, Inc., 1971.

———, Hinz, Jay, and Hinz, Bill. *Creating Design Form, Composition for Artists and Craftsmen.* New York: Doubleday and Co., 1974.

———, and Snow, Lee Erlin. *Creative Stitchery.* Chicago: Henry Regnery Co., 1970.

———. *Weaving Off-Loom.* Chicago: Henry Regnery Co., 1972.

Nordness, Lee. *Objects: U.S.A.* New York: Viking Press, 1970.

Paque, Joan Michaels. *Design Principles and Fiber Techniques.* Shorewood, Wisconsin: Joan and Henry Paque, 1973.

———. *Visual Instructional Macramé.* Shorewood, Wisconsin: Joan and Henry Paque, 1971.

Regensteiner, Else. *The Art of Weaving.* New York: Van Nostrand Reinhold Co., 1970.

Rose, Barbara. *Claes Oldenburg.* New York: The Museum of Modern Art, 1970.

Index

(*C.S.* =Color Section)